Jesus at 2000

Jesus at 2000

edited by
Marcus J. Borg

Westview
PRESS
A Member of the Perseus Books Group

Copyright © 1997 by Westview Press, A member of the Perseus Books Group

Published in 1997 in the United States of America by Westview Press, 5500 Central Avenue, Boulder, Colorado 80301-2877, and in the United Kingdom by Westview Press, 12 Hid's Copse Road, Cumnor Hill, Oxford OX2 9JJ

A CIP catalog record for this book is available from the Library of Congress.
ISBN 0-8133-3252-4

The paper used in this publication meets the requirements of the American National Standard for Permanence of Paper for Printed Library Materials Z39.48-1984.

12 13 14 15 16

For Al Hundere, whose creation of the Hundere Chair of Religious Studies at Oregon State University made Jesus at 2000 possible

Contents

Preface and Acknowledgments

This book is one of the results of "Jesus at 2000," the first nationwide scholarly symposium commemorating the 2,000th anniversary of the birth of Jesus. Convened at Oregon State University on February 8–10, 1996, "Jesus at 2000" not only featured six internationally known scholars in dialogue with a capacity crowd at Oregon State but was also telecast live by satellite to over three hundred downlink sites across the continent. It was a record-setting event: Never before have so many people at one time been part of a scholarly discussion of Jesus and his significance.

"Jesus at 2000" was (and is) a scholarly "taking stock" of Jesus as he turns 2,000. The lecturers–now the authors of this volume–are a distinguished group of scholars and authors representing a variety of scholarly perspectives on Jesus. John Dominic Crossan and I specialize in the study of the historical Jesus and Christian origins, Alan Segal is a Jewish scholar with a special interest in Judaism and Christianity in the first century, Karen Jo Torjesen is a historian of early Christianity from the beginnings to the fourth century, Harvey Cox is an analyst of religion and contemporary culture, and Huston Smith is a philosopher and historian of the world's religions. How does Jesus look from each of these perspectives? Such was the focus of the symposium and now of this book.

Although this book has its origin in the lectures given at "Jesus at 2000," it is not a transcript of what was said on that occasion. It differs in two ways. First, the authors were free to revise their lectures as they adapted them from "oral manuscript" to written presentation in book form. In some cases, the revisions are quite minor; in others, they are more substantial. Second, this book includes an introduction to the historical study of Jesus and Christian origins. As Chapter 8, it is intended to make the book useful for students in undergraduate courses and for "the newly curious," whoever and wherever they may be. Readers for whom the historical study of Jesus and Christian origins is quite new may wish to begin with Chapter 8; readers who are already familiar with this approach may have no need for this material.

One more comment about the nature of this book. Each lecture was followed by approximately thirty minutes of questions from both the on-site audience and the off-site television audience. Persons watching on satellite television were able to call in their questions on an 800 telephone line. These questions and responses are printed at the end of each lecture. They have been edited for reasons of clarity and compactness.

In the rest of this preface, I wish to thank a number of people for their role in "Jesus at 2000." First, I want to thank Trinity Institute of New York City for cosponsoring the symposium with Oregon State. Trinity not only chose to have "Jesus at 2000" as its 1996 annual lecture series but also advertised it widely and televised it on the Episcopal Cathedral Teleconferencing Network. In particular, I thank the Reverend Dan Matthews, rector of Trinity Wall Street; the Reverend Dr. Fred Burnham, director of Trinity Institute; and his staff, especially Laura Crawford and Linda Hanick, who played major roles in the telecast.

I was honored to have Trinity Institute do this from Oregon State University and the "little town" of Corvallis. As I was imagining how the telecast of "Jesus at 2000" might begin, I thought, "Wouldn't it be great if the opening words were, 'Live, from Corvallis, Oregon, home of the Oregon State University Beavers, we bring you Jesus at 2000!'" Well, they were not the opening words, but I managed to say them both in the telecast and now in this preface. So to Trinity Institute: Thank you for your collaboration in televising the symposium across the nation.

Second, I want to thank Al Hundere of San Antonio, Texas, and a 1938 graduate from Oregon State. Just about three years ago, Al, as I have come to know him, created a $3 million chair in religious studies in the Philosophy Department at Oregon State. I am honored to be the first holder of it. "Jesus at 2000" is the first major public event sponsored by the Hundere Chair and Endowment for Religion and Culture. Al Hundere's generosity made this symposium possible and will make much else possible at Oregon State for a long time to come. I and we are very grateful to him.

Third, I want to thank several people at Oregon State who provided indispensable assistance: Lois Summers and Kari Karau of the office staff in the Philosophy Department; Professor Kathleen Moore, chair of the department; Jeff Hale, director of development for the College of Liberal Arts; Larry Pribyl of the Media Center; George Edmonston and Mark Floyd for their help with publicity; and Terry Finch and Sylvia Moore from the Lasells Stewart Center, where the symposium was held. In addition, and above all, I want to thank Mary Streufert, my graduate assistant, on whom fell the burden of taking care of all of the practical details involved in a major event like this. She did so with intelligence, alacrity, and good humor, all of which bode well for her own future in academia. I also want to thank her for her contribution to this book: She transcribed the question-and-response periods that followed each lecture. And I thank Phillip Schlueter of Trinity Episcopal Cathedral in Portland, Oregon, for his help with the mysteries of the computer as I edited this volume.

Finally, I want to thank all of the people who attended. I would have felt very silly if I had planned this commemoration and nobody had come.

Marcus J. Borg

1

Introduction: Jesus at 2000

MARCUS J. BORG

In these opening remarks given before the first lecture, Marcus Borg, organizer and host of "Jesus at 2000," introduced the symposium. He spoke of the current interest in Jesus in our culture, the reason "Jesus at 2000" occurs in 1996 rather than in 2000, the scope of the symposium, the scholarly approach to the study of Jesus, and what can be said about the birth of Jesus.

I am struck by the fact that so many of us are involved in this event and what this says about Jesus. Here in Corvallis, at Oregon State University, the 1,150 seats in this auditorium were sold out two weeks ago. Thousands more are watching live on television at 312 downlink sites across the country. Never before have so many people taken part in a scholarly discussion of Jesus as a figure of history. We are being covered by both print and broadcast media; and after the symposium there will be a follow-up conference on the Internet, for which many hundreds of people have already signed on. Two thousand years after the birth of Jesus, we are still talking about him.

I am reminded of a dark rainy morning about seven years ago when I was driving to the Portland airport in order to fly twenty-five hundred miles to a meeting of the Jesus Seminar, where, among other things, we were to vote on whether the Lord's Prayer goes back to Jesus himself. As I drove along, I was thinking about the fact that about fifty scholars in other parts of the country were also about to board planes for the same purpose. Then on the morning news from National Public Radio on my car radio, the second lead story was about Jesus–specifically, a report about laboratory tests on the Shroud of Turin, that mysterious piece of cloth that some think was the burial shroud of Jesus. And three days later, the voting we did on the Lord's Prayer was a front-page story in over two hundred newspapers.

The combination of events struck me, just as our being here today strikes me. Jesus still makes headlines. It is remarkable, indeed extraordinary, that

1

2,000 years after he lived, a Jewish peasant from Nazareth continues to be a figure of such towering significance.

What was he like? And why and how did he become the single most important person in the history of Western culture? How does he look to us at the turn of the millennium? These are the questions we are here to explore as we gather to commemorate 2,000 years of Jesus.

Why do this in 1996? Why not in 2000? The reason has to do with the most widely accepted date for Jesus' birth: Namely, according to most scholars, Jesus was born not later than 4 B.C. This sometimes surprises people, for how could Jesus be born four years before Christ? The reason has to do with how our present calendar dividing history into B.C. and A.D. came about. It was calculated in the sixth century by a Christian monk named Dionysius Exiguus, whose name translates into English as "Denny the Dwarf." He did a pretty good job, but given our knowledge, we think his calculations were off by about four years.

And so 1996 is the latest we can do this. Very recently, however, it has been argued that Dionysius was closer than we think and that Jesus was born not later than 1 B.C. If this hypothesis should become widely accepted, we'll just have to do this symposium again in 1999. We could call it "Jesus at 2000 II"; sequels are quite fashionable. In either case, this symposium is part of a national and international conversation about Jesus as the year 2000 draws near.

"Jesus at 2000" occurs at a propitious time and not just because the year 2000 is approaching. For we live in an era of renewed interest in the figure of Jesus, both in the scholarly world and among the general public. In the scholarly world, beginning about 1980, there have been a burst of activity and an explosion of publishing, so that it has now become routine to speak of a renaissance of Jesus scholarship and a renewed quest for the historical Jesus.[1] There is widespread public interest as well. In recent years, serious works of Jesus scholarship have become best-sellers. In the last four years, since 1992, five books by Jesus scholars have been on *Publishers Weekly* top ten best-selling list in religion.[2] The renewed quest for the historical Jesus has put Jesus on the cover of all the major news magazines and has generated a number of television programs (often multiple segment) on several cable networks. This widespread public interest in the scholarly study of Jesus is a striking cultural phenomenon and a fact of considerable importance for the church as well. Let me also note that our symposium occurs at a time when there is vigorous and heated controversy in the discipline about what Jesus was like, about the adequacy or inadequacy of various historical reconstructions, and about whether historical reconstruction should be done at all–whether, in fact, it is a mistake.[3]

Thus, "Jesus at 2000" occurs at a time when the question of Jesus–who he was, what he was about, and what his significance is for Christians and for the human quest for the sacred more generally–has again become center stage. Moreover, as the year 2000 approaches, bringing with it many more commemorations of 2,000 years of Jesus, interest in Jesus can only be expected to intensify.

What can be said about Jesus as he turns 2,000? That is the question we will be addressing during this symposium. We do so as scholars speaking from a variety of scholarly perspectives. We will be talking about what we think we can say about Jesus as a figure of history, what his subsequent significance is in Western culture and religion, and how he looks from the perspective of the world's religions.

The scholarly perspective is a limited one, of course. All of us who will be speaking to you are professors, and we have all spent most of our lives in the academic world. We don't have a Dalai Lama or a Mother Teresa or a Desmond Tutu or a saint among us (though I sometimes wonder about one or two of the speakers). The scholarly perspective is a limited one not just because we professors tend to be teachers rather than saints and thinkers rather than doers. It is also limited by the fact that we all (and not just professors, but everybody) see from our particular vantage point in time and space. That is, all of us are profoundly affected by the fact that we all live in this time and place and not in some other time and place. Our seeing is profoundly shaped by the vantage point from which we see.

One of my favorite ways of making this point comes from British historian E. H. Carr. Although he speaks about historians in particular, what he says applies to all scholars. Carr invites us to imagine history as a moving procession or parade and then to imagine the relationship of the historian to the procession. Where is the historian? Historians, Carr suggests, may be tempted to think of themselves as having a vantage point outside of the parade, as if they were in a reviewing stand observing the procession go by. But the truth is that the historian is in the procession itself. There is no vantage point outside of the procession.[4]

This awareness has a twofold effect. First, it underlines that every perspective is a limited one; there is no such thing as a wholly objective perspective (though some do seem to be "better" than others–but I will not now enter the thorny thicket of explaining that statement). It points to the relativity of all historical knowledge–indeed, of all conceptualized knowing.

But second, this awareness has an interesting side effect. Namely, because the historian is part of the procession, and because the procession twists and turns as it moves along, the historian's angle of vision on the past–his or her vantage point–is constantly changing. And we may see "new things" or "things newly" because of that changing vantage point. Moreover, some angles of vision on the past may be better than others for seeing what was central in a particular past, though it is always hard to know when this is the case. In any event, we are all profoundly affected by having lived in the second half of the twentieth century. We–speakers and audience alike–all see very differently because we are alive now rather than a century ago or a century in the future.

Yet though the scholarly perspective is a limited one, it is also important and illuminating. I am convinced not only that we see differently from how our ancestors saw several generations ago, but also that in some respects we see more clearly. How does Jesus look from a variety of scholarly perspectives in the late twentieth century? What do we think we can say about Jesus 2,000 years down the road?

As I move to a description of my own scholarly perspective, one that is shared at least in a general way by the other speakers at this symposium, I am aware that my way of seeing Jesus is very much the product of the fact that I live in the late twentieth century. My approach is interdisciplinary, a quite recent development in the discipline. Had I been doing my scholarly work forty (or even twenty) years ago, I would not have been aware of it.

My approach is shaped by an awareness of religious pluralism and cultural relativism, an awareness that has intensified for most people as the twentieth century has rolled along. This approach is also very much affected by modern historical consciousness, with its awareness of the distinction between "what happened" and "interpretations of what happened"; its awareness of the historically conditioned and historically relative character of all language, including the New Testament and early Christianity's language about Jesus; and its awareness of the relative character of the historical vantage point itself, including my own. And my approach takes seriously a postmodern image of reality, which in many respects is premodern and very much indebted to Huston Smith's work on the primordial tradition. Moreover, my approach is based on the understanding of the Gospels that has emerged in the last two hundred years of scholarship. This understanding of *the nature of the Gospels* is foundational to much of what we will be saying during this symposium, and so I wish briefly to describe it.

I begin with a simple but crucial statement about the nature of the Gospels: They are the developing traditions of early Christian communities. To explain a bit: The Gospels were put into written form in the last third of the first century (from about 70 to 100 C.E.).[5] During the decades between the death of Jesus and the crystallization of the traditions about Jesus in written form, those traditions continued to develop in a process involving adaptation and growth.[6]

As a developing tradition, the Gospels contain minimally two kinds of material. Some is very early, the gist of it probably going back to Jesus himself; some is later and is the product of the community. To use an archaeological metaphor, the Gospels contain early layers of material and later layers of material. Or to drop the archaeological metaphor and move to another, the Gospels contain minimally two voices: the voice of Jesus and the voice of the community. To speak of two layers or two voices is finally too simple, of course. As in an archaeological dig, there are several layers; and because the voice of the community is, in fact, a collection of voices, there are many voices.

This layered and multivocal understanding of the Gospels is nicely illustrated by the work of the Jesus Seminar. Many of you have heard of the seminar, a group of scholars with whom Dom Crossan and I have been associated for the past decade. We are best known (and have become controversial in some circles) for our process of voting on the historicity of traditions about Jesus.[7] Do we think Jesus really said *x?* Do we think Jesus really did *y?*

We vote by casting one of four differently colored beads (red, pink, gray, or black) in a ballot box. The colors represent a scale of historical judgment: Red means "I think Jesus really said (or did) that"; pink means "Sounds like him"; gray means "Well, maybe"; and black means "This does not go back to Jesus but is the product of the community."

The results of our work have been published in *The Five Gospels,* which prints the sayings of Jesus in four colors corresponding to our voting.[8] The display of gospel texts in four colors illustrates perfectly the image of the Gospels as a developing tradition containing earlier and later layers, the voice of Jesus and the voices of the community. In the judgment of the seminar, passages printed in red are close to the voice of Jesus; passages in pink are still close to the voice of Jesus but are beginning to be shaped by the voice of the community; and passages in black are not the voice of Jesus but are the voice of the community.[9]

This multilayered and multivoiced understanding of the Gospels is not peculiar to the Jesus Seminar but has been the common property of New Testament scholars throughout this century. Indeed, it is the defining characteristic of mainline gospel scholarship, though fundamentalist scholars would reject it.

This view of the nature of the Gospels is foundational for an understanding of the quest for the historical Jesus. The quest involves going back to the earliest layers of the tradition, or, to use the voice metaphor, listening for both the voice of Jesus and the voice of the community. Moreover, both voices are important, for the voice of the community tells us what Jesus had become in the experience of those who followed him.

Finally, though the occasion for "Jesus at 2000" is the 2,000th anniversary of Jesus' birth, our focus is not on his birth in particular. But because his birth does provide the occasion for this event, let me conclude this introduction with some remarks about it.

What can we say historically about the birth of Jesus? Not very much, according to contemporary scholarship. His birth probably occurred shortly before the death of Herod the Great in 4 B.C.E. Jesus was probably born in Nazareth, not in Bethlehem. His parents were Jewish, and their names were Mary and Joseph. Jesus was born into a peasant class.

And that's about all. The reason we can't say more is because of how the birth stories are seen by most mainline scholars.[10] The stories of Jesus' birth are found in only two places in the New Testament: the first two chapters of Matthew and the first two chapters of Luke. The apostle Paul, our earliest New Testament author, all of whose genuine letters were written before any of the Gospels, does not mention Jesus being born in a special way. Neither does Mark, the earliest gospel writer. Indeed, no other New Testament author does.

Moreover, Matthew and Luke each tell the story of Jesus' birth very differently. Without trying to be comprehensive, let me list some of the central differences:

1. Matthew has the story of the star and the wise men. Luke has no star and no wise men; rather, shepherds watching their flocks by night receive the news of the birth.

2. In Matthew, Jesus is born at home (the family lives in Bethlehem). Luke has the famous story of the journey from Nazareth (where the family lives) to Bethlehem and birth in a manger because there is no room in the inn.

3. Matthew has the story of King Herod's slaughter of male babies in the vicinity of Bethlehem in an attempt to kill the newborn king of the Jews and Jesus' family fleeing to Egypt to escape. Luke has no story of a slaughter and no journey to Egypt.

4. In Matthew, the central human character is Joseph; Mary doesn't even have a speaking part. In Luke, Mary is the central human character, and Joseph doesn't speak.

5. Matthew traces the genealogy of Jesus back to Abraham (the father of the Jewish people) and from King David onward, through the kings of Judah. Luke traces Jesus' genealogy back to Adam (the father of the human race) and from King David onward, through the prophets of Israel. Moreover, the differences in the genealogies correspond to central themes of each gospel. Matthew stresses Jesus' significance for the Jewish people and sees Jesus as "the king of the Jews." Luke stresses Jesus' significance for Gentiles as well and presents Jesus as a radical social prophet.

For reasons such as these, mainline scholars have concluded that the birth stories are not historical reports but are late-first-century compositions that function as overtures to the Gospels of which they are a part. To use the language of the Jesus Seminar to report a widely shared conclusion, the birth stories are black material; they are the voice of the community, a later layer of the tradition.

To put this both negatively and positively, the birth stories are not historical reports (that's the negative) but symbolic narratives (that's the positive). The virginal conception, the journey to Bethlehem, the birth in a manger, the shepherds, the star and the wise men, and Herod's slaughter of the infants are not facts of history but images and metaphors used by early Christians to speak about the significance of Jesus.

Yet the images and metaphors of the birth stories are, it seems to me, powerfully true, even though not historically factual. As I sometimes put it, I don't think the virgin birth happened, but I think the stories of the virgin birth are profoundly true. They speak of Jesus as, among other things, the light shining in the winter darkness, indeed, as the light of the world. Or as the gospel of John puts it, "The true light that enlightens everyone was even then coming into the world" (John 1.5). And thus the facts of Jesus' birth are shrouded in the mist of history and refracted to us through image and symbol, metaphor and myth. And here we are, 2,000 years later, remembering that birth.

2

From Galilean Jew to the Face of God: The Pre-Easter and Post-Easter Jesus

MARCUS J. BORG

Marcus Borg is Hundere Distinguished Professor of Religion and Culture in the Philosophy Department at Oregon State University. He is the author of seven books, including Conflict, Holiness, and Politics in the Teachings of Jesus *(1984);* Jesus: A New Vision *(1987);* Meeting Jesus Again for the First Time *(1994);* Jesus in Contemporary Scholarship *(1994); and (with John Dominic Crossan and Stephen Patterson)* The Search for Jesus: Modern Scholarship Looks at the Gospels *(1994). Past chair of the Historical Jesus Section of the Society of Biblical Literature and formerly New Testament columnist for* Bible Review, *he is also a fellow of the Jesus Seminar.*

Educated at Concordia College (Minnesota) and Union Theological Seminary (New York City), his doctoral degree is from Oxford. He has held fellowships from the Rockefeller Foundation, the Danforth Foundation, and the National Endowment for the Humanities. Before coming to Oregon State in 1979, he taught at Concordia College, South Dakota State University, and Carleton College. His wife, Marianne Wells Borg, is a priest and canon at Trinity Episcopal Cathedral in Portland.

In his lecture, Borg introduces both the Jesus of history (the pre-Easter Jesus) and the Jesus of Christian faith (the post-Easter Jesus) and addresses the question "How do we get from the historical Jesus to the second person of the Trinity?" He describes the process as involving both "foundational experience" and "metaphorical development."

The title of my lecture describes the central question it addresses. As a figure of history, Jesus was a Galilean Jew. As the central figure of the Christian tradition, Jesus is "the face of God"–the decisive disclosure of God and, ultimately, in the language of the fourth-century Nicene Creed, the second person of the

Trinity. How did this transformation happen? What was the process whereby a Galilean Jewish peasant became "of one substance" with God?

I begin by commenting on the phrases in the subtitle: *the pre-Easter Jesus* and *the post-Easter Jesus*. The two phrases recognize that the name Jesus has two quite distinct referents, referring to two different realities, even though they are also related to each other. On the one hand, Jesus refers to the pre-Easter Jesus, namely, Jesus of Nazareth, a first-century Galilean Jew. On the other hand, Jesus refers to the post-Easter Jesus, or what Jesus became after Easter, which I need to define more fully.

The post-Easter Jesus is the Jesus of Christian tradition and experience. Both nouns–*tradition* and *experience*–are important. Christian tradition includes the Gospels, the New Testament as a whole, and the Christian creeds of the fourth and fifth centuries. The post-Easter Jesus thus includes "the canonical Jesus" (the Jesus of the New Testament) and "the creedal Jesus"; he is also "the composite Jesus" (the product of adding together everything the Christian tradition says about Jesus). The post-Easter Jesus of Christian *experience* refers to the fact that Jesus continued to be experienced after his death as a living reality, from the first century to the present. The post-Easter Jesus is thus not simply an object of belief but also an element of experience.

To explain the distinction between the pre-Easter and post-Easter Jesus further, I present a comparison list, followed by commentary:

The Pre-Easter Jesus	The Post-Easter Jesus
4 B.C.E. to 30 C.E.	30 C.E. to today
Figure of the past	Figure of the present
Corporeal (flesh and blood)	Spiritual, nonmaterial
Finite/mortal	Infinite/eternal
Human	Divine
A Jewish peasant	King of kings, Lord of lords
Jesus of Nazareth	Jesus Christ

The pre-Easter Jesus was born around 4 B.C.E. and executed by the Romans around 30 C.E.; the post-Easter Jesus is Jesus from the year 30 to the present day. The pre-Easter Jesus is a figure of the past, dead and gone; the post-Easter Jesus is a figure of the present. The pre-Easter Jesus was corporeal, a flesh and blood human being; the post-Easter Jesus is a spiritual reality, actual, even though nonmaterial (a difficult combination of words in the modern world, which tends to identify "the real" or "actual" with material reality). The pre-Easter Jesus was finite and mortal, he was limited as all humans are, and he died. The post-Easter Jesus is infinite and eternal; he is "of one substance" with God, to use a phrase from the Nicene Creed, and as such has the qualities of God. Thus, the pre-Easter Jesus was human; the post-Easter Jesus is divine. The pre-Easter Jesus was a Jewish peasant; the post-Easter Jesus becomes King of kings and Lord of lords. Finally, in common scholarly usage, "Jesus of Nazareth" refers to the pre-Easter Jesus, and "Jesus Christ" refers to the post-Easter Jesus of Christian tradition and experience.

To these distinctions, I wish to add two more in order to underline the main theme of my lecture. The pre-Easter Jesus was a monotheistic Jew; the post-Easter Jesus eventually becomes the second person of the Trinity. The pre-Easter Jesus was a Galilean Jew of the first century; the post-Easter Jesus, to use a phrase from my title, is the face of God, a metaphor based in part on Paul's language in 1 Corinthians 4.6. There Paul speaks of beholding "the glory of God in the face of Christ." The metaphor also alludes to Trinitarian thought, in which the second person of the Trinity is God with a human face so that Jesus is the face of God.

Now, how do we get from the pre-Easter Jesus to the post-Easter Jesus? How do we get from a monotheistic Jew to the second person of the Trinity? How do we get from a Galilean Jewish peasant to the face of God? These are the central questions that this lecture addresses.

The Pre-Easter Jesus

Because much of my published work concerns this figure, I content myself here with two compact summaries. The first is my seventy-five-second summary, and I want to tell you how it came about. In 1995 I was invited to be on NBC's *Today Show* on Good Friday. The subject, of course, was Jesus. The producer told me, "We have a big chunk of time—we have a really long segment." I asked, "How long?" She said, "Seven minutes."

That seven minutes rapidly shrank. Two minutes would be used for a video introduction featuring Jesus in the history of art, half a minute would be taken up with comments by the host, and the remaining time was to be divided between two of us (the other scholar was John Meier of Catholic University in Washington, D.C., author of an important multivolume study of Jesus entitled *A Marginal Jew*).[1] I was told what my first questions would be "Well, what would it have been like to have been a companion of Jesus? What was he like?" My time limit: I could have up to seventy-five seconds to respond. And I was told that the average viewing audience was 5 million people.

So I asked myself, "What is my seventy-five-second summary of Jesus? What does one say to 5 million people in seventy-five seconds about Jesus?" I worked very hard on an answer, as if I were scripting a telegram about Jesus. I timed the summary over and over again, finally reducing it to seventy-one seconds. Then the task became memorizing it and yet speaking conversationally so that I sounded as if I were thoughtfully making up a reply as I spoke. On the show itself (which is done live—no opportunity for editing or retakes), I was ready and primed, my carefully memorized response on the tip of my tongue. The host turned to me and said (and remember what my question was going to be), "Well, I imagine that there's a lot that the Bible doesn't tell us about Jesus." I was startled; I thought, "That's not my question!" I wondered what to do—I didn't think I could simply give the response I had rehearsed as if I hadn't heard her question. But making something up on the spot and sim-

ply "winging" it on national television in front of 5 million people seemed per-
ilous; moreover, I didn't think the host's observation was very interesting. So
what I said was, "Yes, that's true, but what it does tell us is very interesting"–
and then went into my prepared response, which I now share with you:

> Jesus was a peasant, which tells us about his social class. Clearly, he was brilliant.
> His use of language was remarkable and poetic, filled with images and stories. He
> had a metaphoric mind. He was not an ascetic; he was world affirming, with a
> zest for life. There was a sociopolitical passion to him–like a Gandhi or a Martin
> Luther King, he challenged the domination system of his day. He was a religious
> ecstatic, a Jewish mystic, if you will, for whom God was an experiential reality. As
> such, Jesus was also a healer. And there seems to have been a spiritual presence
> around him, like that reported of Saint Francis or the present Dalai Lama. And I
> suggest that as a figure of history, Jesus was an ambiguous figure–you could expe-
> rience him and conclude that he was insane, as his family did, or that he was sim-
> ply eccentric or that he was a dangerous threat–or you could conclude that he
> was filled with the Spirit of God.

So that's my seventy-five-second summary. My second compact summary
is one that I have developed in several books: a five-stroke sketch of the pre-
Easter Jesus, with a crucial prologue.[2] As for the prologue: Jesus was a deeply
Jewish figure. Not only was he born and socialized as a Jew, but he also remained Jewish all his life. He did not intend to found a new religion. This
doesn't mean that Christianity is a mistake, but it's not what Jesus had in
mind; rather, he saw himself as doing something within Judaism.

This realization is critically important for two reasons. First, we will not understand much about Jesus if we don't see his Jewishness. Second, Western
culture has witnessed a long, brutal history of anti-Semitism, fueled in part by
a Christian tendency to set Jesus and Judaism against each other–to see "the
Jews" as having rejected Jesus and even holding the Jews responsible for the
death of Jesus.[3]

But historically, that's not the way it happened. The early followers of Jesus
were all Jewish; indeed, all of the authors of the New Testament, with the possible exception of Luke-Acts, were Jewish. Thus, it was not the Jews who rejected Jesus but a narrow circle of the Jewish ruling elites, which, far from representing the Jewish people, are better understood as the oppressors of the
vast majority of the Jewish people in the first century.

To turn now to my five-stroke sketch of the pre-Easter Jesus, each stroke is
a category drawn from the history of religions, that is, from the cross-cultural
study of religions. Each stroke is a religious personality type known in various
religious traditions, as well as in the Jewish tradition. This way of seeing Jesus,
it seems to me, enables us to come up with a reasonably comprehensive
gestalt of the historical Jesus.

1. Jesus was a Spirit person. That is my phrase for a person who has frequent and vivid experiences of the sacred, of God, of the Spirit. Such people are religious ecstatics who in nonordinary states of consciousness have experiences that seem overwhelmingly to them to be experiences of the sacred, of God.
2. Jesus was a healer. The historical evidence that Jesus performed paranormal healings is very strong. Moreover, more healing stories are told about him than about any other figure in the Jewish tradition. He must have been a remarkable healer.
3. Jesus was a wisdom teacher. Wisdom concerns the question "How shall I live?" Broadly speaking, wisdom comes in two forms: conventional and unconventional. Jesus was a teacher of the latter–an unconventional wisdom that challenged the conventional wisdom of his world and, indeed, of every world. Like Socrates, Jesus was a teacher of a culturally subversive wisdom according to which the unexamined life is not worth living. Like the Buddha, Jesus was an enlightened one who taught a subversive and alternative wisdom, the way that in his time, like our own time, was, and is, the road less traveled.
4. Jesus was a social prophet like the great social prophets of the Hebrew Bible. There are thus a political edge and a passion to Jesus. Like Amos, Micah, and Jeremiah, Jesus challenged the domination system of his day, a hierarchical and oppressive social order with sharp social boundaries ruled over by a small class of urban elites.[4] He not only challenged that system; he also had an alternative social vision.
5. Finally, Jesus was a movement initiator, by which I mean that a movement came into existence around him during his lifetime. Moreover, the practice and shape of his movement were not accidental; they were a deliberate embodiment of his alternative social vision, one that was inclusive and egalitarian.

To comment briefly about my sketch in relationship to contemporary scholarship, the greatest areas of agreement–a virtual consensus–would be Jesus as wisdom teacher and healer. Next would be social prophet and movement initiator. Last would be Spirit person, about which there is not really disagreement but mostly silence.

The Post-Easter Jesus

Christian claims about the post-Easter Jesus are extraordinary in character. In the Nicene Creed of 325 C.E., recited by Christians throughout the centuries to the present day, Jesus is spoken of in the most exalted way:

We believe in one Lord, Jesus Christ, the only Son of God, eternally begotten of the Father, God from God, Light from Light, true God from true God, begotten, not made, of one Being (substance) with the Father. Through him all things were made. For us and for our salvation he came down from heaven; by the power of the Holy Spirit he became incarnate from the Virgin Mary, and was made man. For our sake he was crucified under Pontius Pilate; he suffered death and was buried. On the third day he rose again in accordance with the Scriptures; he ascended into heaven and is seated at the right hand of the Father. He will come again to judge the living and the dead, and his kingdom will have no end.

The extravagance of Christian language about Jesus strikes me whenever I sing the great hymns of Christmas and Advent. Listen to these affirmations about Jesus from many different centuries. From the late 300s, here are lines from the hymn "Of the Father's Love Begotten":

> Of the father's love begotten, ere the worlds began to be;
> he is Alpha and Omega, he the source, the ending he,
> Of the things that are, that have been,
> and that future years shall see, evermore and evermore.

From the 1800s, hear again the third verse of "Silent Night":

> Silent night, holy night,
> Son of God, love's pure light
> Radiant beams from thy holy face,
> with the dawn of redeeming grace
> Jesus Lord at thy birth,
> Jesus Lord at thy birth.

From the 1700s comes the second verse of "Hark the Herald Angels Sing":

> Christ, by highest heaven adored; Christ the everlasting Lord;
> Late in time behold him come, offspring of the virgin's womb.
> Veiled in flesh the Godhead see, hail the incarnate deity.
> Pleased as man with us to dwell, Jesus our Immanuel.
> Hark the herald angels sing! Glory to the newborn king.

The transition from the pre-Easter Jesus to the post-Easter Jesus—from a monotheistic Galilean Jewish peasant to one who is praised as Lord, King, and God incarnate—is momentous. How did this happen?

The explanation I find most persuasive requires that I talk about foundational experience and metaphorical and conceptual development. This is the intellectual framework for what follows, derived from Paul Ricoeur's very useful understanding of religious language. Put most succinctly, foundational experience is primary, and metaphorical expression and conceptual development follow. Metaphor (which I understand comprehensively to include symbol, images, and myth) is thus the first language of religious experience. Conceptual thought (including doctrinal development) is the second language, the product of systematic reflection on both the experience and the metaphors generated by the experience.

Foundational Experience

The foundational experience that initiated the transformation from Jesus as a Galilean Jew to Jesus as the face of God and the second person of the Trinity was Easter. By Easter, I do not mean a particular day or an experience confined to a few weeks after the death of Jesus. By Easter, I mean most centrally and simply that the followers of Jesus continued to experience him as a living reality after his death, but in a radically new way. Namely, they experienced him as being a spiritual, nonmaterial reality and, increasingly in the years and decades after his death, as having the qualities of God. (I return to the foundational experience of Easter near the end of this lecture.)

Metaphorical and Conceptual Development

In the beginning was metaphor. More exactly, in the beginning was a multiplicity of metaphors. In the years and decades after Easter, a number of metaphors or images for speaking about Jesus emerged within the Jesus movement. Without seeking to be comprehensive, I list the following: Jesus as the servant of God, lamb of God, light of the world, bread of life, door, vine, shepherd, great high priest, Son of God, Wisdom of God, and Word of God. Over time these metaphors became the subject of intellectual reflection and were abstracted and systematized into a conceptual framework. Some of this abstraction ultimately became doctrine. This whole process is what I mean by metaphorical and conceptual development.

JESUS AS SON OF GOD

What became the dominant way of speaking about Jesus in the Christian tradition—Jesus as Son of God—provides an excellent illustration of this process. Son of God began as a relational metaphor. Within Judaism by the time of Jesus, it had a number of meanings. In the Hebrew Bible, it could be used to refer to the king on the day of his coronation: "You are my son; today I have begotten you" (Ps. 2.7). It could also be used to refer to Israel as a whole: "When Israel was a child, I loved him, and out of Egypt I called my son" (Hos. 11.1). According to Jewish traditions near the time of Jesus, this metaphor could be used to refer to other Jewish Spirit persons. What all of these have in common—the king, Israel, a Spirit person—is a relationship of intimacy with God.

Thus, initially, to call Jesus Son of God was to speak of an intimacy of relationship between Jesus and God. As Son of God developed in early Christian tradition, it moved from being a relational metaphor to being a biological metaphor in the birth stories in Matthew and Luke. In these stories, Jesus is conceived by the Spirit and, if the texts are read literally, is Son of God by virtue of having a divine father rather than a human father. Then Son of God became conceptualized. Specifically, to call Jesus Son of God became an ontological and doctrinal statement about the ultimate status of Jesus, reaching its climax in the Nicene Creed. There, in the language of fourth-century Christian theology, with strong undercurrents of Hellenistic philosophy, Jesus is spoken of as the "only begotten Son of God," "true God of true God," and "of one substance as the Father." Metaphor became doctrine.

A second way to illustrate the claim that Son of God as a phrase applied to Jesus went through a process of development is to ask what may seem like an odd question: When did Jesus become Son of God? Most scholars do not think that Jesus of Nazareth spoke or thought of himself as the Son of God; that was a post-Easter development. So if speaking of Jesus as Son of God didn't begin with Jesus, when did it begin?

A process of development can be seen in the New Testament itself. What may be traces of very early Christian tradition suggest that Jesus became Son of God at Easter. In the mid-50s (and perhaps reporting an earlier tradition), Paul wrote of Jesus as "descended from David according to the flesh, and designated Son of God in power by his resurrection from the dead" (Rom. 1.3–4). An echo of early tradition may also be found in a sermon in Acts in which Peter reportedly said, "This Jesus whom you crucified, God has made both Lord and Christ" (Acts 2.36). Here God made Jesus "both Lord and Christ" *after* his crucifixion.

As the New Testament developed, Jesus' status as Son of God was pushed further and further back into his life. According to Mark, our earliest gospel, Jesus at his baptism heard a voice declaring him to be the Son of God. According to Matthew and Luke, written some twenty years later, Jesus was Son of God from his conception. And in the first chapter of John, that which became incarnate in Jesus was "from the beginning." Thus, Jesus' status as Son of God was finally pushed back into the time before his life. Again we see the process whereby Son of God undergoes a development that moves from metaphor to ontological claim.

JESUS AS WISDOM/SOPHIA OF GOD

Son of God was only one of several metaphors used for Jesus in the post-Easter life of the Jesus movement. Among the others was Jesus as "the Wisdom of God." The phrase can also be translated as "the Sophia of God" because *sophia* is the Greek word for "wisdom." Jesus as the Wisdom/Sophia of God has received much scholarly attention in the last two decades and has recently generated controversy in some segments of the church.

The background of the metaphor is Jewish wisdom literature from before the time of Jesus. In this literature (including Proverbs, Sirach, and the Wisdom of Solomon), Sophia is a female personification for the Wisdom of God. She is brought into the closest possible relationship to God and is sometimes a female image for the divine.

The Gospels and Paul use Sophia language to speak about Jesus. They call him the child of Sophia, the prophet of Sophia, or even the Sophia of God, the incarnation of divine Sophia. Jesus as the Wisdom/Sophia of God was a very early and widespread christological metaphor.[5]

Moreover, the image of Jesus as the Wisdom or Sophia of God is not found only in the very early period of Christianity. Saint Augustine, writing around the year 400, says this about Sophia and Jesus: "She [Sophia] was sent in one way that she might be with human beings; and she has been sent another way that *she herself might be a human being*."[6] The reference, of course, is to Jesus.

If Augustine, not typically seen as a feminist, can speak of Jesus as the incarnation of Sophia, then why is this terminology such an issue for some people in our time? I think one reason for the controversy is that many people take Son of God literally, as if it's not a metaphor but the only really correct way of speaking about Jesus. To them, Son of God and Wisdom/Sophia of God seem like competitive terms, as if Jesus as the Sophia of God is meant to replace Son of God. But Son of God and Wisdom of God are both metaphors for Jesus; properly understood, they do not compete with each other but complement each other.

To return to the main point: We get from Galilean Jew to the face of God through this process of metaphorical and conceptual development. Very important, this process should not be seen as wrong. The process of experience giving birth to metaphors that give birth to concepts is very natural. Moreover, even the full doctrinal expression of Jesus as Son of God in the Nicene Creed continues to reflect early Christian experience. Namely, experiences of the post-Easter Jesus as divine made a doctrine such as the Trinity necessary. How, within the framework of monotheism (which Christians shared with Judaism), could one do justice to the experience of the post-Easter Jesus as a divine reality? One can do so only by affirming that God and Jesus are, in an important sense, one. Otherwise, after Easter there are two gods: God and Jesus. Thus, the Trinity is the conceptual attempt to reconcile monotheism with the Christian experience of Jesus as divine. We grasp the meaning of the Trinity most adequately when we keep it as close as possible to the experience in which it has its origins.[7]

Easter: The Foundational Experience

What can we say about Easter—about what happened, about its meaning, about Easter as the experience of Jesus as a living reality, as a figure of the present and not just the past, as a spiritual, nonmaterial reality who is one with

God? Just as William James spoke almost a century ago of the varieties of religious experience,[8] so I think we should speak of the varieties of Easter experiences. Clearly, there were visions, vivid, subjective experiences of momentarily
seeing the risen Jesus. John of Patmos, the author of Revelation, speaks of having had one. Paul, according to both the book of Acts and his own letters, had
one or more experiences of seeing the risen Jesus. According to Acts, they
were visions involving light (what William James calls "photisms") and an au-
dition (a voice). Alan Segal, one of our speakers today, argues persuasively in
his very important study of Paul that Paul's experience of the risen Jesus belongs to the category of Jewish mysticism.[9]

In the varieties of Easter experience, I also include the kind of experience
that Dom Crossan talks about: After the death of Jesus, his followers continued to experience the kind of power at work that they had come to know
through him. Jesus could also be spoken of as a presence known in the ongoing activity of the Spirit, in the community, and in the breaking of the bread.

It is these kinds of experiences that gave rise to the claim that Jesus after his
death continued to live as a divine reality. Thus, in my judgment Easter need
not involve an empty tomb or anything happening to the physical body of
Jesus. Some scholars disagree. For example, N. Thomas Wright, a scholar
poised on the edge of becoming the most important British New Testament
scholar of his generation, and also a good friend, argues that the truth of
Christianity depends upon whether the tomb was really empty. Wright is not
a fundamentalist but a mainline scholar with conservative-evangelical leanings.[10] So I want to recognize disagreement among scholars even as I say, "I
don't think that's what Easter, or the resurrection, is about."

Why do I not think that? A major reason is the crucial distinction between
resuscitation and resurrection: Resuscitation intrinsically involves something
happening to a corpse, but resurrection in a first-century Jewish and early
Christian context need not. Resurrection means entry into a different kind of
existence, not resumption of a previous existence. Moreover, I don't think the
Easter stories report videocam kinds of events. That is, I don't think they're
speaking about experiences that would have been observable by a disinter-
ested observer; I don't think they could have been filmed.

My favorite story for making this point (indeed, my favorite Easter story) is
the story of the Emmaus road (Luke 24.13–35). The story is familiar to many
of you. Two followers of Jesus are walking on the road to Emmaus on the day
that we call Easter Sunday. They are joined by a stranger, whom we as the
readers know to be the risen Jesus. But they don't know that. The stranger
asks them, "What are you talking about?" They turn to him and say, "Are you
the only person who doesn't know what's been happening these last few
days?" They then tell him. The three of them continue to talk as they walk together for some hours. Yet they still don't recognize him. As they draw near
the village, the stranger begins to leave. They say to him, in wonderfully
evocative words, "Stay with us, for it is evening, and the day is far spent."

Stay with us, for night is falling; the verse is the basis for the great Christian hymn "Abide with Me, Fast Falls the Eventide." The stranger agrees to do so. As they sit at table for the evening meal, the stranger "took bread, blessed and broke it, and gave it to them." *Then*, we are told, "their eyes were opened, and they recognized him."

Then what happens? "He vanished from their sight."

Now with a videocam, how much of this could have been filmed? My strong hunch is that it's not that kind of story. Rather, it strikes me as a metaphorical or symbolic narrative that points beyond itself rather than reporting a specific event that happened on a particular day. Dom Crossan's analysis of this text reaches a similar conclusion: The story of the Emmaus road is "the metaphoric condensation of the first years of Christian thought into one parabolic afternoon." Crossan follows this statement with two short sentences that make the point perfectly: "Emmaus never happened. Emmaus always happens."[11] Emmaus happens again and again. Or, to echo the title of one of my books, Emmaus is a story about meeting Jesus again for the first time.

To speak as a Christian about this story, the truth of the Emmaus road story is that the risen Christ journeys with us whether we know it or not. Yet there are moments when we do become aware of his presence. Moreover, this foundational experience continues to this day. This, it seems to me, is the truth of Easter. The truth of Easter is grounded not in whether the tomb was empty but in the ongoing experience of Jesus as a living reality, as a figure of the present.

As I conclude, I want to return to the pre-Easter Jesus, to the Jesus who was born 2,000 years ago. I want to suggest that for some of his followers even during his lifetime, the pre-Easter Jesus was a manifestation of the sacred, God with a human face. They may have experienced the sacred in his healing powers, in his compassion, and in a spiritual presence that we may imagine they sometimes felt in and around him. Although I cannot demonstrate that the foundational experience of Jesus as a manifestation of the sacred went back, for some of his followers, into his lifetime, it seems intrinsically probable to me. Ultimately, it is this experience of Jesus, whether pre-Easter or post-Easter, as a manifestation of the divine that accounts for this Galilean Jew becoming the face of God.

Questions and Responses from the Symposium

Q: You said that the stories of Jesus' birth are powerfully true and yet not historical fact. How can that be?

A: I don't equate truth with historical truth. In this respect, I am like the Native American storyteller who begins his tribe's story of creation by saying, "Now I don't know if it happened this way or not, but I know this story is true." Not only can the language of metaphor and myth state profound truths, but I think it is also the only way one can really talk about the sacred. Moreover, it's primarily in the post-Enlightenment period (from about the 1700s) that we have developed a fixation about "truth" being "factual truth" or "empirical truth."

Q: If you remove the divinity from Christ, don't you remove the only thing that is unique about Christianity and deny the reason for its existence?

A: I see the post-Easter Jesus as fully divine. So the real question is about the pre-Easter Jesus: If one doesn't affirm that he was divine, does Christianity lose its uniqueness? Maybe it does. But for me, that's a gain. If I had to believe that Christianity is unique in the sense of being the only adequate revelation of God, I could not be a Christian. The claim that God is known only in one religious tradition, which fortunately just happens to be our own, is a product of Christian provincialism. Our ancestors not many generations back lived in a completely Christian world and had no awareness of religious pluralism. There's a natural human tendency to think that one's own group and one's own tradition are the best ones.

I do speak of the pre-Easter Jesus as a manifestation of the sacred: There were moments when his followers experienced him as the presence of the sacred in their midst. But I don't see the pre-Easter Jesus as divine in the same sense that I see the post-Easter Jesus as divine.

Q: You have affirmed the healing miracles of Jesus. What about the nature miracles, such as walking on the water, feeding a crowd with a few loaves of bread, and changing water into wine?

A: In common with the majority of mainline scholars, I see the nature miracles as not historical, but as symbolic narratives. Symbolic narratives can be powerfully true, as in the case of the birth stories.

I think the point of the bread stories is that Jesus is (as John's gospel puts it) the bread of life. Jesus (the post-Easter Jesus) is the spiritual food who nourishes us in the midst of our journeys even now, just as ancient Israel was nourished by manna from the sky during its journey through the wilderness. The story of Jesus coming to his disciples by walking on the sea while they are in a boat at night, in distress and threatened by a storm, affirms that the risen Christ comes to his followers in the midst of difficulty. Regarding Jesus changing water into wine at the wedding at Cana: This story is the first public act of Jesus in John's gospel. It is the author's way of saying, "The story of Jesus is about a wedding feast at which the wine never runs out." That's nicely provocative.

Q: How is your position received by the average person in the pew?

A: To oversimplify, I find two responses to my work among Christians. Our fundamentalist and conservative-evangelical brothers and sisters, numbering in the millions, largely reject what I and my colleagues say. The reason is a foundationally different understanding of the Bible and a fear that if you look at it this way, the whole thing falls apart. I don't think that's the case, but that's where the rejection comes from.

But there is another group of Christians, also numbering in the millions, many in main-line churches, some on its fringes, and some who have left because at some point it didn't make sense anymore. Among that group, the reception is extremely positive and encouraging. My mail and my experiences lecturing on the road suggest that there's an enormous appetite among many mainline Christians for a way of thinking about the Christian tradition that makes sense without ripping the guts out of it.

Q: Do you see the Easter experience as an affirmation of how Jesus lived and died?
A: Yes. Within the early Christian movement, Easter was seen as God's vindication of Jesus, as God's "yes" to Jesus after the rulers of this world had said "no" to Jesus. Thus, Easter is a vindication of how Jesus lived, as well as an overturning of how he died: As God's "yes" to Jesus, it is also God's "no" to the domination systems of this world.

Q: Do you believe that the pre-Easter Jesus believed in the doctrine of original sin?
A: No. The notion of original sin is much later, a fourth- and fifth-century develop-ment. Moreover, Jesus himself said very little about sins; his own passion was not about individual sins that needed to be forgiven or atoned for. Instead, as a wisdom teacher he focused on an alternative way of seeing, and as a social prophet he in-dicted the domination system of his time. Sin and forgiveness as the central dynamic of the Christian life are later.

Q: We tend to emphasize the post-Easter Jesus. Would you suggest some of the power-ful things that we gain by rediscovering the pre-Easter Jesus, the Jewish peasant of subversive wisdom and practice? How might that help this age, whose institutional-ized forms of faith need to be prickled by the powerful and pungent images coming from this peasant with a passion for inclusive justice?
A: You're right: In the history of the church, there has been a much greater emphasis on the post-Easter Jesus than on the pre-Easter Jesus or a blending of the two so that the pre-Easter Jesus virtually disappears. To crystallize compactly some of what I have said about the potential significance of the pre-Easter Jesus in my books, the historical Jesus is a challenge to the modern world and the modern church. He is a powerful testimony to the actuality of the sacred as an experiential reality in an age that has grown skeptical or that tends to think of God as a remote supernatural being "out there." Jesus' alternative wisdom subverts the notion that life is based on requirements and rewards, including forms of the Christian message that say, "Here's what you must do to be saved." Jesus was a deeply sociopolitical figure; tak-ing him seriously would shape our politics and engender a passion for social justice.

Q: In the birth stories, Joseph seems less secure that he is the father of Jesus than mod-ern scholars are. Is it possible that Mary was "compromised," but like other women in the Bible (for example, Tamar in Genesis 38), God used her situation for a divine purpose?
A: Some of you may know Jane Schaberg's *The Illegitimacy of Jesus,* a fine scholarly book that argues that Joseph probably wasn't the father and that Mary was probably the victim of rape. I consider that possible. That is, I take it for granted that either

Joseph was the father or some unknown man was the father. But my own hunch is that Joseph probably was and that the story of Joseph's hesitancy about marrying Mary is not historical fact but is generated by the story of the virgin birth.

Q: According to a Muslim tradition, Jesus survived the cross and went to eastern Asia, where he gathered and taught the ten lost tribes of Israel. What do you think?

A: Stories like this, found in many traditions, misunderstand the meaning of resurrection. They take it as if it means a return to the conditions of normal life. Moreover, these stories are late and seem to reflect the interesting fact that lots of people say, "You know, he was here, too."

Q: I'm wondering about the physical ways in which the resurrected Jesus is portrayed. In John 20–21, "doubting Thomas" is invited to feel the wounds of Jesus, and then Jesus and the disciples dined on bread and fish.

A: As the resurrection stories develop, they begin to include physical details, such as the ones you mentioned. Some of this is because the writers are seeking to express in the language of time and space something that is on the border of the ineffable.

About Thomas: When I was growing up, there was only one thing worse than being a Judas, and that was to be a doubting Thomas; he was virtually a villain. But that's not what the story says. What Thomas desired was his own authentic experience of the risen Christ. There is no condemnation of Thomas in the story. His desire was granted, but I don't imagine that story as the kind that one could have captured on a videotape.

Q: What is the relation between your religious practice and your conclusions about Jesus?

A: I am a deeply committed Christian, raised as a Lutheran and now an Episcopalian. I go to church, receive the Eucharist, say the Nicene Creed, and do so without needing to cross my fingers. For me, the historical study of Jesus and Christian origins has made it possible to be a Christian again.

3

Jesus and the Kingdom: Itinerants and Householders in Earliest Christianity

JOHN DOMINIC CROSSAN

John Dominic Crossan is the premier Jesus scholar in the world today. Author of six-teen books, three of his most recent ones have been on Publishers Weekly *top-ten best-seller list in religion:* The Historical Jesus: The Life of a Mediterranean Jewish Peasant *(1991);* Jesus: A Revolutionary Biography *(1994); and* Who Killed Jesus? Exposing the Roots of Anti-Semitism in the Gospel Story of the Death of Jesus *(1995). Cochair of the controversial Jesus Seminar, he is also chair of the Historical Jesus Section of the Society of Biblical Literature. Often featured in na-tional magazines and on television, he has been on hundreds of radio talk shows, in-cluding twice on National Public Radio's* Fresh Air *with Terry Gross.*

Born in Ireland, he moved to the United States at age seventeen to pursue his edu-cation as a Roman Catholic Servite monk and priest. He returned to Ireland for his doctoral degree and did postdoctoral studies at the Pontifical Biblical Institute in Rome and the École Biblique in Jerusalem. He then returned to the United States and taught at DePaul University from 1969 until his retirement in 1995.

Crossan is known for his interdisciplinary approach to the study of Jesus and his emphasis on the peasant class of Jesus, both of which are reflected in this lecture. The lecture begins with a sketch of the social world of Jesus as disclosed by cultural an-thropology, history, and archaeology. Crossan then speaks about Jesus and the King-dom of God as seen in two of Jesus' most characteristic actions: open commensality (inclusive eating) and free healing. He then moves beyond the historical Jesus to de-scribe the relationship between the itinerant followers of Jesus and settled household-ers in the first century. How were the radical teachings of Jesus to be adapted to peo-ple who continued to live settled lives?

The study of the historical Jesus, now over two hundred years old, has usually been described in terms of finding the Jesus of history rather than the Christ of faith. In the 1906 classic *The Quest of the Historical Jesus,* Albert Schweitzer surveyed the progress of this search up to that time. He distinguished two types of searchers, and his distinction is still valid. There were, first, the dogmahaters, the antitheological ones, the Jesus of history *versus* the Christ of faith group whose "hate sharpened their historical insight. They advanced the study of the subject more than all the others put together." There were, second, the dogma-lovers, the protheological ones, the Jesus of history *equals* the Christ of faith group "who found it a cruel task to be honest. . . . It was fortunate for those men that their sympathies sometimes obscured their critical vision, so that, without becoming insincere, they were able to take white clouds for distant mountains."[1]

For myself, I never formulate the question in terms of the Jesus of history and the Christ of faith. Instead, I formulate the question like this: What did the historical Jesus do and say in the late 20s of that first common-era century that made some people say, "He is criminal; we must execute him," and others say, "He is divine; we must follow him"? How could people look at the same Jesus and judge so divergently? If one cannot explain both those simultaneous reactions, one cannot explain the Jesus who was historically an object of condemnation for some and of adoration for others. That formulation avoids the Jesus/Christ dichotomy, with its twin extremes of pro- or antidogma, theology, or faith that simply skew the discussion in opposite ways.

In this essay, therefore, I begin with a review of my own methodology for historical Jesus research, go on to summarize the vision and program of the historical Jesus reconstructed through that method, and conclude by watching that program at work in one strand of the Christian tradition after his execution—namely, in the relationship between Jesus' itinerant followers and householders who became part of early Christianity.

Method and Model

The methodology I use in historical Jesus research is interdisciplinary and interactive. It involves a four-layer stratification building upward from cross-cultural anthropology, through Jewish history and Galilean archaeology, into the earliest Christian literature. Imagine those layers like transparent overlays laid one upon another so that the one below always shows through and relates to those above just as they relate to it.

Anthropology

My basic layer is not just anthropology but *cross-cultural* anthropology. If I applied an anthropological study of the Irish peasantry under British imperialism in the eighteenth century to the Jewish peasantry under Roman imperialism in the first century, the study could easily be dismissed as irrelevant or invalid.

But *cross-cultural* anthropology derives its broad generalizations from as many situations and locations as possible, and it seeks testable validity across time and place. How do empires and colonies, aristocrats and peasants, exploitation and collaboration, class and gender, usually operate across human history and recorded time? Cross-cultural anthropology produces not immutable laws but global tendencies against which each particular case must be studied, and cross-cultural anthropology must itself be restudied against such individual examples. From cross-cultural anthropology, then, I take two main elements to constitute the fundamental stratum of my interdisciplinary model.

EMPIRE AND PEASANT

The first element combines Gerhard Lenski's analysis of agrarian empires with John Kautsky's division of them into traditional agrarian or commercialized agrarian empires.[2] I term this element the *Lenski-Kautsky model*, and I accept it as no more and no less than it is—namely, a general scenario within which and against which individual contexts and particular players must be described and delineated in all their specific uniqueness. Both authors agree that the Roman Empire in the first common-era century was a commercialized agrarian empire. An *agrarian empire* is characterized by inventions such as the wheel, sail, harnessed animal power, basic metallurgy, and, above all, the iron plow, which produces both huge agricultural productivity and huge social inequality. The peasants produce much more but still live at subsistence level, while the elites now live at far greater levels of luxury. In agrarian empires, for example, 1–2 percent of the population take 50–65 percent of the agricultural productivity. A *commercialized* agrarian empire does not involve business instead of land (that would come only much later) but rather business as well as land for major capital creation. Put bluntly: In a traditional agrarian empire, the aristocracy takes the *surplus* from the peasantry; in a commercializing agrarian empire, the aristocracy takes the *land* from the peasantry. The former devours the peasantry's industry and productivity; the latter, the peasantry's very identity and dignity. Commercialization moves peasants in increasing numbers down the terrible slope from small freeholder, to tenant farmer, to day laborer, to beggar or bandit.

The major advantage of Kautsky's distinction has to do with peasant resistance, revolts, rebellions, uprisings, and revolutions. His thesis is that such events pertain much more to commercialized than to traditional agrarian empires. Land in a traditional agrarian empire is a familial inheritance to be retained by the peasantry. Land in a commercialized agrarian empire is an entrepreneurial commodity to be exploited by the aristocracy. The method is not so much theft as debt, with inevitable land expropriation as debtors become insolvents and mortgages become foreclosures.

Peasant society includes within it not only farmers but also artisans and even fishers. It is quite clear from Lenski that a peasant artisan is lower, not higher, in social class than a peasant farmer. "In most agrarian societies, the artisan class was originally recruited from the ranks of the dispossessed peasantry and their noninheriting sons and was continually replenished from these sources. . . . [But] despite the substantial overlap between the wealth and income of the peasant and artisan classes, the median income of artisans apparently was not so great as that of peasants."[3] That same point is emphasized in the definition of peasantry given by Teodor Shanin. He mentions four points: family farm, land husbandry, traditional culture, and "expropriation of its 'surpluses' by powerful outsiders," but among the peasantry's "major marginal groups" are farmless laborers and "rural craftsmen."[4] George Foster similarly includes in his definition of peasant not only agriculturists but also "other small-scale producers, such as fishermen and rural craftsmen." The reason for this inclusion is his insistence that "like most anthropologists, we agree that peasants are primarily agriculturalists, but we also believe that the criteria of definition must be structural and relational rather than occupational. For in most peasant societies, significant numbers of people earn their livings from nonagricultural occupations. It is not *what* peasants produce that is significant; it is *how* and *to whom* they dispose of what they produce that counts." And that structural relationship is not a very benign one. "Peasants are not only poor, as has often been pointed out, but they are relatively powerless. . . . Peasants know that control over them is held in some mysterious fashion by superior powers, usually residing in cities. . . . It is noteworthy, too, that whatever the form of control held by the elite, they usually drain off most of the economic surplus a peasant creates, beyond the necessity for a bare subsistence living and for local religious expenditures."[5]

As I use the term *peasant,* therefore, it always includes rural farmers, rural artisans, and rural fishers as long as that structural relationship of appropriated surplus is maintained over them by retainer and aristocrat, palace and temple, city and empire. Peasant, from Lenski and Kautsky through Shanin and Foster, is a relational or interactional term. It is not simply a romantic or nostalgic word for rural dwellers, let alone a polite term for rustic, yokel, or country bumpkin. It is, quite simply, a description of a rural and exploited producer.

CLASS AND GENDER

A major weakness of the Lenski-Kautsky model has been pointed out by Marianne Sawicki.[6] Its focus is exclusively on class without any account taken of gender. It is not adequate simply to add on gender distinctions but rather to let *both* class and gender variables interact equally and see how each changes the other. How, for example, does power appear within the *peasantry* when class is crossed with gender? What happens when we talk of power for *peasant women* as distinct from that for peasant men? If, in other words, male anthropologists are basically correct on peasant class, what happens when feminist anthropologists ask questions about peasant gender?

Susan Carol Rogers has focused on that precise problem. She argues, in a first article, that,

> although peasant males monopolize positions of authority and are shown public deference by women, thus superficially appearing to be dominant, they wield relatively little real power. Theirs is a largely powerless authority, often accompanied by a felt sense of powerlessness, both in the face of the world at large and of the peasant community itself. On the other hand, within the context of peasant society, women control at least the major portion of important resources and decisions. In other words, if we limit our investigation to the relative actual power of peasant men and women, eliminating for the moment those sources of power from the outside world which are beyond the reach of either peasant men or women, women appear to be generally more powerful. At the same time, the "symbolic" power of men should not be underestimated, nor can it be left unexplained.

Granted, then, that a peasantry lacks power externally, is it better to have female power-as-control or male power-as-deference internally? And is it *better* from female or male viewpoints? According to Rogers, "Domestic decision-making is of primary importance in peasant societies, because there are few extra-domestic decisions of importance to community life which are within the power of peasants to make. . . . In a domestic-oriented community, the fact that men monopolize high prestige extra-household positions is insignificant. The power attribution in the private, not the public domain, is of primary importance in this cultural context."[7] Furthermore, the actual, if not official, ascendancy of peasant females over peasant males is intensified at least in the *initial* periods of colonization and/or commercialization.

In a second article, based on precolonial West African societies undergoing colonization and traditional European peasant societies undergoing industrialization (that is, advanced commercialization), Rogers argues further that,

> although economic growth induced by colonization initially upset the balance of power in women's favor, there is some indication that with integration into wider economic systems, men may take over and surpass women in the control of formerly feminine resources. They may thus attain a more powerful position than women. . . . As industrialization takes over the countryside, peasant men lose control of their resources, or these are devalued by the group as a whole, with a subsequent rise in the relative value of women's resources, and a power imbalance favoring women. Male control resurfaces, with new resources, most notably those relating to integration in a larger group.[8]

I emphasize once more that Rogers's analysis of gender is done interactively with that of class. She is speaking precisely of peasant gender and specifically at moments of colonization and/or commercialization. That composite class-gender model of a peasantry under imperial commercialization is, of course, peculiarly appropriate for Lower Galilee, the scene of Jesus' primary activity, in the early first common-era century.

I have no presumption that anthropologists are infallible, and I am quite aware that comparative or cross-cultural study is out of favor at the moment as representing a form of intellectual imperialism. But I begin there because it is the most basic general template I can find and because, however it may need correction, its presence is profoundly better than its absence.

History

Over that anthropological stratum I place a second layer from Jewish history, and the contacts with the Lenski-Kautsky model are very close and extremely consistent. By Jewish history, I do not mean that history as separate from the rest of its contemporary world since Judaism, especially in that first common-era century and especially in the Jewish homeland, was in vigorous and variegated reaction to both Hellenistic internationalism and Roman imperialism. I emphasize three points from that magnificent history.

LAND

The Jewish peasantry was prone, over and above the resistance expected from any colonial peasantry, to refuse quiet compliance with heavy taxation, subsistence farming, debt impoverishment, and land expropriation. The peasants' traditional ideology of *land* was enshrined in the ancient Pentateuchal laws.[9] Just as God's people were to rest on the seventh, or Sabbath, day, so God's land was to rest on the seventh, or Sabbath, year: "For six years you shall sow your land and gather in its yield; but the seventh year you shall let it rest and lie fallow, so that the poor of your people may eat; and what they leave the wild animals may eat. You shall do the same with your vineyard, and with your olive orchard" (Exod. 23.10–11). "When you enter the land that I am giving you, the land shall observe a sabbath for the Lord. Six years you shall sow your field, and six years you shall prune your vineyard, and gather in their yield; but in the seventh year there shall be a sabbath of complete rest for the land, a sabbath for the Lord: you shall not sow your field or prune your vineyard" (Lev. 25.2–4).

On that seventh, or Sabbath, year, moreover, Jewish debts were to be remitted and Jewish slaves were to be released:

> Every seventh year you shall grant a remission of debts. And this is the manner of the remission: every creditor shall remit the claim that is held against a neighbor, not exacting it of a neighbor who is a member of the community, because the Lord's remission has been proclaimed. Of a foreigner you may exact it, but you must remit

your claim on whatever any member of your community owes you. ... If a member of your community, whether a Hebrew man or a Hebrew woman, is sold to you and works for you six years, in the seventh year you shall set that person free. And when you send a male slave out from you a free person, you shall not send him out empty-handed. Provide liberally out of your flock, your threshing floor, and your wine press, thus giving to him some of the bounty with which the Lord your God has blessed you. (Deut. 15.1–3, 12–14)

Finally, there was even a jubilee year, the year after seven sets of Sabbath years. In that fiftieth year all expropriated lands and even village houses, but not city ones, were to revert to their original or traditional owners: "You shall hallow the fiftieth year and you shall proclaim liberty throughout the land to all its inhabitants. It shall be a jubilee for you: you shall return, every one of you, to your property and every one of you to your family. ... But if there is not sufficient means to recover it [a piece of property], what was sold shall remain with the purchaser until the year of jubilee; in the jubilee it shall be released, and the property shall be returned" (Lev. 25.10, 28).

It is hard to know now what is ideal and what is real, what is ideological and what is actual in those decrees. Most likely, the jubilee year was not implemented at all by the first century, but the Sabbath year was probably still more or less enforced. My point is that those ancient laws, precisely as ideal vision or ideological promise, refuse to see debt, slavery, or land expropriation simply as business transactions. The land is a divine possession, not a negotiable commodity or, as Leviticus 25.23 put it, "The land shall not be sold in perpetuity, *for the land is mine;* with me you are but aliens and tenants." The Jewish peasantry, as distinct from, say, the Egyptian peasantry, had a long tradition in flat contradiction with a first-century boom economy that saw land accumulation as a sensible business practice and debt foreclosure as the best and swiftest way to accomplish it.

COVENANT

In the first half of the eighth century B.C.E., the prophet Amos insisted that Israel's covenant with God had an economic face, that fidelity to the covenantal God included justice for the marginalized poor. The business of Israel, in other words, was not business but social justice. Again and again he announced doom on those who

> "trample the head of the poor into the dust of the earth, and push the afflicted out of the way" (2.7)
> "oppress the poor, who crush the needy" (4.1)
> "trample on the poor and take from them levies of grain" (5.11)

"trample on the needy, and bring to ruin the poor of the land" (8.4)

"buy the poor for silver and the needy for a pair of sandals, and sell the sweepings of the wheat" (8.6)

In the last quarter of that same century, the prophet Micah proclaimed a rather stunning dichotomy as the very voice of God:

> With what shall I come before the Lord,
> and bow myself before God on high?
> Shall I come before him with burnt offerings,
> with calves a year old?
> Will the Lord be pleased with thousands of rams,
> with ten thousands of rivers of oil?
> Shall I give my firstborn for my transgression,
> the fruit of my body for the sin of my soul?
> He has told you, O mortal, what is good;
> and what does the Lord require of you
> but to do justice, and to love kindness,
> and to walk humbly with your God? (Mic. 6.6–8)

God rejects liturgical worship in favor of social justice. We usually see that as prophetic hyperbole, meaning that God wants *both* ritual and *justice*. Of course. But in the Bible there are several places where God says, in effect, "I reject your worship because you lack justice." There is no place in the Bible where God says, "I reject your justice because you lack worship." Covenant ritual should be, perhaps, the symbolic representation of justice. What we celebrate is a God of radical justice known to us only as social, political, and economic justice.

UNREST

Finally, from the death of Herod the Great in 4 B.C.E. until the First Roman-Jewish War broke out in 66 C.E., there are constant signs of lower-class resistance to Roman imperial power in the Jewish homeland.[10] *Protesters* gathered, again and again, to make unarmed pleas before the second-rank Roman prefect of Palestine or the distant but first-rank Roman governor of Syria. Sometimes the protesters were effective; sometimes they were slaughtered. *Prophets* gathered large groups of followers and led them out in the desert so that they could cross the Jordan into the promised land, which God would then give back to them from the Romans as of old from the Canaanites. Since these groups were expecting divine deliverance and not human violence, they were usually unarmed. Always they were slaughtered. *Bandits* increased as farmers were forced off their lands through debt or disaster and chose the option of banditry in the hills rather than beggary on the roads. *Messiahs* arose invoking the ancient ideal of David as the once and future king and proclaiming war against Rome in the name of God. It is probably false to see Jewish peasants as seething with rebellion and moving inevitably toward open revolt against Rome in that first common-era century. It is probably equally false to imagine anyone seriously interacting with them and not facing that situation of imperial oppression and colonial resistance.

Archaeology

I next overlay archaeology on those two preceding substrata, but I do not intend to subordinate material to textual remains in so doing. Material remains must speak for themselves and not serve simply to prove or disprove textual data. I place archaeology in third place, but actually material and textual data should always be treated with equal importance and kept in creative tension with each other. In this case, however, I have to wrestle somewhat with Galilean archaeologists whose social interpretations of their material discoveries raise very serious problems. I am thinking, for example, of how James Strange can use a serenely benign expression like *urban overlay* even though he knows full well about "the city as a symbol of power."[11] A *fact* of power, also.

Christopher Seeman has asked a terribly obvious question, terribly obvious, that is, once he had asked it:[12] Why was it that the Jesus movement emerged in Lower Galilee during the reign of Herod Antipas rather than at some other time and place? Why in Galilee rather than in Judea and why in Lower, rather than in Upper, Galilee? Why under Antipas rather than under his father, Herod the Great, who ruled from 37 to 4 B.C.E., or under his half-nephew Agrippa I, who ruled from 40 to 44 C.E.? And since Antipas ruled between 4 B.C.E. and 39 C.E., why in the late 20s rather than in any other period of that long reign? Why precisely there? Why exactly then? Or, to broaden Seeman's question, why did *two* movements arise in the late 20s of that first common-era century in the *two* separated regions of Antipas's territory, John's Baptism movement in Perea east of the Jordan, and Jesus' Kingdom movement in Galilee to the northwest? Seeman finds the answer in Antipas's urbanization program for Lower Galilee, where two cities, Sepphoris (started around 4 B.C.E.) and Tiberias (finished around 19 C.E.), were rebuilt or built from scratch within twenty years and twenty miles of each other. That is, of course, exactly what anyone using the Lenski-Kautsky model could have expected. Commercialization leads to peasant unrest, and Roman commercialization involved urbanization.

When one turns, however, to recent Galilean archaeology, a somewhat different picture emerges, not because its material data are incorrect but because its social interpretations are naive. It is particularly interesting to compare the social conclusions of Galilean archaeologists with those of other archaeologists working on the Roman Empire. Susan Alcock, for example, makes the following generalization from her work in Roman Greece:

> Today, instead of focusing upon the perquisites of the victor, archaeologists are engaging with the effects of imperialist expansion upon subject peoples, generating a new kind of "archaeology of imperialism." A battery of archaeological techniques is being turned upon issues such as shifting levels of exploitation, changes in economic and social behavior, acculturation, and resistance. Settlement studies, often made possible for the first time as a result of archaeological survey, have in many cases proved particularly crucial indicators of the life of a conquered population.[13]

Is this generalization true of Galilean archaeology in the early Roman period? I take two examples from recent Galilean archaeology to illustrate its social conclusions.

CITIES

In a series of very instructive works, Jonathan Reed has estimated that Sepphoris and Tiberias had a population of about twenty-four thousand inhabitants apiece. "In terms of food alone, the agricultural practices of Galilee were completely realigned and stretched with the foundation of these two cities. The picture of numerous self-sufficient farms or hamlets in Galilee radically changed. The entire agricultural focus turned to feeding Sepphoris and Tiberias. . . . How would the indigenous Galilean population react to Sepphoris and Tiberias? The attitudes and sentiments are not discernible in the archaeological record."[14] But are they not discernible or simply not discerned?

An alternative example from across the Roman Mediterranean is again important. In studying "'Romanisation'–the effects that Roman rule had on the economics and societies of the ancient Mediterranean," John Patterson focuses on two mountainous regions, Samnium in the central Italian Apennines and Lycia in southeastern Turkey, to test the hypothesis that there is a general structural relationship among "three important facets of town-country relations–public building in the towns, settlement change in the countryside, and the mobility shown by those members of elites who acquired their wealth in the countryside, but spent it principally in the towns." I focus here on that second element, on rural settlement change as small peasant freeholders yield before "the increasing agglomeration of rural estates" owned by urban elites. "The problem then arises of what this change actually meant in practice for the common people who owned or occupied these estates. Various possibilities could exist: that the peasants remained on the land as tenants of the larger proprietors, living in poor and squalid circumstances; or that they left the land to become bandits . . . or departed the land altogether to go to the city."[15] I presume, speaking systemically rather than individually, that none of those three options is a particularly happy one for the peasants involved. But once again, could Sepphoris and Tiberias be treated like Samnium and Lycia? And even if not, could Galilean archaeology be more sophisticated in its general social and economic comments?

CERAMICS

David Adan-Bayewitz's 1985 doctoral dissertation (at Jerusalem's Hebrew University) has shown that most of Galilean pottery came, for half a millennium, from two villages: Kefar Hananya, on the border between Upper and Lower Galilee, and (Kefar) Shihin, identified in 1988 with some ruins about one mile northwest of Sepphoris. Maybe, then, the arrival of two cities, rebuilt Sepphoris and newly built Tiberias, was not bad news for the Galilean peasants. Was it simply an opportunity for increased trade, for larger markets? Should we imagine not unhappy peasants but happy potters, not oppressed farmers but enhanced traders? That is Adan-Bayewitz's *social* conclusion from his *material* data: "It may also be noted that the distribution pattern of Kefar Hananya ware does not seem consistent with the picture, common among scholars, of the exploitation in the early Roman period of the Galilean peasant by the urban wealthy."[16] Is that social conclusion correct? Do these pottery data change the general picture of peasant exploitation in Galilee? What, in other words, is the relationship between pottery production and agricultural land? Does the peasant potter deliberately and willingly abandon the life of a peasant farmer for the presumably more lucrative possibilities of entrepreneurial activity? Here, once again, cross-cultural anthropology questions the social conclusions but not the material discoveries of Galilean archaeology.

In a cross-cultural anthropological work *Ceramic Theory and Cultural Process*, Dean Arnold proposes as a "general principle" that "when a population exceeds the ability of the land to sustain it (and thus exceeds its carrying capacity), there is movement into other occupations like pottery making." Thus, for example,

> it is not unusual that pottery making and other crafts are a secondary choice to agriculture and resorted to by people with poor quality, insufficient or no land. While agriculture provides food directly to a family, craft production does not, but requires additional labor and greater risks than agriculture. . . . It is not unusual, then, that pottery making, as an indirect subsistence technique, is the result of population pressure and not a desirable occupation for most farmers . . . [so that] once there is a better living with agriculture or more secure or steady work, pottery making is abandoned.[17]

Whether one looks to cross-cultural anthropology, to Roman archaeology elsewhere, or to ancient economists, it seems that Galilean archaeology needs seriously to rethink its comments on the social, economic, and political implications of early Roman imperialism in that area. I can place its material data atop my other two layers only by correcting those social conclusions.

Gospel

My fourth and final overlay is the Jesus tradition itself. But here a very special problem intervenes: The Jesus tradition includes everything in canonical and noncanonical Gospels said or done by Jesus and said or done to Jesus. But there is a massive scholarly consensus that this tradition includes successive layers of materials, first from the historical Jesus, then from the developing tradition, and finally from the gospel writers themselves. There is also a massive *nonconsensus* on what belongs to what layer. We are back again, in other words, with stratigraphy, but now within the Jesus tradition itself. One can find almost anything imaginable within that tradition so that without disciplined stratigraphy and methodological consistency, there is hardly even a basis for discussion among scholars. Disagreements are not just about the interpretation of the same units but even about what units are to be interpreted. In this situation method is everything. And I mean method, not just criteria. Criteria do not constitute a method unless they are organized on some theoretical basis into some operational system that can be used by anyone.

I give one example of what happens when historical Jesus research is undertaken with neither criteria nor methodology. Ben Witherington III has recently written a review of about twenty scholarly studies of the historical Jesus. They all fail, he says, because they see a *part* rather than the *whole*. But the whole, for Witherington, is the full Jesus of the complete canonical tradition. In one sense, of course, that is absolutely correct (except that I would add the noncanonical tradition, too). That is the *whole*, but it is also not the question, which is, What of all that whole goes back to the historical Jesus? Since Witherington ranges freely across all the layers of the tradition indiscriminately, he has to reconcile a message from Jesus that says the Kingdom is present, the Kingdom is future, the Kingdom is imminent, and the Kingdom comes I know not when (Mark 13.32). When all of that data, all clearly present in the divergent *gospel* Jesuses, are put together on the lips of the one *historical* Jesus, Witherington quite logically and consistently concludes that Jesus said all of this, and he also repeats it thrice: "Even the coming Son of man sayings do not have to be read as proclaiming a *necessarily* imminent end, but only a *possibly* imminent one. . . . Jesus did not proclaim that the end was *necessarily* imminent. At most he could only have spoken of its possible imminence, something which I believe he did do."[18] In other words, Jesus' eschatological message announced that the end of the world was coming soon, maybe. I repeat: Without the strictest possible methodology, scholars will disagree not only on the interpretation of any given text but also on what texts are in the original historical Jesus layer of the tradition to be interpreted. What, in other words, is one's method for determining that original layer?

My own method, in fastest summary, begins by distinguishing *formal procedures* from *material investments* so that they can be discussed and used separately. Somebody, for example, could agree on the former while disagreeing completely on the latter. I am thinking of how lawyers agree in court on formal procedure (innocent until proved guilty beyond a reasonable doubt), even while they disagree on material investment (this person is innocent or guilty). My formal procedures are, first, begin with a *full inventory* of the entire Jesus tradition divided according to *successive strata* and *independent attestation*. Second, presume that everything in the earliest stratum is original until the opposite is proved; in other words, there must be a strong argument for removing anything. Third, build upward from multiple independent attestation in that earliest stratum. Fourth, bracket anything with only a single attestation as a safeguard against mistakes. None of these procedures, or anything else, can guarantee truth, but they are a method, a discipline, a process open to discussion even before one gets to disagreements on what sources exist, how to date them, and so on. Apart from some such method, clearly divided between formal and material components, one can find whatever one wants about the historical Jesus or earliest Christianity, not because one is dishonest, but because whatever one wants is already there somewhere in the tradition.[19]

Vision and Program

This section presumes the full application of my method for the Jesus tradition already published in several books between 1991 and 1996.[20] I emphasize here only two very basic conclusions concerning the *vision* and the *program* of the historical Jesus. I separate those terms because it is possible to have a vision, a theory, or an idea but no operational social program for realizing it. My point is that Jesus had both and that they should not be separated.

The Kingdom of God

The vision of Jesus was that of the Kingdom of God, of the will of God to be done on earth as in heaven. Heaven, however, then as now, was, and is, in very good shape. It was earth, then as now, that was, and is, problematic. The term *Kingdom of God* must be understood within, first, that absolute conjunction of religion and politics characteristic of the ancient world in general and, second, that situation of imperial domination and colonial exploitation characteristic of the Jewish homeland in particular. The phrase evokes an ideal vision of political and religious power, of how this world here below would be run if

God, not Caesar, sat on its imperial throne. As such the term always casts a caustically critical shadow on human rule. It focuses not just on personal or individual evil but also on systemic or structural evil.

A preliminary note on terminology is needed because a confusion or equation of eschatology and apocalyptic, that is, of a genus and a species, continues to bedevil our exegesis. The term *eschatology* refers, literally, to discussion about the *eschata*, the last things of earth, the ending of human existence in this world, and it normally includes the idea that such an ending comes through divine or transcendental causality, be it from angels or ancestors, spirits or demons, gods or God. At first glance, then, eschatology means the same as *apocalypse*. That term refers, literally, to a special divine *revelation* about the imminent end of the world, and it normally includes the idea of goodness vindicated and evil eliminated. Contemporary scholarship, therefore, regularly uses the adjectives *eschatological* and *apocalyptic* to designate exactly the same phenomenon. But that same contemporary scholarship speaks also of *realized eschatology* or of *present eschatology*, which it must be differentiating from some other type of eschatology, and usually that is *apocalyptic eschatology*, even when that latter phrase is not used. This confusion shows up as well in the use of *apocalyptic* as both noun and adjective. As noun it can stay equal to eschatology, but as adjective it must be subordinate to eschatology or at least to something else that it qualifies.

What has happened, as I see it, is a confusion between a genus-level term (eschatology) and a species-level term (apocalyptic). I find that I need *some* genus-level terms and *some* species-level terms beneath them. I emphasize this point to avoid useless disagreements over words and terms rather than useful ones over ideas and concepts. As upper- or genus-level terms I use more or less interchangeably these words: basic, fundamental, radical, utopian, countercultural, or eschatological refusal of the world as it is presently run, but, of course, those judgments must be divinely or transcendentally based, justified, and proclaimed. I use all those adjectives interchangeably but insist that, whereas eschatology has to do etymologically with an ending of a world, such world-endings or world-negations come in many different forms. There are, for instance, apocalyptic, sapiential, cynic, gnostic, monastic, hermitic, anarchic, or even nihilistic eschatologies. The former two are of immediate present importance.

Apocalyptic eschatology announces the *apocalypse* (Greek for revelation) of imminent and cataclysmic divine intervention to restore peace and justice to a disordered world. Whether thereafter there will be heaven on earth or earth in heaven is left rather vague, but the evil *they* will be gone forever, and the holy *we* will be in charge under God. An example of apocalyptic eschatology's divine revelatory promise is, from the ancient world, John of Patmos, author of the book of Revelation, and from the modern world, David Koresh of Waco, Texas. *Sapiential eschatology*, in contrast, emphasizes the *sapientia* (Latin for wisdom) of knowing how to live here and now today so that God's present power is manifestly evident to all. An example of sapiential eschatology's radical lifestyle challenge is, from the ancient world, Diogenes of Greece living in his barrel, and from the modern world, Mohandas Gandhi of India living in nonviolence. Apocalyptic eschatology is world-negation stressing imminent divine intervention; sapiential eschatology is world-negation emphasizing immediate divine imitation. In apocalyptic eschatology we are waiting for God to act, but in sapiential eschatology God is waiting for us to act. In apocalyptic eschatology there is private revelation announced secretly to the righteous. In sapiential eschatology there is public challenge announced openly to the courageous. *Both* appeal to God and faith, but apocalyptic radicalism speaks in private, sapiential radicalism in public, discourse. The former is the message of John the Baptist; the latter, that of Jesus. Both have to do with religio-politics or politico-religion here and now in this world. But they are different visions demanding necessarily different programs.

Reciprocity in Eating and Healing

The aphorisms and parables of the historical Jesus often bespeak a radical egalitarianism, but were they accompanied by any social program? Was his message all an act of ecstatic imagination and rhapsodic vision, or did it also contain policies, plans, and procedures for communal implementation? My affirmative answer is based on three independent sources, two of which date from the earliest stratum of the Jesus tradition, and all of which contain an emphasis on *eating* and *healing*.

> His disciples asked him and said to him, ". . . What diet shall we observe?" . . .
> When you go into any country and walk from place to place, when the people receive you, *eat* what they serve you and *heal* the sick among them. (Gos. Thom. 6.1d, 4.4)

*   *   *

> [After this the Lord appointed seventy others and sent them on ahead of him in pairs to every town and place where he himself intended to go.]
> Carry no purse, no bag, no sandals; and salute no one on the road. Whatever house you enter, first say, "Peace be to this house!" And if a son of peace is there, your peace shall rest upon him; but if not, it shall return to you. And remain in the same house, *eating* and drinking what they provide, for the laborer deserves his wages; do not go from house to house. Whenever you enter a town and they receive

you, *eat* what is set before you; *heal* the sick in it and say to them,
"The kingdom of God has come near to you." But whenever you
enter a town and they do not receive you, go into its streets and say,
"Even the dust of your town that clings to our feet, we wipe off
against you; nevertheless know this, that the kingdom of God has
come near." (Q Gospel in Luke 10.[1], 4–11 = Matt. 10.7–14)

*   *   *

He called the twelve and began to send them out two by two, and
gave them authority over the unclean spirits. He charged them to
take nothing for their journey except a staff; no bread, no bag, no
money in their belts; but to wear sandals and not put on two tunics.
And he said to them, "Where you enter a house, stay there until you
leave the place. And if any place will not receive you and they refuse
to hear you, when you leave, shake off the dust that is on your feet
for a testimony against them." So they went out and preached that
men should repent. And they cast out many demons, and anointed
with oil many that were sick and *healed* them. (Mark 6.7–13 = Matt.
10.1, 8–10a, 11 = Luke 9.1–6)

Jesus called his practice and program the presence of the Kingdom or, better, the Rule of God, but that expression must be interpreted primarily in the
light of those actions. It did not mean for Jesus, as it could for others, the imminent apocalyptic intervention of God to set right a world taken over by evil
and injustice. It meant the presence of God's Kingdom here and now in the
reciprocity of open eating and open healing, in lives, that is, of radical egalitarianism on both the socioeconomic (eating) and the religio-political (healing)
levels. Six elements of that program are still discernible in those texts: The first
three are reflected in all of them, the next two in the Q Gospel and Mark, and
the final one only in Mark.

EATING

All three sources indicate that we are dealing not just with almsgiving but also
with an open table. Anthropology uses the term *commensality* for those decisions about what we eat, where we eat, when we eat, and, above all, with
whom we eat, all of which form a miniature map of our social distinctions and
hierarchies. But Jesus, in rejection of this cartography of discrimination, advo-
cates instead an open commensality. His companions do not carry a bag because they do not beg for alms or food or clothing or anything else. They
share a miracle and a Kingdom, and they receive in return a table and a house.
Here, I think, is the heart of the original Jesus movement: a shared egalitarianism of spiritual and material resources where materiality and spirituality, fac-
ticity and symbolism, cannot be separated. The mission we are talking about is

not, like Paul's, a dramatic thrust along major trade routes to urban centers hundreds of miles apart. Yet it concerns the longest journey in the Greco-Roman world, maybe in any world: the step across the threshold of a peasant stranger's home.

Shared home and common meal must be seen against the cross-cultural anthropology of food and commensality.[21] But I cannot emphasize one point too strongly: Commensality is not almsgiving; almsgiving is not commensality. Generous almsgiving may even be conscience's last great refuge against the terror of open commensality. For Jesus, however, commensality was not just a strategy for supporting the mission. That could have been done by alms, wages, charges, or fees of some sort. It could have been done, for instance, by simple begging in good Cynic fashion. Rather, commensality was a strategy for building or rebuilding peasant community on radically different principles from those of honor and shame, patronage and clientage. It was based on an egalitarian sharing of spiritual (healing) and material (eating) power at the most grassroots level. And for that reason, dress and equipment appearance were just as important as house and table response.

HEALING

Open eating and open healing are reciprocally linked in all three sources. I understand healing within the basic distinction made in cross-cultural medical anthropology and modern comparative ethnomedicine between doctors who *cure disease* and those others who, under whatever name, *heal illness.*[22] Disease is the organic, physical ailment. Illness is the disease's effect on patient, family, and community. This distinction applies on two levels. On the one level, we are dealing with mind over matter or with faith over pain, with those cases where it is almost impossible to distinguish disease from illness. Those are, in general, the types of cases well documented from ancient Epidaurus or Pergamum (healing shrines of the god Asklepios), to modern Fatima or Lourdes (healing shrines of the Virgin Mary). Faith heals—but only for certain people with certain diseases in certain circumstances. That is as certain as human affairs can ever be. But we still need to explain why anyone had faith in Jesus and his companions (as distinct from Asklepios). On the other level, think of AIDS, for example, and of the movie *Philadelphia*, in particular. The *disease* is the virus's effect on the patient's immune system and the consequent vulnerability to infection. The disease can be *cured* only if medication were available to destroy the virus. The *illness* is the effect of the disease on the sufferer himself, on spouse and family, on employers and job, and on society and jury. That can be healed negatively by a fundamental resistance to society's rejection and positively by a fundamental acceptance of an alternative community. At that point both levels coincide in Jesus and his companions. Their radical and transcendental critique of oppressive imperial society begins an ideological healing without which no other is possible.

What exactly is the logic of that reciprocity? It might be clear why itinerants who have nothing would need eating, but why would householders need healing? Is it just a presumption that there would always be somebody sick in every house? Or is it something more profound and precise? I propose that Jesus' deliberate conjunction of itinerants who need eating and householders who need healing points the Kingdom of God at that terrible line between Galilean poverty and destitution, not just at that general one between poverty and wealth. On one side of that line stand the terror and contempt of the poor householder for itinerant destitution, and on the other stand the envy and hatred of itinerant destitution for the poor householder. But the line is absolutely clear: If a peasant still has the family farm, he is poor; if he has lost it, he is destitute. Jesus' program involves those two groups facing each other and attempting to restore peasant society by that conjunction.

It is also worth noting that the *Our Father* prayer (the Lord's Prayer) asks for enough bread for today and no debt for tomorrow. The one who needs bread is destitute. The one who needs debt forgiven is only poor. Usually the eternal peasant cry is for land without debt, but here things seem much worse: Bread without debt would suffice. The Kingdom invokes the radical justice of God, but it points that radical justice at the major terror of first-century Galilean peasants—namely, the slippage from householder to itinerant, from farmer to beggar, from poverty to destitution.

Jesus and his companions healed illness. They never, in my opinion, cured disease except when and if it happened indirectly through that former and much more important process. And, of course, when such actions got Jesus into very serious trouble, it was certainly not, as the authorities would have understood very clearly, for practicing medicine without a license. Finally, in the Jesus movement the healers make house calls. Healing is shared freely in the only way that is truly free for a peasant: It comes to him or her.

ITINERANCY

This element also appears in all three sources. Ever since the groundbreaking studies of Gerd Theissen in the early 1970s, the itinerant radicalism of Jesus and of the original Jesus movement has been a major topic of discussion and controversy. Itinerant radicalism means that one's itinerancy or even vagrancy is a programmatic part of one's radical message. But what did it mean for Jesus and his followers? If it was meant to send a message of being homeless within an alien world, such a message is far better sent by staying in one place and living, like Diogenes, in a barrel.

The itinerancy of Jesus' movement was radical because it was a symbolic repudiation of the hierarchical system that was the celestial and terrestrial, heavenly and earthly, supernatural and natural heartbeat of the Roman world.[23] For Jesus, God was not a patron of whom he was the broker and his followers the clients. Neither Jesus nor his followers were supposed to settle down in one place and establish there a brokered presence. And even though we would expect them, as healers, to have stayed in one place, established around them a group of followers, and had people come to them, they instead went out to people and had, as it were, to start anew each morning. If Jesus was a well-known magician, healer, or miracle worker, first his immediate family, and next his village, would have expected to benefit from and partake in the handling of that fame and those gifts. Any Mediterranean peasant would have expected an expanding ripple of patronage, brokerage, and clientage to go out from Jesus, through his family and his village, to the outside world. But Jesus refused to stay either in his family's home at Nazareth or at Peter's home at Capernaum because only itinerancy could symbolize unbrokered egalitarianism available openly and freely to all alike.

GENDER

In Mark 6.7 "the Twelve" and in Luke 10.1 "the seventy others" are sent out "two by two" or "in pairs." Why? We know that rabbis often traveled on official business in twos, but that was much later, after the destruction of Jerusalem's Temple in 70 C.E. There is no evidence of such a procedure at the time of Jesus. There are, however, two other texts that may clarify what is happening. One is a highly symbolic story in which two followers of Jesus travel from Jerusalem to Emmaus on Easter Sunday (Luke 24.13–35). One of them is identified as Cleopas, a male; the other is left unidentified. I presume, in such a combination of named and unnamed pairs, especially in Mediterranean society, that the second person was a woman. She is not, however, specified as *his* wife. The other text is 1 Corinthians 9.5, in a context where Paul is discussing his own missionary activities: "Do we not have the right to be accompanied by a believing wife [*adelphen gynaika*], as do the other apostles and the brothers of the Lord and Cephas?"

That translation makes the problem a simple one of support for both the missionary and his wife as long as she, too, is a Christian. The literal Greek "sister wife" is translated into English as "believing wife." But is Paul talking about real, married, Christian wives, and if so, how exactly are we to imagine what happened to their children in such situations? And, more specifically, how could the unmarried Paul be accompanied by his wife? My proposal is that a sister wife means exactly what it says: a female missionary who travels with a male missionary as if, for the world at large, she were his wife. The obvious function of such a tactic would be to furnish the best social protection for a traveling female missionary in a world of male power and violence. Was that the original purpose and focus of the "in pairs" practice—namely, to allow for and incorporate safely the possibility of female itinerants?

I am utterly aware of how tentative this suggestion must remain. But I am convinced that it must be made for two reasons. First, Paul's expression *sister wife* must be given some more adequate interpretation than *believing wife*. Second, if, as suggested earlier, Jesus advocated *open* commensality, that would have involved both women and men. If, then, the itinerants included women, how could that possibly have worked in the context of Galilean peasant society? I do not think they could have gone out to houses alone, and a sister wife relationship might have been not only the best but also the only way to effect it. If society had got wind of this arrangement, the term for such women would have been *whores,* the standard description for any women outside normal social convention or outside normal male control. Jesus, of course, would then have been consorting with whores.

DRESS

The final item, dress or dress code, also occurs only in the Q Gospel and Mark. It seems, however, so closely linked to those more secure themes that, at least in working hypothesis, I consider it also as part of Jesus' original program. I focus, for here and now, on only one single prohibition from that dress code: The itinerant followers of Jesus are not to carry a *bag,* or what we might term a *knapsack.* What is most striking about that injunction is that, although much of the remaining dress code agrees with that of Greco-Roman Cynics, it was precisely a bag that Cynic preachers carried as a symbol that all they needed could be carried on their hip.

Cynics preached to ordinary people in marketplaces and temple courtyards a radically countercultural lifestyle that attacked not just Greco-Roman society but also civilization itself. As followers of Diogenes of Sinope, who lived from about 400 to about 320 B.C.E., their title *cynic* came from *kyon,* the Greek word for "dog," originally a derogatory term for the provocative shamelessness with which Diogenes deliberately flouted basic human codes of propriety and decency, custom and convention. They preached, in other words, by their deeds as much as by their words, by their dress and lifestyle as much as by their ideology and philosophy. And ordinary people who might miss the Cynics' theoretical arguments could hardly miss their symbolic provocations. What is clear, however, is that if the heart of Jesus' program was the reciprocity of eating and healing, the symbolic dress and equipment of his itinerants should have been not bag but no bag, not a bag to symbolize their self-sufficiency but no bag to symbolize their interactive dependency.

THE TWELVE

In the three fundamental texts, reference to the Twelve is present only in Mark. First, the Gospel of Thomas, with 14.4 as the displaced response to 6.1, simply says that the group to which the instructions were given was Jesus' followers or disciples. Next, Mark names them as "the Twelve," which is his usual term for the group of disciples (3.16, 4.10, 9.35, 10.32), but it is clear from 3.14, where Jesus "appointed twelve, whom he also named apostles, to be with him, and to be sent out to proclaim the message," and 6.30, where "the apostles" return after their mission, that Mark understands "the Twelve" as "the Twelve apostles." Finally, the Q Gospel is more complicated because, as is so often the case, Matthew conflates Q Gospel and Mark together in his account, whereas Luke keeps them separate, with his 9.1–6 from Mark and his 10.1–11 from the Q Gospel. Both Matthew 10.1 and Luke 9.1, therefore, follow Mark 6.7's mention of the Twelve. But, in their Q Gospel sections, Matthew 9.37 has "the disciples," and Luke 10.1 has "the seventy." The second half of Luke 10.1 is so specifically Lukan ("to every town and place where he himself intended to go") that one is tempted to dismiss the entire verse as Lukan redaction. But that "in pairs" gives me pause since it is also present independently as "two by two" in Mark 6.7. Maybe, therefore, "the seventy" was in the Q Gospel. For Mark 6.7, the companions of Jesus are explicitly the Twelve Apostles, but that is found only in Mark. But is he equating those possibly far more general and numerous companions from the time of the historical Jesus specifically with the Twelve Apostles?

The point of twelve is that Jesus' community forms a New Israel in miniature, a new people of God with twelve new patriarchs to replace the twelve sons of Jacob from the Old Testament. The question, however, is whether such an institution derives from the time of the historical Jesus or was created after his death among certain early Christian groups. I accept that second alternative for two reasons. One is that I find it almost impossible to imagine thirteen men traveling around together among the small villages of Lower Galilee in the first century. Imagine that group arriving in a hamlet with all the men out working in the fields and only women and small children at home, especially in an honor and shame culture divided along gender lines. Jesus surrounded by the Twelve would fit well as a sort of philosophical school in a city but is incredible among the tiny hamlets of rural Galilee. That, however, is a very general objection.

The second and more immediate one is that whole groups in the early church seem never to have heard of this most important and symbolic institution. Paul mentions a tradition about the Twelve in 1 Corinthians 15.5, but he distinguishes them from "all the apostles" in 15.7, and they never appear as any sort of an authoritative source or group in his epistles. Neither the Gospel of Thomas nor the Q Gospel ever mentions them. The *Teaching*, or *Didache*, a catechetical, liturgical, and disciplinary manual whose earliest sections may go back between 50 and 70 C.E., knows only of apostles in the sense of itinerants who are given temporary hospitality as they pass through to found new communities elsewhere. The eleventh-century manuscript that alone contains this complete text is entitled, first, *The Teaching of the Twelve Apostles* and, then, *The Teaching of the Lord Through the Twelve Apostles to the Pagans*. Neither of those external titles reflects the text's internal understanding of apostles and must be considered as later additions. Neither do the Twelve Apostles appear in First Clement, a letter written around 96 or 97 C.E. from the church at Rome to that at Corinth. Finally, they are not mentioned in the letters that Ignatius of Antioch, traveling under guard to martyrdom in Rome between 110 and 117

C.E., wrote to various Christian communities along his route. If the institution of Twelve Apostles, with all its profound symbolic connotations, had been established by Jesus during his lifetime, it would have been more widely known and noted. I conclude, therefore, that the connection between Jesus' companions and the Twelve in Mark 6.7 is due to Mark himself and not to the historical Jesus.

A Companionship of Empowerment

I have no presumption that what is primary is always better than what is secondary, that what is original is better than what is derivative. The historical Jesus, as reconstructed by our best endeavors, could well be a figure to be opposed from our contemporary viewpoint. It is neither his gender nor his title but his vision and his program that are determinative for that judgment. And what must be asked most specifically is whether the Kingdom of God denotes a realm of domination or of empowerment. His companions can do exactly what Jesus himself was doing. The Kingdom is not his monopoly; it is for anyone with courage enough to accept it. Jesus announces its presence, its abiding, permanent possibility. He does not initiate its existence. He does not control its access.

Imagine, as an alternative example, that Jesus had settled down with his family at Nazareth or with Peter at Capernaum and sent out disciples to bring or send back to him those in need of healing or teaching. That would have symbolized a God of domination and a Kingdom of control and mastery, and, if that was the historical Jesus I discovered, he would have to be understood as promoting domination, kinder and gentler to be sure than Caesar's, but still domination and not empowerment. Even the term *disciples* is probably not the proper term for that inaugural community. It presumes a master and students, a teacher and pupils. And even though teaching can be empowerment rather than domination, it can also be the opposite.

I prefer, therefore, in the light of those three seminal texts, to describe the Kingdom of God not as a *discipleship of equals,* with Elisabeth Schüssler Fiorenza,[24] but as a *companionship of empowerment.* Disciples (or students) can all be equal with one another and still subordinate to a teacher. The root question is whether God and hence the Kingdom of God and thence Jesus as the announcer of its permanent availability are to be seen within a model of domination or one of empowerment. Jesus' program was one of empowerment, and that meant one could not destroy it by executing its founder. Easter was built into the program of the Kingdom from the beginning.

Itinerant and Householder

Gerd Theissen, in those studies mentioned previously, distinguishes in earliest Christianity between *wandering or itinerant charismatics* and *settled or local sym-*

pathizers.[25] I take my distinction of *itinerant* and *householder* from his pioneering work, but I use my own particular terms to emphasize the complete and equal reciprocity that I imagine between those two groups. They stem from that eating and healing dyad at the core of the Kingdom program, and I do not want in any way to subordinate one to the other. It is their interaction that counts. But to have an interaction, *both* parties must exist and be present to each other. What I study here is how that interaction continued after the death of Jesus.

Theissen's term *ethical radicalism* is a very good description for that program. But I understand the term in a very specific sense, and I distinguish it from, say, ascetical or apocalyptic or esoteric or gnostic radicalism. In a *systemically* evil situation of injustice and oppression, only the destitute are structurally innocent. Ethical radicalism is, above all else, a political statement of dissociation from a systemically unjust situation. If, for example, a minister today started to live on the streets with the homeless, that is ethical, and not just ascetical, radicalism. On the one hand, therefore, that mission by immediate lifestyle obviated any need for a theoretical schooling process before those first companions could themselves live the Kingdom just as well as Jesus. On the other hand, there was necessarily a *paradoxical relationship* between itinerants and householders. Were all supposed to become itinerants? Was that the point of the mission so that, as Theissen proposes, the householders were but sympathizers, supporters, and admirers at best? Was there a tendency for the itinerants to see itinerancy as an end in itself rather than as a symbolic catechesis of mission? How did itinerants and householders interact in practice and not just in theory?

Theissen also notes that "the synoptic speeches sending out disciples and the Didache contain direct statements about early Christian itinerant charismatics. In the first are rules for early Christian missionaries, in the second rules for how to treat them."[26] I focus, therefore, on the Q Gospel and the Gospel of Thomas to hear the voice of the itinerants and their reproaches against the householders who accepted them, and I focus on *Didache* to hear the response of the householders who accepted the itinerant's mission but also defended themselves against its too radical implications. In all of this I am deeply indebted to lines of research from James Robinson to John Kloppenborg on the Q Gospel and from Helmut Koester to Stephen Patterson on the Gospel of Thomas.[27]

The Common Sayings Tradition

The Q Gospel is a hypothetical document proposed, on the presupposition that Mark was used by Matthew and Luke, to explain the parallels in order and content between them but not derived from that Markan source. The Gospel of Thomas is an actual document known from the turn of the century in Greek fragments from Oxyrhynchus and since 1945 in a Coptic translation from Nag Hammadi. There are six very striking parallels between Q and

Thomas. First, their literary forms contain much more saying or dialogue than incident or narrative. Second, their overall structures are very loose between the units or at least between groups of units. Third, their common genre is a wisdom or sapiential one, the Sayings of the Sages, in Robinson's terminology. Fourth, that wisdom is not conventional but subversive. Koester speaks of "realized eschatology" in both Gospels, Kloppenborg speaks of the "radical wisdom of the kingdom" in the Q Gospel, and Patterson speaks of the "social radicalism" of the Gospel of Thomas. Putting the terms together, I see in both Gospels *an eschatology realizable in the wisdom of social radicalism.* Fifth, that eschatology is quite different from the death and resurrection of Jesus eschatology usually considered the only early Christian one available, as both Koester and Kloppenborg emphasize. It is a not a future or apocalyptic eschatology but a present or sapiential one. Sixth, about one-third of each document contains a common sayings tradition, that is, 36 out of 100 units in the Q Gospel and 36 out of 132 units in the Gospel of Thomas. Those units are redacted toward apocalyptic eschatology in the former case but toward ascetical eschatology in the latter. It is still possible, however, by looking at each text's particular materials and also at how each redacts its common materials to discern what was there before redaction began. Some units, for example, are redacted by each in those two divergent directions, some are redacted by one but not the other, and many are not redacted in either direction, except, of course, by general context.

Those redactions raise the following questions: Why did both those Gospels start with a common base in sapiential radicalism and then move, one toward apocalyptic, biographical, and exegetical traditions in the Q Gospel, and the other toward ascetic, esoteric, and maybe even incipiently gnostic traditions in the Gospel of Thomas? What happened and happened so early to create those developments away from the common tradition? My working hypothesis is that the householders both accepted and domesticated (pun intended) the radicality of the itinerants, who responded by moving from social radicalism to apocalyptic radicalism in the Q Gospel and ascetic radicalism in the Gospel of Thomas.

The Itinerants Speak Out

One example will have to suffice for now, from the Q Gospel's inaugural speech by Jesus. It opens with a fourfold beatitude as programmatic introduction: for destitution, hunger, sorrow, rejection (in Luke 6.20b–23 = Matt. 5.3, 6, 4, 11–12). Next follow two more fourfold clauses. The first commands "you" (plural) to love, do good, bless, and pray for enemies (in Luke 6.27–28, 32–33, 35a = Matt. 5.44, 46–47). The second commands "you" (singular) to turn the other cheek, give both shirt and cloak, go the extra enforced mile, and give without hope of return (in Luke 6.29–30, 34,3 5b = Matt. 5.39–42).

Think, now, of those admonitions in terms of itinerants and householders. The beatitudes are simply accurate descriptions of the itinerants (as of Jesus himself), and they assert the Kingdom's presence in their lifestyle. But what of the householders? They certainly could not have accepted the beatitudes in exactly the same sense as did the itinerants, or else they would no longer have been householders but itinerants. And the Jesus movement would have been primarily a caste of itinerants with sympathizers as no more than a support system. Could householders have followed any of those admonitions at all, or did they simply admire and ignore them? Turn, then, to the end of that inaugural speech of Jesus in the Q Gospel (in Luke 6.46–49 and Matt. 7.21–27):

[1]Why do you call me "Lord, Lord," and not do what I tell you?

* * *

[2]Every one who comes to me and hears my words and does them, I will show you what he is like: he is like a man building a house, who dug deep, and laid the foundation upon rock; and when a flood arose, the stream broke against that house, and could not shake it, because it had been well built. But he who hears and does not do them is like a man who built a house on the ground without a foundation; against which the stream broke, and immediately it fell, and the ruin of that house was great.

The first saying distinguishes between invoking the Lordship of Jesus and not obeying his commands. The second distinguishes between hearing and doing and hearing and not doing. Those, however, are distinctions *within* the Christian community, within those who have already accepted Jesus. They are not distinctions between those inside and those outside that community. They are distinctions, within acceptance, between *acceptance with practice* and *acceptance without practice*. We hear in those specific warnings the reproach of itinerant to householder, the reproach of one who has given up everything against the one who has not given up enough. And it will require much more study to see what, between everything and nothing, *enough* might mean. How, in other words, did the radical and absolute counterculturalism of the itinerant translate into the relative and pragmatic counterculturalism of the householder? If the householder did not drop everything and join in itinerancy, how was *acceptable acceptance* to be calculated for such a person? Would some itinerants ever be satisfied with householders? I propose that the crucible for the earliest tradition about the words of Jesus was the necessarily paradoxical tension between itinerants and householders, with the former justifying their lifestyle with "Jesus said" and the latter replying, in effect, "Yes, but."

Look once more at those short lists of Jesus' sayings in his inaugural sermon according to the Q Gospel and especially at those fourfold smaller units within them. There would have been very little point in citing them to those first hearers challenged to either accept or reject the itinerants. To say that one's countercultural lifestyle is based on that of Jesus only impresses those who have already somehow accepted Jesus. No, their first challenge was that the Kingdom of God was here and now present in their own words and deeds, their own performances and practices, their own healings and exorcisms. Thereafter, with some minimal acceptance already obtained, it might be possible to speak of Jesus. It might be possible, for example, to cite sayings in justification both of his and their own lifestyles and of what he and they were asking people to do. For "Jesus said" was clearly important to both Q Gospel and the Gospel of Thomas. The itinerants were not ready, even though they had been themselves empowered to proclaim the Kingdom's presence, to speak only on their own individual authority.

My argument is not that they had memorized all or even any of Jesus' sayings. The continuity is not in mnemonics but in mimetics, not in remembrance but in imitation, not in word but in deed. They were living, dressing, and preaching as physically similar to Jesus as was possible. More simply, most of them were originally as poor or destitute as he was. When they quoted him, we can never now be absolutely sure whether they had memorized an aphorism or summarized an attitude. But it is the *continuity of lifestyle* between Jesus and itinerants that gives their tradition its validity, even if we were ready to accept every single aphorism or parable we now have as reconstructed summary or redacted expansion. But that insistence on "Jesus said" warns us that the itinerants were meeting with resistance even or especially within the Christian communities. To hear the voice of that resistance, I turn to another document, *Didache,* or *Teaching.*

The Householders Talk Back

Didache is a document discovered in 1873 by the Greek Orthodox Metropolitan Philotheos Bryennios in the library of the Most Holy Sepulchre Monastery in Constantinople's Phanar quarter. It was part of a vellum codex dated to June 11, 1056. Tiny fragments dated to the late fourth century have also been found among the Oxyrhynchus papyri. Its basic composition has been dated by scholars from as early as 50 to as late as 100 C.E. There is also a disagreement on whether it is independent of or dependent on the canonical Gospels. In my earlier work I presumed it was totally independent of them except for the later insertion of that Sermon on the Mount–like section in *Didache* 1.3–5, but I am now persuaded, especially by the work of Willy Rordorf, Aaron Milavec, and Ian Henderson, that it is totally independent even or especially for that precise section.[28]

The constitutive moment of its composition was in response to a pressing social crisis within the network of rural households for whom and to whom it spoke. Some members, called "hypocrites" in *Didache* 8, have broken away from *Didache*'s groups because, apparently, Gentile converts were not observing Torah in both its ethical and ritual obligations as the breakaway members considered they should. In response, *Didache* proposes an initiation program for all future (and especially Gentile) converts that would both precede Baptism and serve as a weekly confession of faults before the community Eucharist. But how does this internal organization, this official and agreed-upon teaching, stand with regard to itinerant authority?

PROPHETS

Itinerant authorities come, for *Didache*, in three types: apostles, prophets, and teachers. One could almost describe *Didache* as the slow and careful ascendancy of teacher or, better, "teaching" over prophet and apostle–but very slow and very careful. Notice, by the way, that these figures represent a different problem from "travelers," who, in *Didache* 12.2–5, are to be helped as much as possible but who must stay at most two or three days. If they settle down, they must work; else they are, in a bitingly accurate epithet, a *christemporos*: a Christ-peddler or Christ-hustler.

Itinerant teachers and apostles are easily contained. Teachers, according to *Didache* 11.1–2, must conform to the moral and liturgical teaching just laid down in *Didache* 1–10: "Whoever then comes and teaches you all these things aforesaid receive him. But if the teacher himself be perverted and teach another doctrine to destroy these things, do not listen to him, but if his teaching be for the increase of righteousness and knowledge of the Lord, receive him as the Lord."

Apostles are, by definition, prophets on their way to found new Christian households or communities elsewhere and are supported by already established ones on their way. They can, according to *Didache* 11.4–6, stay only one or two days and take only bread until the next night's lodging: "Let every Apostle who comes to you be received as the Lord, but let him not stay more than one day, or if need be a second as well; but if he stay three days, he is a false prophet. And when an Apostle goes forth, let him accept nothing but bread till he reach his night's lodging; but if he ask for money, he is a false prophet."

Prophets, however, are much more difficult, and the text returns to focus on them repeatedly in 10.7, 11.7–12, and 13.1, 3–7. I look only at 11.7–12, a marvelously delicate and intricate dance of containment. The basic principle concerning itinerant prophets is very clear. Notice its emphasis on *behavior* (literally: ways), a term that should be taken not just as ethically good behavior but also as continuity with Jesus' own ethically radical behavior. Here is the core principle, in *Didache* 11.7–8: "Do not test or examine any prophet who is speaking in a spirit, for every sin shall be forgiven, but this sin shall not be forgiven. But not everyone who speaks in a spirit is a prophet, except he have the behaviour of the Lord. From his behaviour then, the false prophet and the true prophet shall be known."

Next follow four examples, in *Didache* 11.9–12. The first two are easy and give criteria by which one can judge a prophet to be false: "And no prophet who orders a meal in a spirit shall eat of it: otherwise he is a false prophet. And every prophet who teaches the truth, if he do not what he teaches, is a false prophet." The third one is very hard to understand, but it helps us see the difference between prophet and teacher. With a prophet we are looking primarily at performance, at lifestyle, at symbolic catechesis, and not just at a teaching, a word, a saying, even one backed by divine revelation. "But no prophet who has been tried and is genuine, though he enact a worldly mystery of the Church, if he teach not others to do what he does himself, shall be judged by you: for he has his judgment with God, for so also did the prophets of old."

That is much more complicated. What does it mean "to enact a worldly mystery of the Church"? It clearly has to do not just with prophetic words but also with prophetic deeds, actions, or lifestyles, with ways that both imitate the ways of the historical Jesus and symbolize externally the hidden mystery of the church. That is why one must be so careful with those radical itinerants: Something immensely important is at stake here. It is fascinating to watch *Didache* handle the problem: Do not dare to judge them, but do not learn to imitate them either. Gently, delicately, and carefully, lines are being drawn between itinerant and householder, between the symbolic catechesis of the former and the settled *didache* of the latter.

The fourth example, like the first two, is also relatively straightforward: "But whosoever shall say in a spirit 'Give me money, or something else,' you shall not listen to him; but if he tell you to give on behalf of others in want, let none judge him." Again, that delicacy. Do not give for the prophet's own benefit; but for others, do not judge. Does that mean to give or not to give? *Didache* leaves the question open and would probably answer, if directly asked, "*Do what you can,*" as in 6.1 on teaching, 6.2 on food, and 12.2 on hospitality.

These householders, networked together by the consensual documentation of their *Didache*, can both accept and contain the radical message of itinerant apostles, prophets, or teachers. Their *words* and *ways* must agree. Their words must agree with *Didache,* and their ways must be admired rather than imitated.

SAYINGS

Imagine itinerants (like those visible in the Q Gospel) insisting that Jesus said this and Jesus said that as they preached to resident householders, like those of *Didache.* We have just seen how to contain the spiritual pyrotechnics of an itinerant prophet, of one programmatically imitating the lifestyle of Jesus himself, but how do we contain the sayings they have quoted to us? How do we live *with* if we cannot totally live *by* those most radical Jesus sayings themselves?

The teaching in *Didache* 1–6 is a typical "Two Ways" teaching, which describes two ways of living. It contains a catalog of virtues and vices, a stereotyped list of things to do and live or things to do and die. But it has two fascinating elements unusual in such an instruction, totally absent from both pre-Christian Jewish models and other Christian parallels and therefore indicative of the redactional activity of the *Didache*'s constitutive moment. These elements occur, respectively, at the start and at the end of the instruction. We begin with the one at the end, which is appended to 6.1 as 6.2: "See that no one makes you error from this way of the teaching, for such a one teaches you without God" (6.1). "For if you can bear the whole yoke of the Lord, you will be perfect, but if you cannot, do what you can" (6.2).

The first sentence (6.1) is from the Two Ways source and is typical of the either/or tenor of that pattern. The second one (6.2) breathes another world and invites us to wonder what exactly from the preceding Two Ways might be omitted with loss of perfection but not of God. Surely, "do what you can" does not apply, for example, to murder, adultery, sodomy, and so on.

That question about the redacted *ending* in 6.1–2 forces us back to review the redacted *beginning* in 1.3b–2.1. Does 6.2 refer precisely to 1.3b–2.1? That insertion has two parts, and in them we hear, respectively, the voice of the itinerants and the response of the householders.

The first part, in 1.3b–4, is composed of twin fourfold injunctions: (1) bless, fast for, pray for, love enemies—with a plural "you"; (2) turn other cheek, go other mile, give both garments, give your possessions—with a singular "you." That is precisely the same syntactically disparate (singular/plural you) combination seen earlier in Jesus' inaugural sermon from the Q Gospel. And that is, I think, too much coincidence for oral memories simply recalling isolated sayings of Jesus. Somewhere within the delicate interface of orality and literacy, lists of radical Jesus sayings are being assembled from separate units or even multiplied from a single unit. They are still very close to lists, but they are also already evincing a common theme and even a common form. My present tentative hypothesis is that the itinerants started at a fairly early stage to organize, within what I have called the delicate interface of orality and literacy, short lists of Jesus sayings justifying their lifestyle and presented as such to their householder converts. And if we hear their voices in 1.3b–4, we hear that of the householders in 1.5–7.

The second part of the insertion, in 1.5–7, immediately follows and comments on that preceding final unit of that second foursome, "If anyone will take what is yours, do not refuse it, for you cannot," as follows:

> Give to everyone that asks you, and do not refuse, for the Father's will is that we give to all from the gifts we have received.
>
> Blessed is he that gives according to the mandate; for he is innocent.
>
> Woe to the one who receives; for if anyone receive alms under pressure of need he is innocent;
>
> but he who receives it without need shall be tried as to why he took and for what, and being in prison he shall be examined as to his

deeds, and he shall not come out thence until he pay the last far-
thing.

But concerning this it was also said, "Let your alms sweat into
your palms until you know to whom you are giving."

What is happening here? Those twin foursomes are never designated as
stemming from Jesus. They are, even granted their pride of place, simply part
of the Two Ways teaching. Thus, the syntactical inclusion of 1.3b–2.1 within
Didache 1–6 mirrors the jurisdictional subordination of itinerant prophet (even
or especially armed with Jesus sayings) to the resident teacher with *didache*.
But it is all done so very delicately, gently, firmly, and even serenely. Hence,
the radical dispossession advocated in 1.4e ("Do not refuse one who takes
what is yours–for you cannot do so") is contained somewhat by this absorp-
tion within the Two Ways teaching. But it is also deradicalized in a more
telling fashion by the subsequent long interpretative gloss in 1.5–7.

There is no way to think that the speaker of 1.3b–4 is not the same as that
of 1.5–7. Hence, that interpretation is as authoritative as what it glosses. And
that glossed interpretation is known also to the *Shepherd of Hermas* in *Mandate*
2.4b–7. Clearly, early Christians found people who were abusing the mandated
generosity, and 1.5–7 tries for an even balance between commanding almsgiving to those who can give and warning those who take that they must be in
need to do so. Jesus' injunction demanding readiness for radical dispossession
on the lips of those itinerant prophets who had nothing in any case is here
carefully and quietly deradicalized by householders into ready almsgiving despite the possibility and probably past experience of abuse. And it is, I propose, precisely to that inserted beginning that the inserted ending "do what
you can" applies. Here, say those householders, is where "perfection" lies, and
here also is where one's best is enough.

Kingdom?

The social radicalism of the itinerants has not been denied or rejected, but the
householders have transmuted it into serious and heavy almsgiving. And that
raises some profound questions, ones that go far back and deep down into the
vision and program of the Kingdom of God. As those householders seek to
contain the radicality of the itinerants, should we mourn the Kingdom's
demise? Does the Kingdom stand or fall with the itinerants? Or does the Kingdom stand or fall with the creative interaction of itinerant and householder,
charisma and institution, radicalism and pragmatism? The dyadic relationship
of eating and healing, of itinerant and householder, was constitutive for the
earliest Kingdom companionship, as far back as I can discern its presence
within our extant texts. Maybe, then, the Kingdom was always to be found in
that dialectic. If, however, we opt for interaction, we must be able to find the
presence and conjunction of both parties. Where, today, are the householders,

and where, today, are the itinerants? Where, now, are the pragmatists, and where, now, are the radicals?

Conclusion

I have been told, as have many other historical Jesus scholars, that in our re-search we do but look down a deep well and see our own faces reflected in its waters. That could be dismissed as a cheap crack since it is seldom used by those who apply it to others against themselves. I accept it, however, as the most accurate description I can imagine of historical reconstruction of the past. Such reconstruction can be subjective, though it may deny being so; can-not be objective, though it may claim being so; but should be interactive, though it may fight being so. Present and past intertwine creatively, and the best we can ever hope for is to keep that interaction as even, balanced, and honest as possible. That, to return to this paper's beginning, is what method is about. Method, at its best, guarantees the fullest interaction of self and other, past and present.

It is rare to find a deep well. It is more rare to look down it long and hard. It is most rare to see your own reflection at the bottom. Your reflection there will be strangely different and differently strange. It is extremely rare, as Mar-cus Borg might say, to meet your own face again for the first time.

Questions and Responses from the Symposium

Q: How do you reconcile Jesus' words "The poor you will always have with you" with the claim that he had a deep concern for the poor, which you talk about a great deal?

A: The question concerns the story in Mark 14.3–9: A woman anoints Jesus with ex-pensive nard a few days before his death; after somebody complains that her action was extravagant and that the money should have been used to help the poor, Jesus says, "The poor you will always have with you."

First of all, I don't think this literally happened as reported in Mark. As far as Mark is concerned, what is important is that this woman is the first Christian. Jesus has been telling the disciples all the way from Galilee that he's going to die and rise. And they say, "Yeah, yeah. Whatever." Now this woman says, "I believe it. And so if I want to anoint you at all, I must anoint you now." She is, for Mark, the first Christian. That's why, whenever the gospel is told, Mark says, she will be remembered: She is the first Christian. For her, Easter came early that year.

Q: Do you believe the book of Revelation has merit for the year 2000?

A: Apocalyptic eschatology means that we (a small group, whoever we are) believe that God is going to slaughter everyone else except us. I want you to hear very clearly that apocalyptic eschatology is not just an innocent statement that the end of the world is coming soon and that if the statement's wrong, well, that's all right. Apocalyptic eschatology can corrupt the human imagination profoundly in that it imagines a God whose solution to the problems of the world is slaughter. I call it "divine ethnic cleansing." It's much better than human ethnic cleansing because it really does the job. We should take it out into the open and take a good look at it. No, I don't think it applies to the year 2000. I think it applied originally to the Roman Empire around the year 100. And I don't think it was the solution to the Roman Empire that Jesus had in mind.

Q: Could you speak a bit about the voice of Jesus in our time and connect it to the dialectic you spoke of between the itinerant and the householder?
A: As I understand the Kingdom of God from Jesus, it has very little to do with personal or individual sins, as Marcus Borg has also said. That doesn't mean they're not important. It means there's something even more important, which is structural or systemic evil. That's what Jesus was talking about. An example of an individual sin would be beating your slave. Jesus would ask why we have slaves at all–that's a systemic question. The Kingdom of God in the twenty-first century asks us, in America, today, where are all of us (I'm including myself, the churches, everyone) entrapped in systemic, structural evil? That's the first question Jesus is asking. It's a question for which nobody has a simple answer. Personal and individual sins are relatively easy to understand. Structural evil is like the air we breathe. It's all around us.

Q: In your book *The Historical Jesus,* you locate Jesus in the peasant class and refer to him as an illiterate peasant. What are the grounds for seeing Jesus that way?
A: According to experts on literacy in the ancient world, the literacy rate in the Jewish homeland in the first century was about 3 percent. That in itself doesn't tell me about Jesus. But he is from a peasant village, Nazareth. So the burden of proof shifts: How do you prove he was literate? If we could take Luke 4.16–21 historically, where Jesus goes into a synagogue, takes up a scroll, finds his way around an unpointed Hebrew text of Isaiah, and exegetes it, then, of course, Jesus was not only literate but a scholar. And that's the way Luke sees him. I think it would probably horrify Luke to think that Jesus was a peasant because Luke would probably make the mistake (which our country made in this century, too) of thinking peasants were dumb. Peasants are not dumb. They simply can't read. Jesus was orally brilliant. That's quite clear for me: in his use of metaphor, in his use of image, in his use of story, in his use of aphorism. But I don't find evidence for saying Jesus was literate; he was a peasant talking to peasants.

Q: Could you tell us how the historical Jesus can help us with the environmental crisis facing the twenty-first century?
A: I'm not going to try to say that Jesus has the answers for everything. That would be condescending to everyone involved. But it's very clear to me that the Kingdom of God has to do with (as Matthew puts it in the Lord's Prayer) *the will of God being done on earth.* The Kingdom of God is not about heaven. Heaven is in great shape. That's not the problem. It's really about the will of God for earth. What Jesus could see in his day was the injustice that was being perpetrated by imperial expansionism

and the economy in Lower Galilee; that's what he was focusing on. For us today, we see a far wider structural evil. It's as big as the world. That's what we have to deal with. You can get very easily, if you start with structural evil, to ecological crisis. If you start with personal evil, personal sin, it's very hard to get anywhere because certainly I'm not doing something personally that's going to pollute the world, but I am part of something that is. So think structurally, think systemically, and think about the Kingdom as being on earth.

Q: What do you think is most striking, appealing, or disturbing about Jesus?.

A: What is most striking about Jesus, for me personally, is that what is most appealing about him is most disturbing. If Jesus had settled down at Nazareth, as I think his family wanted him to do, and sent out followers to bring everyone to him, in effect saying, "Bring them to me, and I will teach them here; I will heal them here," then I would have to say that Jesus is part of the problem. He is part of the domination system, no doubt a gentler, kinder one, of course, than Caesar's, but still part of the problem, not part of the solution. He would not be part of human empowerment, but part of human domination. So it's crucially important for me that Jesus kept moving all the time, that there was no hierarchy of place symbolizing and masking a hierarchy of person. If Jesus had said, "I am the Kingdom of God," or "I bring the Kingdom of God; it was not here before me; it will not be here without me," then Jesus, too, I would have to criticize.

Jesus did not do that. I think he could have sat down with Amos in the Mediterranean sun, under an olive tree, surely with wine and bread, and they could have agreed that what Amos might have called the covenant of justice, Jesus called the Kingdom of God. They were talking about the same thing. Now what I find disturbing–indeed, terrifying–about that is I don't really think that what's being said here is, "You people run the world this way, and God has an idea for a better way; but if you don't do it, well, it's kind of all right, though you might get a bit punished." The Kingdom of God means for me the fabric of the universe, the only way it will work. It will not work any other way. Now behind that I begin to see something that terrifies me more than the Kingdom of God, which is the patience of God. I do not think that God intervenes in any sense, not because God could not; I make no such statement. God does not. And that frightens me more even than the radical justice of God. I am completely convinced that if we set out to destroy ourselves, God will not intervene to stop us, and God will settle eventually for the grass and the insects. That terrifies me.

4

Jesus and First-Century Judaism

ALAN F. SEGAL

Alan Segal is professor of religion at Barnard College and Columbia University in New York City. A well-known Jewish scholar, he is the author of six books, including Two Powers in Heaven: Rabbinic Reports About Christianity and Gnosticism *(1977),* Rebecca's Children: Judaism and Christianity in the Roman World *(1986),* The Other Judaisms of Late Antiquity *(1988), and* Paul the Convert: The Apostolate and Apostasy of Saul the Pharisee *(1990). His next book,* Writing the Hereafter, *will be on life after death.*

Segal received his bachelor's degree from Amherst College, graduate degrees from Brandeis and Hebrew Union College, and his doctorate from Yale. He has held prestigious fellowships from the Woodrow Wilson Foundation, the American Council of Learned Societies, the National Endowment for the Humanities, and the Guggenheim Foundation. Before moving to Columbia, he taught at Princeton University and the University of Toronto.

In his lecture, Segal does a number of things as he offers a Jewish perspective on Jesus. He first shows the important but limited use of the criterion of dissimilarity in establishing the historical existence of Jesus. Then he turns to what else can be said about Jesus with varying degrees of probability. He argues that the biblical texts used by early Christians to speak of Jesus' resurrection suggest that there is a strong apocalyptic stream in early Christianity and that Jesus himself was an apocalyptic figure who believed the end was at hand. Segal then turns to some concluding comments about Jesus' relationship to Jewish groups of the first century.

I recently heard of a new book by a contemporary Jesus scholar whose interpretation of Jesus was carefully nuanced. "Jesus is almost entirely a mystery to us from an historical perspective," he said. "All we know about him is that he was a feminist and a postmodern critic of society."

Well, we all understand the problem. The New Testament advises us to imitate Jesus; religious communities, which include scholars as well, constantly and often unconsciously revalue Jesus as the exemplar of the goals of our current social agenda. So besides remaking our lives in the image of Jesus, we are constantly remaking Jesus in our own image. He needs to be the very best we can imagine we should be. This is a warning to historians, for it makes doing history very difficult, if not impossible, as the postmoderns advise us. As historians we need to be most suspicious when we begin to come up with a Jesus who seems comfortably acceptable to our values. We may simply be succumbing to our own, often unconscious, prejudices.

My gift for this 2,000th birthday (if it happened two years ago, consider this a belated present) is to provide some perspective on the Jewish background of Jesus. Much scholarship has, in effect, overlooked this important aspect of Jesus' life: his undeniable Judaism. Even as I admire the acumen and courage of the so-called third search for the historical Jesus, I think we are no further along in discovering Jesus the Jew than we were a decade ago.

The reason for our lack of progress, more than anything else, comes from the very admirable and justifiable methods by which Jesus' life can be teased from its context. In the eighteenth and nineteenth centuries, the truth of the gospel stories was brought into doubt by the philosophies of the Enlightenment. Intellectuals asked, "What makes the stories of the Old or New Testament any more historically probable than Aesop's fables or Grimm's fairy tales?" It was the same inquiry that eventually brought all authority into question. Unfortunately, the truth of the New Testament depends either on divine authority or entirely on its own record. It is the only historical source that tells us much about Jesus at all. Although the New Testament contains four different accounts of Jesus' life and significance in the four Gospels, it basically counts as one source because there is no non-Christian witness to the events of the New Testament. When this became obvious in the nineteenth century, New Testament scholars needed to study the text in a whole different light.

Dissimilarity and Historicity

As a way of combating the Enlightenment's cultured critique of religion in general and Christianity in particular, scholars in the nineteenth and twentieth centuries developed criteria for judging the historical reliability of a source like the New Testament, which was written from the perspective of people who had already accepted the truth of its major propositions. A number of important criteria emerged, including Jewish background and multiple and early attestation. But they are all logically subordinate to what scholars call "the criterion of dissimilarity."[1] It is the most important arrow in our scholarly quiver on the issue of the historicity of Jesus.

In plain English, the criterion of dissimilarity means that to arrive at an undoubted fact in the life of Jesus, one must eliminate as possibly nonhistorical everything that is in the interest of the early church to tell us or that it could have taken over from Judaism. Conversely, for a fact or saying to be held historical, it must not be in the interest of the church to tell it; to be blunt, for a tradition to be indubitable, it must be an embarrassment for the early church. Thus, the criterion of dissimilarity is more or less identical with what is sometimes called "the criterion of embarrassment."

This is a very hard test. Many things Jesus is reported to have said or done will be eliminated by this criterion because we cannot demonstrate them to be free of the bias of the early church. Furthermore, and this is where this criterion most affects me, it almost completely negates Jesus' Jewish background. When Jesus says things that are also said by the early rabbis (such as the Golden Rule, which Rabbi Hillel is reported to have said in the generation before Jesus), the criterion requires that we suspect that the church has appropriated a famous saying for its most important wisdom teacher. This necessarily denies the possibility (and even the probability) that Hillel and Jesus both may have said similar things. Thus, the criterion of dissimilarity implies dissimilarity from early Christianity and from the Jewish environment as well. Yet logic seems to demand that any authentic Jesus would have to be thoroughly Jewish. Why, then, use this criterion if it involves us in a logical conundrum?

The answer is that the criterion was designed not to make it possible to write a biography of Jesus but to answer the challenge of the cultured despiser of Christianity as to whether *anything*–including Jesus himself–is historical in the Gospels. The criterion was designed to sift through the Gospels for indisputable facts so that scholars could be sure that the Jesus tradition is, at least in part, historical. The criterion also has a secondary and very important function, if I may be allowed an outsider's observation, of cautioning persons of different Christian denominations away from overconfidence about seeing their own beliefs as grounded in authentic New Testament facts; the criterion suggests that very few facts are indisputable.

So what passes this very hard criterion? Does anything? The answer is yes. Very few things pass (which is just what we would expect), but some do. Of course, this is the most important reason for using the criterion, for if some things pass, then we know that Jesus existed. Jesus was baptized by John (a great theological problem), Jesus preached the end of the world (which did not come), he opposed the temple in Jerusalem in some way, and he was crucified (a disreputable way to die, and the inscription on the cross implies a presumed political crime). No one actually saw him arise, but evidently his disciples almost immediately felt that he had.[2]

Gone are his Davidic ancestry, the birth stories, and many (if not most) of his sayings and his healings. Clearly, scholars are not saying that these events did not happen, though there are differences of opinion on what exactly failing the criterion means about the historical factuality of particular passages. Minimally, scholars are saying that if we cannot be (let's say) 99 percent sure that these things happened, then they cannot be used as evidence for the historical existence of Jesus.

Many Jews have intuitively understood the import of the challenge of nineteenth- and twentieth-century rationalism and would be very surprised to hear a Jewish scholar say that the existence of Jesus has been proved beyond a rational doubt. But I think we have to give the criterion its due. It has served its purpose in answering the question "Did Jesus really live?" The answer is yes. We can be as sure of Jesus' historical existence as we are of anything in history.

This does not mean that we have the 100 percent certainty of the faithful, who are always completely sure and whose minds cannot be changed by any argument. Our arguments are necessarily based on percentages of doubt, and our confidence in them must necessarily change as new evidence and arguments are adduced. Most likely Jesus lived; we are 99 percent sure he lived, let us say. That is, of course, a very different thing from saying that he was resurrected, that his resurrection is a historical fact in the way that other events are facts, or that the empty tomb is a historical fact.

To say Jesus lived means that the cultured despiser of Christianity is answered: The New Testament is not Grimm's fairy tales. However, it is not *The Congressional Record* either. As a historical document, the New Testament is subject to critique and analysis, as any document of that period must be. As many scholars have shown, the Gospels are not biographies but are missionary documents whose purpose is to convince hearers of the truth of the Christian message.

Many important New Testament scholars leave the issue there: We know only a few sure facts among the many things reported in the Gospels. Why go onto unsure ground? Why risk discourse bound to start interdenominational polemics? Why not settle for no biography if every biography is bound to be wrong or misleading?

Yet summarizing the matter with the few facts that pass the criterion of dissimilarity is not the only possible place to end up. It is almost always a dissatisfying place to be. Christians find it dissatisfying to be left with a mysterious Jesus with few, if any, preachings or healings, who stands against a black background, a constant cipher. For Jewish scholars, this place is also very frustrating because, as I mentioned earlier, it prevents us from saying very much about Jesus' Judaism. I want to go beyond these hard and important facts because virtually everything about Jesus' Jewish background has been eliminated by the criterion of dissimilarity. Moreover, no historian contents herself merely with what can be completely demonstrated. It is quite legitimate to argue and speculate about what may have happened, provided the scholar is prepared to describe the reasons and the level of confidence in the arguments.

But caution is in order. We leave the area of securely known facts and enter an area where we know much less, have less confidence, and the value of our arguments is more relative than the ones just discussed. We enter into an area where we must be satisfied with less than surety. To people whose faith depends on the reality of Jesus in their lives, this lack of certainty can be very confusing. But even nonbelievers encounter the same snare. Everyone, believer or nonbeliever, necessarily must deal with the issue of bias. We must be honest. The discussion of what Jesus was like is unsure and unsettling, even though Jesus is, ironically, one of the most written about persons of the first century, in spite of his humble beginnings and his life being almost entirely outside of the great events of history.

What Is Most Certain

So how would I place Jesus within his Jewish environment? We must begin with the early church and extrapolate backward to what is most likely to have existed in the pre-Easter setting. We must keep close tabs on what passes the criterion of dissimilarity. We must begin with several assured or virtually assured conclusions: Jesus lived and died as a Jew for his Judaism, and some of his Jewish convictions evidently impressed Rome and possibly some of the Judean ruling class as politically dangerous. He was the leading figure in a small movement of Jews who saw his death as a martyrdom like many previous Jewish martyrdoms.

It was evidently his earliest disciples who saw a victory in the Easter event and interpreted it as a sign that Jesus had been resurrected from the dead and ascended to heaven to sit next to God. I feel sure that the earliest Christians experienced the continued presence of Jesus in their lives not in some vague form but exactly in a form that combined a resurrected messiah, angel of the Lord, and Son of Man who was enthroned next to God.[3]

I begin with the scriptural support that the early church almost universally used to articulate its convictions about Jesus' resurrection. Not only is this use of Scripture very interesting, but it also provides a clue as to what may have been present in the Jesus tradition before Easter. Scripture for the earliest Christians was the Hebrew Bible, probably mostly as translated into Greek. The passages that seem to be at the center of the church's narrative of Jesus' resurrection and exaltation are somewhat strange from a Jewish point of view because they are not traditional messianic prophecies. Indeed, they are passages that no one has yet found combined in the same way in a non-Christian source.

Three passages are particularly important: Daniel 7.13–14, Psalm 110:1–4, and Psalm 8:

> I saw in the night visions, and behold, with the
> clouds of heaven there came *one like a son of man*,
> and he came to the Ancient of Days and was presented
> before him. And *to him was given dominion and glory
> and kingdom*, that all peoples, nations, and languages
> should serve him; his dominion is an everlasting
> dominion, which shall not pass away, and his kingdom
> one that shall not be destroyed. (Dan. 7.13–14)

* * *

The LORD says to my *lord*: *"Sit at my right hand,*
till I make your enemies your footstool."
The LORD sends forth from Zion your mighty scepter.
Rule in the midst of your foes!
The LORD has sworn and will not change his mind,
"You are a priest for ever after the order of
Melchizedek." (Ps. 110.1–2, 4)

* * *

What is man that thou art mindful of him,
and *the son of man* that thou dost care for him?
Yet *thou hast made him little less than God,*
and dost crown him with glory and honor.
Thou hast given him *dominion* over the works of thy
hands;
thou hast put *all things under his feet.*
O LORD, our Lord, how majestic is thy name in all
the earth! (Ps. 8.4–6, 9)

These passages were read in the early Christian movement as a kind of prophecy that turned Jesus' death into a victory punctuated by Jesus' ascension and enthronement in heaven as the Son of Man figure mentioned in Daniel 7.13, to whom is given authority to judge the nations at the last judgment. Psalm 8 adds the notion that the enthroned Son of Man is just a little less than God, crowned with glory and honor. Psalm 110 adds a messianic note as God is talking to God's "son" David; it also suggests that the enthroned figure is to be understood as LORD, at least in Greek, where *Kyrios* is equivalent to the sacred name of God in the Hebrew Bible, the tetragrammaton YHWH.

This consistent pattern of Jesus' glorification in heaven is present in most of the New Testament.[4] Moreover, the Gospels show that the identification of Jesus as Son of Man is early and important. In them, the resurrected Jesus becomes the figure mentioned in Daniel 7.13, a figure now explicitly called "the Son of Man," but prior to this Christian use, the phrase is better understood only as a reference to "a manlike figure in heaven" and not as a title at all. No other Jewish group had seen these passages as prophesying this enthronement or functioning in a similar light. It appears that these passages are the background of the post-Easter church's claim to the resurrection, messiahship, and divinity of Jesus, now understood as the beginning of the apocalyptic judgment foretold in Daniel 7.13.

The three passages together can almost be read as a narrative of the resurrection and ascension of Jesus as the figure enthroned next to God. We don't know why the Gospels make this identification, except that the phrase *one like a son of man* was part of a very famous apocalyptic document, the visions of Daniel 7–12, the first time resurrection is mentioned unambiguously in the Hebrew Bible and promised to martyrs: "And many of *those who sleep in the dust of the earth shall awake*, some to everlasting life, and some to shame and everlasting contempt. And those who are wise shall shine like the brightness of the firmament; and those who turn many to righteousness, like the stars for ever and ever" (Daniel 12.2–3).

It seems clear that the Christian use of this passage depends on Jesus' prior identification as a martyr and so cannot be earlier than the crucifixion. But is it possible that Jesus spoke of himself as the manlike figure of Daniel 7.13? It is unwise, given the evidence, to venture a guess, except to say that it is more likely that Jesus may have called attention to the vision of judgment in Daniel 7.13 without necessarily identifying himself with the manlike figure.

Whether we can take this identification back a few years and posit that this portion of Daniel figured prominently in Jesus' teaching is difficult to know. Even today it is difficult to know when a figure is quoted by a newspaper what exactly the figure said. According to the Gospels, Jesus was remembered as having identified himself with the figure on the throne, but this is highly problematic. However, neither Psalm 110 nor Psalm 8 appears to be as crucial to the combined tradition as is Daniel 7.13. The identification of Jesus with the manlike figure of Daniel 7:13 is crucial to the whole notion and, indeed, to all subsequent Christianity.

This combination seems impossible to explain without an apocalyptic (and not just eschatological) content in Jesus' preaching. Jesus preached repentance because he saw the end of the world coming soon and recommended a radical change of behavior as the only way to prepare for this event. He was, in the words of my colleagues Marcus Borg and John Dominic Crossan, an eschatological Jesus. But I think he was also an apocalypticist, which makes my view different from that of both Borg and Crossan. Jesus seems to me not just a Jew who believed that God would bring an end to the world but also a millennialist prophet. He was the chief inspiration in a religious movement against oppression, the likes of which we can sometimes see today among oppressed groups wherever a traditional worldview is being deeply challenged by a different and usually oppressive religious, political, or economic system. In short, Jesus was the leader of an apocalyptic movement.

We know something about movements like the Jesus movement. They are not uniform. They can be primarily symbolic and religious or primarily political, but they are always both at once in some mixture. We cannot adequately describe the mixture in the Jesus movement before Easter. However, in the contemporary world these millennialist movements always have political implications, especially in the eyes of the ruling classes, against which the hostility of the group is focused. But the language is almost always determinedly religious, not political. More often than not, the movement's political and religious aims are easily disconfirmed when the expected end does not happen, but sometimes only the political aspect of the future life is disconfirmed, and the group survives religiously.

Christianity is one of these rare movements in world history whose possible revolutionary political ideology (if it was there at the beginning) was disconfirmed by the crucifixion but continued as a more carefully defined religious movement. The Sabbatian movement among seventeenth-century Jews is another such movement. Some of the followers of Sabbatai Zevi thought that he would go to Istanbul to take the crown from the head of the sultan. But even when Sabbatai Zevi failed and even converted to Islam, many of his followers followed his example, seeing in his anomalous actions a revelation that the true Jewish mystic, like the mystical messiah, must take upon himself the fallen world in order to find the divine sparks within it and redeem it. The movement evidently still exists in rural Turkey today, albeit in minuscule numbers.[5]

To return to the case under consideration, whatever Jesus' followers may have expected of him, when Jesus was arrested, he evidently did not fight his incarceration. He was crucified by the Romans, who meant to insult not only him and his movement but through him also the entire Jewish community, which yearned to be free of Roman occupation. The inscription on the cross, "King of the Jews," shows exactly what the Romans wanted to convey to the Jewish people by crucifying him. (This inscription, by the way, passes the criterion of dissimilarity; even though it states Jesus' messianic status, it does so in a mocking way and has little to do with the titles with which the church proclaimed Jesus.) It was a ferocious and cruel way to show the restive Jews that revolt was hopeless and their expectations for a king ludicrous. The effect of the passion narrative is to disconfirm the political expectations of any disciples who may have harbored them. Jesus had eschewed political insurrection against Rome. The later church increasingly saw its future in appeasing Rome and blaming the Jews for the crucifixion.

Yet Jesus' crucifixion was a martyrdom within Judaism, at least as far as the Jewish populace would have seen it. Here was a Jew, like many other Jews, who died keeping his faith and died *for* keeping his faith, no matter how misguided many Jews would have thought him. His martyrdom was not at all unique at the time; crucifixions of Jews were very common under Rome. Yet it was not Jesus' death as a martyr but the Easter experience of resurrection and exaltation that transformed the demoralized group of early Christians into a new religious movement. The disconfirmation of political and religious hopes was revalued by the early church's experience of resurrection into a new apocalyptic religion of salvation.

That apocalypticism, like similar movements all over the world, could not long continue without the arrival of the apocalyptic end. The history of Christianity is a history of defusing the original millennialism or channeling it into more normative aspects of the church. Intellectual developments in later Christianity show this; attention to the immortality of the soul instead of to the apocalyptic resurrection of the body is but one of the foremost examples of how the church transformed itself from an apocalyptic movement into a mainstream one. In so doing, the church designed a program for survival since almost all apocalyptic movements observable today are characterized by their quick demise. Apocalyptic motifs tend to dissolve over history. If we are interested in the roots of Christianity, we must, at least at the outset, analyze these apocalyptic aspects. Since normative doctrines replace apocalyptic sentiments, we should look for the earliest aspects of Christianity, and perhaps even some of the teachings of Jesus, in the apocalyptic statements attributed to Jesus. They may not all be authentic; we must subject them to the same test as other traditions. But we should be careful to start with the apocalypticism of the earliest church.

It is no longer fashionable among Jesus scholars to maintain that Jesus was a millennialist or an apocalyptic Jew. But given the criterion of dissimilarity and the apocalyptic character of the early church, I think we have no other choice. The apocalyptic statements of Jesus pass the criterion of dissimilarity. What interests me specifically are the predictions of the end that did not come true. They are attributed to Jesus and speak of the end of time coming soon. Since they talk about an event that did not happen, it is understandable that they are neither very common nor repeated in later documents.

> For the Son of Man is to come with his angels in the glory of his Father, and then he will repay everyone for what has been done. Truly I tell you, *there are some standing here who will not taste death before they see the Son of Man coming in his kingdom.* (Matt. 16.27–28)

*   *   *

> When they persecute you in one town, flee to the next; for truly I tell you, *you will not have gone through all the towns of Israel before the Son of Man comes.* (Matt. 10.23)

The first passage meets the criterion of dissimilarity. It could not have been created by the evangelists around the year 70 because it was already manifestly false by then. Indeed, we can account for it only by assuming that it was said by Jesus and hence had come down from the very earliest tradents.

The second saying may not be authentic. Unlike the first, it presupposes a persecution of the movement that happened not during the lifetime of Jesus but only after his death. Yet it indicates an important continuity of apocalyptic sentiment between the early church and Jesus' own movement. The church's experience of pariah existence is given significance: It was foreseen by the master. Although reported as prophecy from the mouth of Jesus, this saying actually flows out of the post-Easter experience of the church. Thus, I see within these difficult passages a demonstration of Jesus' own apocalypticism and also the early church's continuation of it, at least for a time. For me, there is but one convenient way to explain why these sayings remain part of the corpus of Jesus' words: Jesus actually predicted that the end would come fairly quickly. This has a very clear context within Judaism and is understandable in the social world that Jesus inhabited.

There is also the evidence of other Son of Man sayings. Certainly in Mark, the influence of apocalypticism is apparent in these strange sayings, and I find the fact that they do not explicitly identify Jesus as the manlike figure of Daniel 7.13 to be evidence of their early origin: "Those who are ashamed of me and of my words in this adulterous and sinful generation, of them *the Son of Man* will also be ashamed when he comes in the glory of his Father with the holy angels" (Mark 8.38; see also Matthew 16.27 and Luke 9.26). Jesus is reported to have spoken of the Son of Man in the third person as if referring to a figure other than himself.

Scholarly opinions about the use of Son of Man in the Gospels vary widely. Some scholars think that only the future Son of Man sayings (such as this one) are authentic. Others are convinced that only the self-referential or present sayings (such as "Foxes have holes, and the birds of the air have nests; but the son of man has nowhere to lay his head" [Matt. 8.20 = Luke 9.58]) go back to Jesus. Still others think that none of the sayings can be attributed to Jesus but are generated by the post-Easter experience of the risen and glorified Christ, understood as the manlike figure on the throne of Daniel 7.13. But I am convinced that Jesus could have said something about the figure from Daniel that was later and retrospectively understood to be a self-prophecy, in part because there is not much record of speculation about that passage before Jesus.[6]

At least this particular Son of Man saying seems to me to be authentic, precisely because it does not identify Jesus with the heavenly manlike figure. Certainly, even if not all the Son of Man sayings are from Jesus' own mouth, they come from his immediate environment and before Easter because after Easter Jesus is clearly the Son of Man. Nor could these sayings have come from later because the church drops the title *Son of Man* almost immediately. If statements of this kind are not original, they must be so close as to come from Jesus' immediate followers on the basis of Jesus' own message of the coming Kingdom. There is no plausible way for them to enter Christianity afterward. Mark is a witness to this apocalypticism, Paul is imbued with apocalypticism, and the Q source is more eschatological and influenced by apocalyptic wisdom than is usually admitted.

In short, apocalypticism is rampant in earliest Christianity. It passes the criterion of dissimilarity. Moreover, I can't see how it could be absent in Jesus' message, present in the early community, and then wane and peak again in the early forms of the Gospels. It is far more rational to suppose that apocalypticism was there in Jesus' message and became an embarrassment to the church by the time of the gospel writers and certainly later.

That would seem to put me on the extreme opposing position to my friends here. But I do not think so, or at least I do not think that we must necessarily argue on every point. Of course, Marcus Borg has argued strenuously for a more balanced, less eschatological Jesus than the one I have drawn as emerging from the criterion of dissimilarity. He sees Jesus' preaching of the Kingdom to be important but not the central, defining, or dominant texture of the movement. I agree that Jesus does not seem to have preached his own return, and I would say that he does not seem to have identified himself with the apocalyptic Son of Man either. As I said, I don't think that there was such a title before Christianity because that is not the way in which Jewish exegesis or expectations of the future were expressed. Jews understood events by appeal to biblical quotations, not to preexistent figures. So probably Jesus used the term to refer to the whole scene in Daniel and not specifically to himself as the manlike figure.[7] Later tradition, which was less aware of the distinction and sure that Jesus had survived death to have ascended to heaven enthroned next to God, reunderstood the "human figure" as a preexistent messiah. This was a Christian, post-Easter innovation. Yet there is no question in my mind, using the criterion of dissimilarity, that the apocalyptic end was part of Jesus' message; and a reference to Daniel 7.13 would have been appropriate in that context. Apocalypticism was not at all atypical of first-century Jewish movements if we read Jewish history under Roman domination carefully.

Beyond What Is Most Certain

Apocalypticism is the central fact in our understanding of the historical Jesus because of the scholarly filter that we have had to use to demonstrate the historicity of Jesus. It cannot be ignored that Jesus predicted the end fairly quickly. But it is not the whole story. No one who taught only about the end would have garnered Jesus' following. There are numerous ancient and modern examples of persons who continually preached the end and only the end. They are tragicomic figures who do not attract a following. Successful contemporary apocalypticists do not only or always talk about the coming end. Every successful leader, even of a small group, must also make important sense for the present or be bereft of any followers. We are not free to deny apocalypticism, but unlike the *eschaton,* we do not have to end with it. Although apocalypticism is clearly part of the Jesus movement, it is not sufficient to explain either Jesus' message or why he attracted a following.

So what else can be said? Recently, some scholars have used categories drawn from other cultures to characterize Jesus. Some have argued that he was a Hellenistic Cynic sage.[8] The Cynics, a type of Greek philosopher, were

radical cultural critics whose short witty sayings and lifestyle (including itinerant homelessness and lack of possessions) poked fun at and ridiculed the con-
ventions by which most people lived. Granted, the wider Hellenistic culture
could have seen Jesus in terms like this because he was itinerant, attracted a
following, and may have favored Cynic values such as *autarkeia* (autonomy,
independence) and *parresia* (free speech). He may have lived for a time without the solace of home or family.

But is this not just as much of an imposition as calling Jesus a magician, to
cite another category used by some contemporary scholars?[9] There may have
been people who called Jesus "Magos," but is this the term that his own culture and he himself would likely have used to describe his mission? Jesus was
called a magician by his Jewish detractors, but not by his Jewish followers.
Similarly, Jesus would not have been characterized as a Cynic philosopher except in a purely Hellenistic context, which belongs to a later period.

Of course, it is always possible to paint a portrait of Jesus from a distant
point of view; but isn't it more accurate to attempt to get at the close-up? If so,
aren't we committed to finding a credible way to describe Jesus Jewishly? Calling Jesus a Cynic philosopher dissolves his Jewish identity. Any subversive
leader of the first century might have had some of the characteristics of a
Cynic philosopher; indeed, not just Cynics but also other philosophers affected the *autarkeia* of Diogenes. But Jesus was not a card-carrying member of
any Hellenistic philosophy. He may never even have heard of them. I would
sooner believe that Paul could have been seen as a Cynic, for Paul was a Jew
who was at home in more than one cultural world, and he seems to have used
Cynic-style diatribes in many contexts.[10]

Although I can identify the problem, I'm not sure that I want to attempt an
equally cogent but opposing portrait. But I think an outline can be suggested.
Jesus clearly was a leader of a not insignificant Jewish movement of the coming Kingdom. Certainly, Jesus would have needed all the skills of pastoral sayings and dominical sayings to have been a successful Jewish leader. But we
could go in many different directions from this core.

Does Jesus fit into any of the Jewish sectarian movements of his time? Was
he a member of the Dead Sea Scroll community at Qumran (probably to be
identified as Essenes) or close to it? There is no evidence that he was but some
evidence that he shared some points with the community. He had in common
with it the conviction that the end was near. Like those belonging to the community, he was not very interested in spelling out detailed apocalyptic systems, as the writers of some apocryphal and pseudepigraphical works were.
But Jesus was not very interested in the priestly or communal agenda of Qumran. Nor was he, like John the Baptist, especially ascetic or monastic. Nor was
he a baptizer, which characterized both John and the Essenes.

Was Jesus a Pharisee? In some respects he seems close to the scriptural
agenda of the Pharisees. With them (and the Essenes), he believed in resurrection. Some Pharisees talked about angels as Jesus did. The Pharisees af-

firmed on oral tradition of Torah, and some of Jesus' sayings imply an acceptance of some kind of oral tradition. Clearly, Jesus' early followers endorsed
Jesus' own sayings as an oral tradition and especially the love commandment
as a key for interpreting Scripture. He studied Torah and critiqued wrong interpretations of it, as all the groups did. He had a similar notion of how to
demonstrate life after death (Matt. 22.23–33). But Jesus, despite his legal
sense on occasion, seems inimical to the communal life and purity regula-
tions of the Pharisees and a social class away from them in education, sophis-
tication, and urbanity.

Jesus interpreted purity very differently from the Pharisees. It is not, as
many have supposed, that Jesus was opposed to purity rules, while the Pharisees fostered them. Rather, Jesus (somewhat like the Qumran sectarians) interpreted all purity obligations in the moral realm and therefore preached the
ones that furthered avoidance of sin (not necessarily egalitarianism). In this
Jesus resembled the Essenes, though they had a much greater agenda in purity
than the Christians, as they lived communally, baptized daily, gave priests a
great deal of deference, and generally lived as if they needed to enter the temple daily. The Pharisees (and the rabbis after them) separated the two spheres
of sin and impurity radically. Sin was still sin and punishable or forgivable according to its own rules. But the rabbinic tradition, reflecting different periods
in Jewish history, tended to make purity into an almost totally separate system
that in many cases operated without any necessary connection with sin.[11] Although this distinction between sin and impurity makes a great deal of sense
from the rabbinic point of view, it is easy to see how this could be seen as
hypocrisy by other Jewish groups, including both early Christians and Essenes. The Pharisees, and the rabbis after them, did not live in strict communities as the Essenes did, nor did they share belongings; rather, they provided
for charitable institutions for the common good. The early Jerusalem church
apparently did treat property communally, though this practice was quickly
abandoned, especially in the Gentile mission.

In short, even though Jesus endorsed a program similar in some respects to
that of the Pharisees, I think he would have been closer to the critique of the
Pharisees found in the Qumran community: The Pharisees were hypocritical
sayers of "smooth things." The New Testament calls them hypocrites, and the
Qumran community appears to have called them "slick" exegetes. Jesus'
much-debated sayings about oaths and vows fit this pattern of eschewing the
subtle legal solutions of the Pharisees in favor of plainspoken, morally unim-
peachable behavior, a standard that was very high: "Be perfect, therefore, as
your heavenly Father is perfect" (Matt. 5.48), and "Jesus said to him, 'If you
wish to be perfect, go, sell your possessions, and give the money to the poor,
and you will have treasure in heaven; then come, follow me'" (Matt. 19.21).

Jewish teachers, of course, preached morality and high standards of behavior. But perfection, as here outlined, is a still higher, more sectarian standard
that entails embracing communal life and eschewing wealth, as the Essenes

did. It is the mark of a millennarian group that it shares property in just this way. This social ideal is also a direct attempt to emulate the coming paradise on earth as it approaches.

Jesus' role as the leader of a small social movement is as important a definer of his identity as anything else we can find. Movements of this sort in Jewish life in the first century most often relied not just on exegesis but also on direct prophetic inspirations as to the meaning of Scripture. This leads me to a final speculation. Of special interest to me is the frequency with which reports of religiously altered states of consciousness appear in early Christianity. I think Jesus was a mystic, but not exactly in the sense of a person who studiously sought visions by disciplined contemplation. It would have been very hard, if not impossible, to be an apocalypticist without being a visionary in Jesus' Jewish culture. So I think Jesus may have been a kind of religious visionary who experienced religiously altered states of consciousness. With this I stand firmly with Marcus Borg, though I think it is the early Christian connection with apocalypticism that most demonstrates that Jesus was a mystic.

We must be willing to argue back from the behavior of the early church to the Jesus movement, searching for plausible connections. There is no question that Paul received visions and revelations of Christ and that he saw himself in a prophetic role in acting upon these visions and preaching upon them. Peter is said to have received visions that guided his actions with regard to the food laws. Indeed, the transfiguration scene in the Gospels resembles nothing so much as a revelatory experience of Jesus in the post-Easter church.[12] It may reflect the kinds of experiences early Christians had more than something that happened in the life of Jesus. There are events in Jesus' life that seem to resemble apocalyptic revelations, such as the healings and the desert temptation, which has been discussed at greater length by Marcus Borg in his books.[13] This characteristic of early Christianity seems to fit apocalypticism and popular wonder-working very closely, but not to fit the Cynic philosopher hypothesis at all.

I think my admittedly incomplete portrait of Jesus is still mysterious because of its unfinished nature and because of the difficulty we have in appreciating Jesus' apocalypticism. Jesus' apocalypticism most challenges us as scholars and likewise most challenges believers who wish to emulate Jesus. Like all apocalypticists, he set very high standards and insisted that his followers live as if already in the new world order that was shortly to arrive. It appears that one way in which his followers transformed his preaching was a consequence of seeing his resurrection and glorification as the sign that the *eschaton* had arrived. Although its arrival was not yet evident, it would shortly be disclosed to all. That is surely Paul's understanding of time, and he is our earliest named Christian writer.

Because of this resurrection and ascension, Paul clearly identifies Jesus as divine. So also does the book of Hebrews by linking sonship with a divine name of God: "But of the Son he says, 'Your throne, O God, is forever and ever, and the righteous scepter is the scepter of your kingdom'" (Heb. 1.8). Here we see that Elohim (a name of God) is identified with Jesus as the Son of God. In this early report we have a very clear example of how the process of explicating Jesus' post-Easter divine nature continued.[14]

I do not think that Jesus preached his own divine status. On the contrary, I think such preaching is historically impossible. But Jesus was not just a philosopher or a wisdom teacher or a political revolutionary. He did not live in a community that argued philosophically. He lived among people who looked to Scripture to understand how God would vindicate the downtrodden righteous. His wisdom sayings, healings, and mysticism all seem to me to naturally fall out from this basic fact. That, in turn, seems to lead directly to the appreciation of his role as the leader of an apocalyptic group. Otherwise, he is just a preacher of return to Jewish piety. But even more important, if we were to give up the apocalypticism of early Christianity, we would give up our basic claim to have shown Christianity's historicity because inherent in the apocalyptic claim is the core of sayings that pass the criterion of dissimilarity.

My portrait is not very different from the one that the New Testament gives us of John the Baptist, who lived and died a Jew in everyone's opinion. What changes the portrait are the events of Easter. After the Easter events and Jesus' presumed resurrection, the Jesus movement began to work out a Christology of a human raised to divine status. That event also initiated the end of time, which the movement expected to come to conclusion very quickly. That it did not necessitated many changes in the movement's thought structure, which evolved over centuries and takes us away from my topic today.

So my portrait of Jesus is similar to that of my colleagues in that it is a challenging and not particularly comforting portrait of Jesus. We cannot "domesticate" Jesus into a person with whom we can be entirely comfortable. It is, unfortunately, also necessarily an unfinished portrait. One thing is sure: I would be very suspicious of my own method if I came up with a Jesus who was not particularly Jewish but looked a lot like a professor of religion of the late twentieth century—even if I could put a name such as Cynic philosopher upon that portrait. Instead, I think a millennialist Jesus who was a religious innovator in a Jewish religious context is the Jesus I find historically plausible. I don't think you have to be Jewish to appreciate a Jesus who is somewhat other, strange, maybe wonderful, but still mysterious and incompletely understood. But it helps.

As scholars or persons of faith, we all face the same issue because of the epistemological problems of the twentieth century: We cannot make history serve to remove our doubts about faith. We can be sure of a few things in the 90 percent range. This is not much solace. It is not like digging up a piece of the true cross or Noah's ark. But these are fools' expectations in our world. Those who naively trust these kinds of frauds are justly confounded.

The great Jewish philosopher and theologian Martin Buber said it best: The true person of *faith* lives in a state of *holy insecurity*. Buber meant that anyone who believes in God in the twentieth century must be prepared to admit that there are no objective criteria to demonstrate that belief. To be 100 percent sure of one's life and faith is, Buber says, *fanaticism*. Unfortunately, there are many people who flock to the side of fanaticism for the strong sense of security and moral simplicity that it provides. But in the end, it is against discussion and tolerance. Anyone who demands certainty with no doubt is merely valorizing intolerance. We should not leave the historical study of Jesus to naive historians and readers who come up with a Jesus who is a tool of intolerance. The method, and not the conclusions we reach, is the real importance of our historical inquiries.

Questions and Responses from the Symposium

Q: Professor Crossan said he wanted to know, "What was there for Paul to persecute?" Do you have a response?

A: I think the pre-Christian Paul shows that the early Christian movement must have been perceived as dangerous. It must have been apocalyptic and eschatological because all movements of reform in that day were both political and religious. If Jesus had not been against some of the things he saw in his society, there would have been no reason for Paul to be worried as a Pharisee. But I think it's also likely that Paul was one of those right-wing Pharisees who were likely to be more intolerant than some of his brothers, at least before he became a Christian, and that his Christianity was a way of doing away with that intolerance.

Q: I would like you to say more about the purity code because it seems to me to be a central aspect of Jesus' teaching that at least parts of the purity code excluded people.

A: Marcus Borg has looked at that of late, and I think he is correct that Jesus did a critique of the purity code. It's surely true that if Jesus said, "The pure in heart will see God," that he was saying some aspects of purity, namely, those aspects necessary to gain a religious vision, can be safely done away with. And I think that if Jesus were looking for a justification for that statement, he would have looked to some of the prophets of the Hebrew Bible.

On the other hand, I don't believe that the purity codes, or the purity laws in the Hebrew Bible, necessarily operated to oppress people. We may not like observing them, and we may find them oppressive in a personal sense, but that's not what I'm talking about. I don't think women were oppressed by the purity laws, nor were Jewish men. On the whole, Gentiles were not part of this purity issue—at least the rabbis eventually decided that Gentiles weren't. So I don't think that it automatically excluded people from religious life.

People became pure or impure in the course of daily living, and impurity is not the same as sinning. In fact, it rarely is the same. It is only the same when one deliberately goes against a purity law in order to break it. If one were to walk inside the temple in an impure state, that would be a deliberate sin. Some people have claimed that Jesus did that, but I don't see any evidence. Impurity as a result of contact with certain substances or because of one's married sexual life is in no sense sinning. Although sexual relations bring about impurity, it doesn't mean that sexual relations are wrong or forbidden. Impurity is the natural by-product of them in the minds of those people, and all that is required to remove the impurity is bathing afterward. So becoming impure did not exclude one from society. In fact, most of the society would have been impure as a matter of course and would have seen the observance of purity rules as an opportunity to raise their sanctity.

Q: You spoke about the relationship of Jesus to the different Jewish groups of his day, but some scholars have claimed that Christianity would have remained a minor Jewish sect if it hadn't been for the apostle Paul. What is your view of Paul's role in turning a minor Jewish sect into a successful new religion?

A: I think there's some truth in that claim. But it's an ironic truth because I don't believe that Paul thought of himself as a success in his own day. I think he fought desperately for the inclusion of his group of proselytes, namely, the Gentiles, those with whom he had most success, into the growing community of Christianity. Of course, the term is anachronistic because Paul didn't use "Christianity" but referred to members of "the way" or whatever he was calling his new group. I think Paul thought of himself as an embattled minority voice. On the other hand, I think history has shown us that his writings have been most responsible for justifying a Gentile Christianity. But I don't think it's exactly what Paul intended. In fact, I think if you look at his letter to the Romans, he intended something much greater: the inclusion of Jews and Gentiles in one community, with equal voices for both. That, so far, hasn't happened.

Q: My question deals with the purity laws and women's menses. Within the Jewish tradition, are the menses of a woman so powerful as to make her presence cancel out any kind of ritual power, for instance, of men in the community?

A: The menstrual cycle of a woman makes her impure, in the technical sense of the word, until she has undergone a ritual of cleansing and, of course, until the menses have stopped. We are not to think of this as in any way sinful. A woman's menses also makes a man impure, so husband and wife would seek to stay apart during her period. It is also true that a man's sexual emissions make both of them impure. All of these kinds of impurity are remedied through immersion and, in Jesus' day, through sacrifice. Possibly, Jesus opposed the heavy understanding of sacrifice—that may be one of the things that disturbed him about the temple scene, for certainly people coming to Jerusalem for the Passover would need to purify themselves in order to eat the paschal meal. It may be that he found that difficult. If so, he was not alone in Judaism among Jewish thinkers of that day.

The evidence in the New Testament is somewhat ambiguous, in part because the gospel writers did not understand the issues very clearly. It is easy to see their mistakes. When Mark says that all Jews washed their hands for purity reasons, it's an exaggeration. The Bible commands only priests to do so, although the Pharisees advocated that ordinary people take upon themselves priestly obligations. So it was a kind of pietistic and holiness movement that said that ordinary people could become as priests if they practiced the same kinds of purity. Rather than creating an oppressive situation, the Pharisees were a religious purity-equalizing kind of movement.

Q: This talk has been particularly interesting to me because it's the first time I've heard a Jewish scholar speak about Jesus, and, as a Christian, Jesus and his Jewish background are very interesting to me. What sort of response have you had from Jewish audiences? Are they interested in hearing about Jesus from a Jewish scholar?

A: That's a very good question, and there isn't a single answer. There are many Jews who prefer not to talk about Jesus because they feel that he is the central symbol of a faith that has not been particularly tolerant of Jewish society. There are many Jews who know nothing about Jesus. It may be quite a surprise to you to discover that most Jews grow up in the United States without ever having read a word of the New Testament. Therefore, Jesus may just be irrelevant. And yet there are many more who are intrigued by Jesus and would like to see him as a member of Jewish tradition but don't know exactly how to do so. And I think I'm one of those.

5

"You Are the Christ": Five Portraits of Jesus from the Early Church

KAREN JO TORJESEN

Karen Jo Torjesen is Margo L. Goldsmith Professor of Women's Studies in Religion at Claremont Graduate School. A well-known scholar of early Christian history, she is the author of over a score of articles. Her 1985 book Hermeneutical Procedure and Theological Structure in Origen's Exegesis *treats the important early Christian theologian Origen. Her widely read 1993 book* When Women Were Priests: Women's Leadership in the Early Church and the Scandal of Their Subordination in the Rise of Christianity *has been translated into German. Currently, she is working on books tentatively titled* From Housechurch to Imperial Church *and* The Invention of Woman: A History of the Doctrine of Woman's Nature. *Before moving to Claremont, she held teaching positions at Mary Washington College (Virginia) and Georg August Universität (Göttingen, Germany).*

She has received a number of prestigious fellowships, including ones from the National Endowment for the Humanities and the American Council of Learned Societies. She earned her bachelor's degree at Wheaton College, her master's at the School of Theology at Claremont, and her Ph.D. at Claremont Graduate School.

In her lecture, Torjesen describes the emergence of christological thinking about Jesus during the crucial and formative first three centuries of the Christian era. Central images such as Sophia (Wisdom), Victor, Teacher, Logos (Cosmic Reason), and Pantocrator *(Ruler of All) were borrowed from Jewish and Hellenistic culture as a way of expressing who Jesus had become in the experience, thought, and practice of the early church.*

When Christians of the second and third centuries struggled to articulate the true identity of the Galilean prophet executed by the Romans, they drew on the rich resources of Mediterranean religions and philosophies. It was their naming of the person of Jesus and their language about his divine work that have reverberated across the centuries. To these early Christians we owe the portraits of Jesus as Divine Wisdom (Sophia), Jesus as Victor over Death, Jesus as Divine Teacher (*Didaskalos*), Jesus as Cosmic Reason (Logos), and Jesus as World Ruler (*Pantocrator*). The details of each of these portraits of Jesus reflect the distinctive insights of the communities that crafted them.

A quick overview of these communities shows that Jewish Christians steeped in the traditions of Divine Wisdom, Sophia, saw in her a divine partner in the work of creation and a divine guardian who instructed and nurtured the Israelites through their long history; these Christians interpreted Jesus as Sophia's messenger and then as Sophia's incarnation. For early Christian communities that faced martyrdom and whose burial rituals were often celebrated in the catacombs, the image of Jesus as Victor over Death articulated the power of Jesus as transcending the authority of the state and the daimonic powers behind it. The apologists defending Christianity to the persecuting emperors portrayed Jesus as the Divine Teacher whose powerful teachings could make of even the despised classes of potters, fullers, and miners respected and virtuous citizens, a feat that the best philosophers had failed to perform. Christian intellectuals trained as philosophers put Jesus at the center of the cosmos, explaining him as the Logos incarnate, a cosmic principle accounting for the goodness, order, and rationality of all created things. When in the 300s the first emperor converted to Christianity, the cosmic Logos gained political significance, and Jesus became World Ruler, exercising an authority that flowed through the emperor to the populace and through the bishops to the church. These are the portraits of Jesus that I trace as they unfold over the first three centuries.

Popular Cosmology

Each culture has its own distinctive concepts and categories for thinking about the divine, articulated at times in a cosmology, at others in a mythology. Early Christian communities shared with their contemporaries common notions of the divine and used them as a framework within which to fashion their particular Christologies. The societies of the ancient Mediterranean imagined the relation between the human and the divine as a continuum stretching from this physical world across a vast distance to the realm of the most perfect, most pure, most blessed, and most beautiful—the divine.[1]

The earth was both at the center and at the periphery of the ancient cosmos, imagined as concentric spheres. It was peripheral because it belonged to the lowest realm; it was central because it was the reference point. The sphere most distant from its heavy center was that of the fixed stars, those perfect, timeless, luminous bodies inhabiting the perfect, tranquil, divine realm of rarefied intelligence. The Jewish god, the Christian god, and the divine of the Platonic tradition lay beyond the realm of the fixed stars.

Below the fixed stars and yet still a part of the upper realm suspended in the rarefied realm of ether were the seven planets (which included the sun and moon), whose regular circuits exemplified a stable, perfect, and unchanging motion. Both the fixed stars and the planets were understood to be divine and perfect beings; their luminescence was a manifestation of their divinity. The moon formed the lower boundary of the upper world, and below it were the teeming realms of change and time.

Still divine but somewhat ambiguous were the powers of the sublunar realm: the intermediate daimons, angels, principalities, and powers; the ruling daimons of peoples; the daimons of the elements; and the tutelary daimons attached to souls at birth. These were the powers that governed the physical world, human society, and the underworld.

This two-tiered cosmos, of the unchanging divine and the realm of changeable matter, framed the ancient world's notions of the human person. The eternal soul and its reasoning parts (the mind) consisted of the same ethereal material as the upper world. From this realm the soul descended or fell into the heavier, darker realm of the lower world, became enclosed in a material body and encrusted with passions (lust, anger, greed, domination, and arrogance). Each of the following portraits of Jesus places him somewhere within this cosmology.

Jesus as Divine Wisdom (Sophia)

The earliest Jewish-Christian traditions about Jesus proclaimed him as a prophet of Sophia, Divine Wisdom. Jesus as a street preacher is called an emissary of Sophia. "Therefore also the Sophia of God said I will send them prophets and apostles, some of whom they will kill and persecute" (Luke 11.49).[2] When the message of Jesus to the poor and the outcast was derided, he responded by appealing to Sophia: "Sophia is justified by her children" (Luke 7.35).[3] Paul calls the crucified Christ the power of God and the Sophia of God (1 Cor. 1.22–24).

Who or what is Sophia? For the preceding four centuries, Sophia was a familiar figure in Diaspora Judaism and Mediterranean Judaism. "Sophia strides into the book of Proverbs with a noisy public appearance. She is a street preacher, a prophet who cries aloud in the market and at the city gates a message of reproach, punishment and promise."[4] She prepares a banquet at which she is both the benefactress and the teacher: "Come eat my bread and drink the wine that I have mixed" (Prov. 9.5). She is a teacher of righteousness, knowledge of God, and justice.[5]

In the book of Proverbs the figure of Sophia appears as a preacher, teacher, and prophet, but most important, she is given a role in creation: "The Lord created me at the beginning of his work, the first of his acts of old. Ages ago I was set up, at the first, before the beginning of the earth. . . . Before the mountains had been shaped, before the hills I was brought forth. . . . When he marked out the foundations of the earth I was beside him like a master work-man and I was daily his delight, rejoicing before him always, rejoicing in his inhabited world and delighting in the human race" (Prov. 8.22–31).

The cosmic role of Sophia, who is present at the creation, is that of a master architect shaping the world order according to wisdom. In the book of Sirach Sophia says of herself: "I am the Word which was spoken by the Most High; it was I who covered the earth like a mist. My dwelling place was in high heaven; my throne was in a pillar of cloud. Alone I made the circuit of the sky and traversed depths of the abyss. The waves of the sea, the whole earth, every people and nation were under my sway" (Sir. 24.3–6). A heavenly figure, she guides both the cosmos and human history.

In the Wisdom of Solomon, from around 50 B.C.E., she is spoken of as a guardian and savior of God's people. Sophia/Wisdom protected Adam when he was first formed. She delivered Adam from his transgression, whereas Cain perished because he abandoned her. She saved Noah, rescued Lot from the burning cities, guided Jacob, and protected Joseph in the dungeon. She was the cloud by day and the fiery pillar by night, the guardian who led the op-pressed Israelites out of Egypt and punished the Egyptians. She gave them water from a rocky cliff.[6]

The writers who built on the earlier Sophia traditions invested Sophia with all the cosmic operations the ancient world associated with the realm of the divine. Sophia knows and teaches all of the "cosmic secrets," "the alterations of the solstices," "the changes of the seasons," "the natures of animals," "the powers of spirits," "the virtues of plants." She is the fullest manifestation of the divine:

> For in her there is a spirit that is intelligent, holy, unique, manifold, subtle, mobile, clear, unpolluted, distinct, invulnerable, loving the good, keen, irresistible, beneficent, humane, steadfast, sure, free from anxiety, all powerful, overseeing all and penetrating through all spir-its that are intelligent and pure and most subtle. For Wisdom/ Sophia is more mobile than any motion; because of her pureness she pervades and penetrates all things. For she is a breath of the power of God and a pure emanation of the glory of the almighty, for she is a reflection of eternal light, a spotless mirror of the working of God and an image of his goodness. Though she is but one she can do all things and while remaining in her self she renews all things. Every generation she passes into holy souls and makes them friends of God and prophets. (Wisd. of Sol. 7.22–27)

The writer of this beautiful passage praises Wisdom/Sophia in terms that show that she belongs to the highest realm of the divine: She is of the purest, finest substance; her realm is the realm of intelligence and knowledge; she ex-ercises power and oversight over all that is below. In short, Sophia encompasses all aspects of the divine associated with the resplendent domain of the fixed stars and planets. Furthermore, she has saving functions as the one who reveals God. She actively sustains and renews the created world and unites herself with those who belong to God.[7]

An early hymn to Christ found in the New Testament letter to the Colossians casts Jesus in the role of the cosmic Sophia: "He is the image of the invisible God, the first born of all creation; for in him all things were created in heaven and on earth, visible and invisible, whether thrones or dominions or principalities or authorities—all things were made through him and for him. He is before all things and in him all things hold together" (Col. 1.15–17). Jewish Christians would recognize in this hymn the claim that Jesus was the incarnation of the cosmic Sophia. Or as Paul says, "For us there is one God the father, from whom are all things and for whom we exist; and one Lord Jesus Christ through whom are all things and through whom we exist" (1 Cor. 8.6). In this passage, Paul applies to Jesus Christ the unique creative role of Sophia and thus attributes to him a cosmic significance "extending far beyond the observable influence of the crucified prophet from Nazareth."[8] Elizabeth Johnson observes that John's portrait of Jesus is shaped by the Sophia tradition more than any other gospel: "Like Sophia, Jesus calls out in a loud voice in public places, speaks in long discourses, invites people to come eat and drink using the symbols of bread and wine and teaches divine truth."[9]

Like Sophia, he is identified with Torah, and he promises gifts of life and light. John's prologue celebrating the Word/Logos ("In the beginning was the Word, and the Word was with God, and the Word was God" [John 1.1]) reads like a hymn to Sophia. When John reveals that Jesus is the Logos by making life and light central attributes, John is shaping Jesus in the image of Sophia.[10]

Communal Setting.   What meaning did Christ as Sophia have for the worshipping community? Were there distinctive forms of worship that reflected an understanding of Jesus as Divine Wisdom? Wisdom for first-century Christians represented a distinctive kind of knowing. It was closely allied with prophecy. Paul described wisdom as the knowledge of the divine realm that lay beyond the realm of chance, fate, and the daimonic powers that govern the created world.[11] Paul's Divine Wisdom is, in fact, hidden from the powers that rule the visible cosmos, those lower powers that control the material world. Wisdom is the knowledge of God's secret purpose, of God's nature, of the depths that are beyond seeing, hearing, and imaging. Knowing wisdom glorifies and dignifies the knower.[12]

In fact, this kind of knowing is possible only for those who possess the divine nature that Christians have received through the new birth. Such Christians are spiritual persons, and they are able to interpret spiritual truths.[13] Paul dramatizes the potency of this kind of knowing by quoting the rhetorical question in Isaiah 40.13, "Who can know the mind of the Lord?" which anticipates the humble response, "No one can know the mind of the Lord." But,

Paul counters, not only can we know the mind of the Lord; we, in fact, also *possess* the mind of Christ. Spiritual persons are among the perfect, and this superiority places them above judgment. Although they are capable of judgment and discernment, they are not subject to judgment.[14] These spiritual persons are rich in wisdom/knowledge (*gnosis*), rich in speech (*logos*), and rich in gifts (*charismata*).

In the worship of the Corinthian church, all participated in speaking God's wisdom to one another in a mystery.[15] They sang, they prayed, they prophesied, they praised, they taught, they exhorted, and they spoke in angelic languages. Through interpreting spiritual things, they disclosed the mind of Christ in a multiplicity of forms.[16] Their speaking in each of these forms was inspired by the Divine Spirit, and through their worship the boundaries between the divine and human realms became fluid and porous. They experienced themselves in their new identity as spiritual persons, at home in a spiritual realm, having been given a new spiritual identity through their baptism into Christ, their putting on of Christ, and their possessing of the mind of Christ.[17] In the Corinthian context the figure of Divine Wisdom who calls all and invites all to her banquet and becomes the teacher of all was identified with Christ, who invites everyone–Jew and Greek, slave and free, male and female–to participate in Divine Wisdom.[18]

Jesus as Victor over Death and the Powers

The periodic outbreaks of persecution that wracked the churches during the first three centuries forged powerful links between the crucifixion of Christ and the execution of the martyrs. Out of this experience of martyrdom another powerful image of Christ was crafted. For the church of the martyrs, Christ was a savior, a hero, and, most important, a victor. Christians who experienced the political and judicial oppression of Roman power used political and military metaphors to assert that Jesus was not an executed criminal but a victorious hero. The story of Christ as Victor was recreated in the drama of martyrdom, and it was there that the story found its most potent expression.

During the Decian persecution in the mid-200s, an African noblewoman, Perpetua, was arrested.[19] While imprisoned, she had a series of visions that interpreted both martyrdom and the "victor" Christology. Shortly before her execution in the amphitheater where she was scheduled to fight with the beasts, she had a vision. In this vision she is led into the arena, but now as a gladiator, a warrior, stripped and oiled and ready to fight. It is not wild bulls and bears that come out to fight her but a "fearsome Egyptian of great height."[20] In fierce hand-to-hand combat Perpetua defeats her opponent, triumphs over him by placing her foot on his head, and is led out through the gate of life, victorious, a hero having won the prize of life. The crowd cheers her victory as she is awarded the prize of the contest, a laurel wreath. By this Perpetua knows that her contest will be with the devil and victory will bring her eternal life.

Perpetua's vision reinterpreted her arrest and execution in a theology of martyrdom that reversed the meaning of state judicial violence and turned it into a celebration of victory over death and over the powers of the state. The church of the martyrs knew that Jesus was the victor over death and the salvation that he brought was immortal life. The drama of the arrest, interrogation, torture, and execution of the martyrs reenacted the events of the arrest, interrogation, and crucifixion of Jesus.

To the callous eye of the idle spectator, the events surrounding the crucifixion told the story of a Jesus who was a victim. In the story of Jesus' arrest in the Garden of Gethsemane, Jesus was a wanted man, a fugitive hiding in an orchard outside the city. The secret police penetrated the garden, the fugitive himself was betrayed by a follower, and his friends put up a feeble resistance and were scattered. In the trial he was caught in the machinery of justice, a victim of the violence of the judicial process, subjected to chains, scourging, beating, and, finally, execution by the cross. The crucifixion was an event of suffering, aloneness, and a final succumbing to death. Not until the resurrection was there a message of deliverance from death that transformed the meanings of the ordeal.

The reversal of this story, which casts Jesus as the victor, tells the "real" story from the standpoint of the persecuted church. Gethsemane was a preparation for the contest with death. Jesus prepared like an athlete, praying, gathering strength, building concentration to be ready for the moment of the contest. When death came stalking him in the garden in the persons of soldiers and a band of rabble-rousers, the enemy was engaged, and the contest had begun. In the trial each of the instruments of death was met and mastered–the chains, the whips, the rods, and the cross.[21] Even the surrender to death itself became a turning point in the contest, for by submitting to death, Jesus overcame it. The resurrected body, like the victor's crown, was the victor's trophy over death. It was the evidence that death could be conquered and that it could not overpower divinity.

Christ the Victor was more than a savior from death. He was also a liberator from the hostile powers of the sublunar cosmos–that vast hierarchy of spiritual authorities and rulers that controlled events in the world of change.[22] Paul himself speaks of conversion as a liberation from the tyranny of these intermediary powers of the cosmos: "We were in bondage to the ruling spirits of the cosmos," who, in comparison to Christ, are "weak and beggarly" (Gal. 4.3, 4.9). In fact, Christ not only is superior to these ruling spirits of the cosmos, but he also has conquered them and leads them bound as captives in his victory parade. A victorious emperor or general celebrated his triumph and demonstrated his victory over his enemies by forcing them to march in chains in his victory parade. It is this image of a victorious Christ leading all the ruling powers of the cosmos as captives in his triumphal procession that Paul invokes.

Here the work of salvation is portrayed as a cosmic drama in which Christ the Victor fights against and triumphs over the evil powers of the cosmos that hold humankind in bondage.[23] This vision of Christ the Victor eventually was elaborated into a soteriology that identified victory over the daimons with victory over death and the devil, who had rights over humankind because of sin. As the fourth-century theologian Epiphanius puts it, humanity "harmed by the serpent would have been abandoned to death but Christ the second Adam found the strong one, spoiled his goods and annihilated death, bringing to life humanity who had become both the devil's possession and subject to death."[24]

The image of Christ as Victor proclaims a powerful reversal in which the vulnerable, the captive, and the tortured become the conqueror, the victor, and the hero. The drama of the martyr's death recapitulated Christ's victory over death and over the daimons. In so doing, it renewed the powerful vision of Christ as Victor.

Communal Setting. In what settings did the early church celebrate Christ as Victor? What were the forms of worship that rehearsed this image of Christ? Christian burial rites and memorial services for the deceased provided the ritual context for a profound appreciation of Christ as Victor. Early Christians followed Roman burial practices by celebrating a common meal with consecrated bread and wine on the anniversary of a death.[25] When held for those who had died a martyr's death, these annual celebrations became the feasts of the martyrs, often celebrated at night in a vigil by the tomb. In the course of prayers, petitions, and a eucharistic meal, the stories of the martyrs were retold. In them the church celebrated the reversal from victim of persecution to victor over death, as the martyrs reenacted Christ's first contest with death.

Jesus as Divine Teacher (*Didaskalos*)

Although it was primarily street preachers and wandering prophets who populated the religious landscape of the Roman Empire, those who wore the mantle of respectability were the few educated elites. They had learned to read and write by studying Homer, trained in rhetoric by reading classical literature, and underwent rigorous intellectual training by attending the philosophical schools. Only these educated elites, it was thought, were capable of achieving moral perfection (it was a common tenet of aristocratic empires that those with higher status also possessed moral virtue). Through a rigorous exercise of the mind, they disciplined the irrational and errant passions. Their discourses and deep reflections on the beauty, goodness, and eternity of the divine realm further refined their moral sensibilities.

Celsus, a second-century detractor of Christianity, scoffs at Christians as rude, illiterate, lower classes that gathered to discuss their superstitions in the backs of shops. But in this very ridicule the early defenders of Christianity found a way to show that Christianity contributed to Roman society, in spite of the fact that Christians refused to participate in important civic and religious rituals. To defend Christians from ridicule and persecution, the apologists created an influential portrait of Jesus as Divine Teacher who succeeded where the philosophers had failed. Philosophers, whose teachings were accessible only to the educated elite, could lead only a few to the moral life, but Jesus the Divine Teacher had succeeded in leading people from all social classes into the moral life, a feat that no philosopher before him had achieved.[26]

Not only had philosophers failed to raise the masses to the level of morality that Roman society admired, but also Roman laws could not do it. Christ the Divine Sage taught an even higher morality than that observed by the Romans. Justin, a second-century Christian apologist, argues, "For what human laws could not do, that the Word [Christ], being divine, would have brought about if the evil daimons had not scattered abroad many false and godless accusations [resulting in the persecution of Christians]."[27] Justin's evil daimons were the gods who demanded ritual sacrifices offered at the Greek and Roman temples and the administrative daimons who manipulated rulers and public officials to suppress the teachings of the Christians. In Justin's cosmology, the role of the daimons in world governance included preventing people from escaping daimonic control by converting to Christianity. If the Roman emperor Hadrianus Antoninus, to whom Justin wrote, would protect Christians instead of persecuting them, these are the transformations he would see:

> Those who once rejoiced in fornication now delight in continence alone; those who maintained use of magic arts have dedicated themselves to the good and unbegotten God; we who once took more pleasure in the means of increasing our wealth and property now bring what we have into a common fund and share with everyone in need; we who hated and killed one another and would not associate with men of different tribes because of differing customs now after the manifestation of Christ live together and pray for our enemies and try to persuade those who unjustly hate us, so that they, living according to the fair commands of Christ, may share with us the good hope of receiving the same things from God.[28]

Why would the emperor continue persecuting Christians when he understood that these same Christians could bring a moral revolution to his empire? In Justin's portrayal of Jesus, he has the powers of a philosopher and miracle worker. He is the Son of God because of his own miracles and the miracles associated with his birth. At the same time, Justin argues that Jesus' wisdom and the divine nature of his teachings are sufficient to identify him as a Son of God [29]

The portrait of Jesus as Divine Teacher had a natural home in Roman culture, which believed that the potency of the divine could actually reside in a teacher.[30] The study of philosophy is directed toward the changeless, timeless, and invisible realm of pure intelligibility. "This divine realm enters into society in the person of the teacher."[31] The presence of the divine in the sage is so enlightening, so compelling, that it is like a fire that kindles in the disciple such a passion to know that the disciple models himself on the teacher. This imitation of the divine in the teacher gives birth to the divine in the disciple. Origen of Alexandria, a third-century Christian theologian, describes Christ the Logos/Word as just such a teacher: "And the soul is moved by heavenly longing when, having clearly beheld the beauty and the fairness of the Word of God, it falls deeply in love with his loveliness and receives from the Word himself a certain dart and wound of love. For this Word is the image and splendor of the invisible God. . . . [The soul] will suffer from the dart himself [Logos] a saving wound and will be kindled with the blessed fire of his love."[32]

When Origen develops his concept of Christ as the Logos, it is Christ the Divine Teacher who lies at its heart. Christ is the Divine Teacher who leads the soul to its own divinization by firing it with heavenly love. A bonding takes place between the teacher and the followers. Through that bonding, a moral transformation is set in motion, and over a period of maturation the follower is assimilated into the divine. Consequently, the bonding of the students to the teacher is salvific. The presence of divinity in the teacher engenders the powers of interpretation, understanding, communication, and instruction that guide the students in the quest for the divine. Through a process of maturing, the students eventually become assimilated into the divine and attain divine status themselves. This is how Origen understands what it means to become "sons of God."

Because in Roman society there were two different teaching functions, that of the tutor (*paidagogos*) and that of the master teacher (*didaskalos*), the image of Christ as Divine Teacher produced two distinct portraits. Well-born families employed a tutor to be responsible for the moral formation of a child. The tutor inculcated good manners, taught proper aristocratic bearing, and, most important, helped form in the child Roman character and virtues. The tutor guided the process of formation that created the religious, social, and class identity that embodied the values of Roman culture.[33] The term *didaskalos* was used for the teacher who instructed students in the higher sciences and for the master who taught a group of disciples. The social role of the tutor lies behind the portrait of Christ as pedagogue who undertakes a similar moral formation for young Christians just entering the faith. When they are more mature, Christ the *Didaskalos* who mediates the higher wisdom of the divine will be their guide.[34]

A second-century Christian theologian from Africa, Clement, makes this distinction between Christ as *Paidagogos* and Christ as *Didaskalos* central to his ideas about salvation. As *Paidagogos* Christ provides guidance for the day-to-day life of Christians. The simplicity of his dress and eating habits serves as a model for their lives, and his moral teachings form their character. When Clement speaks of the "higher wisdom" (*gnosis*) that the master imparts to the advanced souls on their way to perfection, Christ is a *didaskalos*, a master.[35] For Christian intellectuals like Clement, conversion only began the process of becoming Christlike; it would not be completed until the soul bore the perfect image of its maker. In the words of Friedrich Normann, "This same teacher is also the one who became human in order to encompass all of humankind in his school of the church where the goal of formation and education is a process of assimilating to the divine."[36]

Communal Setting. What is the Christian communal context in which Christ as Divine Teacher is encountered? Christ the pedagogue whose work is moral formation is encountered in catechetical instruction. By the third century, it took three years of apprenticeship in the Christian life to become a Christian. Christ was also experienced as pedagogue in the moral discipline that the church imposed on its members. In its early years this was done through mutual correction and in the third century by the disciplinary authority of bishops, priests, and widows.

Christ as *Didaskalos* was deemed present, above all, in Christian schools, such as Alexandria in Egypt, that featured teaching on Christian doctrines and lectures on Christian philosophy. In fact, one of the ways in which converts from the educated upper classes were brought into Christianity was through the Christian schools.

Jesus as Cosmic Reason (*Logos*)

There are actually two contexts for encountering Christ as the master: the Christian schools and the scholar's study. Origen of Alexandria is the representative, par excellence, of the scholar's study for third-century Christianity. Building on the work of earlier theologians who identified Christ as the Logos, Origen developed an extended portrait of Christ as Cosmic Reason, one that was philosophically sophisticated and biblically based.[37] One could think of it as a companion piece to today's scholarship on the historical Jesus because the Christ who is Cosmic Reason answers the questions that troubled Christian intellectuals in antiquity.

In the philosophical schools, ancient thinkers imagined the entire cosmos as deriving from a single source or principle that stood outside of the visible world of change and chance and beyond the worldly categories of knowing.

For a human mind whose knowledge was mediated by the material world manifest to the senses, the source of all was difficult to know and impossible to express. The perfection of the first principle of the cosmos required that it remain utterly free from contact with the visible world of time and change. To explain how this distant, unknowable, yet perfect source (God) still ordered the cosmos, the philosophers proposed a mediating principle that could interact with the material world of time and change and still remain part of that timeless realm of pure divinity. Depending on the philosophical system, this principle was called Mind (*Nous*) or Reason (*Logos*). By ordering the cosmos and making it rational, this mediating principle also made the cosmos intelligible and therefore knowable.

The problem for Christian intellectuals such as Origen was this: If Jesus is the Son of the creator God who is the source of all, how could he have any part in bodily and temporal existence? The solution was to claim that the historical Jesus was also the cosmic Logos.[38] The philosophical idea of a mediating principle became a very effective way for Christian intellectuals to explain to their educated and cultured despisers who the historical Jesus was. The historical Jesus was simply the cosmic Logos incarnate.

For the Christian philosophers to identify Christ as the Logos was a way of claiming the preexistence of Christ and explaining that Jesus was divine in a philosophically meaningful sense. The historical person Jesus is the eternal Logos incarnate in time. Christ as Logos is God's mind or intelligence and thus the image of the invisible God. Therefore, the cosmic Logos is the basis for all truth and the foundation for all knowledge. The historical Jesus, who is the cosmic Logos visible in the flesh, is the one who mediates knowledge of the divine.

The whole created order is an expression of the order, purpose, meaning, and rationality of the Logos; therefore, Christ as Logos is present in every created thing. Because Christ as Logos encompasses all the wisdom of the philosophers, every quest for truth and every search for wisdom will lead to Christ the Logos. For Origen, Christ the Logos as the embodiment of philosophical wisdom and Christian truth is the hidden spiritual meaning of every Scripture.

Furthermore, Christ as Logos is present in every human being as a capacity for rationality. The universal presence of the Logos in every rational being means all creatures created through the Logos have knowledge of the universal Word. What this means is that everyone has the potentiality to recognize the Logos Christ, who becomes a universal savior, not just because he preaches the gospel to all peoples but also because he is an intrinsic part of the very structures of existence.

Jesus as World Ruler (*Pantocrator*)

Our last portrait reveals Christ as World Ruler.[39] When the martyrs were tried before provincial governors, they were ordered to sacrifice to the gods and obey the emperors. In this practice the interests of the state in religion come sharply into focus. Prayers and honors shown to the gods on behalf of the emperor were essential for the welfare of the empire. The Roman state supported the performance of rituals, paid the salaries of the priests, and financed the festivals because honoring the gods was essential to secure their continued patronage of the city and the empire. This understanding of the patronage of the gods becomes an important aspect of Christology in the fourth century.

The story of the emperor Constantine's conversion in the early 300s includes an account of a vision that Constantine interprets as Christ's offer to become Constantine's new patron and secure for him victory in battle. When Constantine carries into battle a standard bearing the first two letters of the name *Christ,* he enters into a new relationship with this god, and Christ becomes the new protector of the empire.

Constantine's conversion had great significance for the church, for when Constantine took Christ as patron, suddenly the rituals honoring this new god (which, of course, were Christian liturgies) now became essential for the welfare of the empire. Consequently, Constantine returned the properties that had been confiscated during persecution to the church, subsidized the clergy, passed laws against doing business on Sunday, and eventually persecuted the enemies of the church.

Out of Christ's role as patron emerged a new image of Christ as World Ruler. Imperial titles such as savior, shepherd, physician, God, and father were transferred to Christ in this new role as patron of the Roman Empire. A new image of Christ as a heavenly emperor came to dominate Christian art. In this new iconography Christ appears wearing the imperial purple, a color reserved for the emperor alone; Christ is attended by high government officials on either side (the archangels); enthroned on the cosmos, he receives gifts and honors from figures representing both church and state.

Communal Setting. With this image of Christ as world ruler, a new space for Christian worship was created: the basilica. The basilica (which became the classic architectural shape for church construction) was taken over from Roman political life. It was, in effect, a throne room. With an apse that housed the bishop's throne, the basilica was modeled on the ceremonial hall in which an emperor received dignitaries. New rituals of worship borrowed from imperial ceremonies gave liturgical expression to the new Christology of Christ as the heavenly emperor. Many of the rituals of honor for the emperor designed to convey a sense of the emperor's distance, formality, and even transcendence (such as prostration before the emperor, processions with his portraits, and the burning of incense before them) found a place in Christian worship.[40]

What happened in the fourth century was of momentous significance, for the cosmic order became fused with the political order. The image of Christ as Cosmic Reason merged with the image of Christ as World Ruler. The claims of early Christianity that Christ is a universal savior were fully realized in this new Christology, for Christ now functions as the cosmic principle and source for the entire universe and simultaneously as the ultimate political authority behind both the state and the church. Although this development gave great honor to Christ, it also over time became the basis for providing theological legitimation for hierarchical and oppressive social orders and political systems. Christ as World Ruler was often to become the legitimator of dominant culture rather than its subverter.

Thus, by the fourth century the primary christological images had been honed and polished by a rapidly growing church seeking to explain to itself and the society in which it matured the meaning of this Jesus who was central to the church's faith. These early images and the theological concepts they engendered have formed the vocabulary with which Christians have spoken of Jesus ever since. Christian theology in subsequent centuries has typically sought to integrate these images and concepts into a single system, more often than not subordinating them to the Trinitarian language of Father, Son, and Spirit, whose dominance in Christian thought is also a fourth-century development, the product of the imperial church's definition of its beliefs at the Council of Nicea in 325 C.E. But behind this dominance of Christian thinking about Jesus by creedal language is a tapestry of rich diversity. The images of Christ as Sophia, as Victor over Death, as Divine Teacher, as Cosmic Reason, and as World Ruler, coming from the earliest Christian communities, can continue to provide a pluralistic context for Christian theological reflection today.

Questions and Responses from the Symposium

Q: Some people believe Jesus spent time before his public ministry in India, studying with the Hindus. The idea is not totally absurd; long before Jesus, Alexander the Great marched his armies from Greece to India. What are your thoughts on that?

A: I'm intrigued with the India connection, but I don't see any reason to connect it particularly with Jesus. There is an India connection in Alexandria in Egypt. Pantinius, the head of the first Christian catechetical school in Alexandria, was a missionary to India. There is some interesting work on the intellectual exchange that might have gone on between India and the Christian and philosophical schools in Alexandria.

Q: Do images of Christ as "the good shepherd" in early Christian art predate the image of Christ as *Pantocrator* (King)? And what would be the liturgical setting for those?

A: The good shepherd images (and there are an enormous number of them) are associated with funerary art, Christian and non-Christian. The state of the blessed is imagined as very pastoral and idyllic; shepherd and the sheep, green pastures and posies and water, are consolation images. But there's quite a bit of debate about whether these images in Christian funerary art really reflect what second-century Christians thought. Did they see Christ as the good shepherd? You don't find that motif a great deal in the written sources.

Q: Would you compare and contrast Sophia and Logos?

A: The figure of Sophia and the figure of the Logos are, by many ancient Jewish and Christian intellectuals, developed side by side. The figure of Sophia is a gendered image that is easily seen as a female figure. The Logos figure is more easily seen as a male figure. What basically happens is that the Sophia image and the constellation of functions connected with it gradually evolve into a Logos image, and the Sophia image gets essentially eclipsed by the Logos image. The Logos image is, I think, more abstract and philosophical. It seems to me less rich than the Sophia image, which gathers a whole domain of wisdom, experience, and practice and can be legitimately associated with maternal wisdom. That is absent from the Logos image.

Q: Given such a rich and varied set of images of Christ and Jesus, why do you think the church is so resistant to some of the claims and directions of postmodernism, which functions as a way of relativizing all images?

A: The answer, I suppose, is fairly obvious. Let me talk about what I call the life cycle of a doctrine. An image begins by being born out of profound religious experience. Then it gets articulated by a community and perhaps synthesized by an individual in a creative process. Then it becomes an image with which a community can really resonate; it takes root, as it were, in much broader circles. As it takes root in these larger circles, it begins to function normatively; it begins to establish boundaries and to define power relations. Eventually, when an image is in its last stage of the life cycle and about to die, it then becomes very authoritarian, formal, and rigid, loosed from its context in life, where it originated. Finally, it collapses under its own weight. But at that stage we're dealing with power relations. Because an image functions to cement power relations, there is resistance to change.

Q: Would you expand on the transition or relationship between Sophia and Logos?

A: A lot of my recent work is on issues of gender in the development of early Christianity. I seem to be tracing out a process that I will call the masculinization of Christianity—a very long process propelled by a whole variety of causes and sources. In that process there was a shift from Sophia as a female figure (with which ancient society was very comfortable) to the figure of the Logos. Ancient society was much more comfortable with maternal power than contemporary society because of the difference in family structure in antiquity. In the writings of Philo (a first-century Jewish philosopher who lived in Alexandria), you can see some of that transition. Although Philo speaks of both Sophia and Logos, he is very ambivalent about any kind of a female figure; whenever he uses female imagery, he always makes clear that it's subordinate to male images. He was very anxious that the gendered imagery conform to gender hierarchy. Forces like that led to an eclipsing of the figure of Sophia.

Q: We started the morning talking about Jesus as the peasant teacher who taught to peasants and for peasants. Early images of Christ the Savior and Christ the Liberator connect with the peasantry, but later images of Christ as philosophical teacher and as *Pantocrator* seem much more masculine and hierarchical and connect to the upper classes rather than to the peasantry. Are these later images maybe even antithetical to what Jesus said?

A: With any image, literary or artistic, and with any cultural production, one of the most important, and probably the first, question to ask is, "Who's producing it?" When you see mosaics, or when you see basilicas built on a very grand scale, you know that wealthy people were responsible for them and that they produced the images out of the patterns of social relations that characterized their world. They used the symbols that moved them, and so you have a class trajectory from the second to the fourth century in symbols.

Q: How did second-century Christians reconcile their picture of Christ as the cosmic Logos with the New Testament picture of Jesus as finite and suffering and mortal? Do you think these pictures are compatible?

A: That's very well formulated, and it was the dilemma of Christian intellectuals a few centuries later. It's important to understand (and I think we keep missing this point) that in the worldview of antiquity, the claim that Jesus was divine and the Son of God was an important claim but also a credible claim. It was almost an ordinary claim. Within the framework of our worldview, the claim is very radical, but it's not that radical in that period. The dilemma emerged when it became a question of how to integrate the Logos Christ (the Christ who had become divine in the fully philosophical sense) with the human person of Jesus. And you don't really get to that dilemma until the Council of Nicea (325) and, more than a century later, the Council of Chalcedon (451). So that was really not yet a question in the second century.

6

Jesus and Generation X

HARVEY COX

Harvey Cox is Thomas Professor of Divinity at Harvard University, where he has taught for over thirty years. His 1965 book The Secular City *became a best-seller and made him a household name in academic and church circles. He has published many other well-known books, including* On Not Leaving It to the Snake *(1967);* Turning East *(1977);* Religion in the Secular City *(1984);* The Seduction of the Spirit *(1985);* The Silencing of Leonardo Boff: Liberation Theology and the Future of World Christianity *(1988);* Many Mansions: A Christian's Encounters with Other Faiths *(1988); and, most recently,* Fire from Heaven: The Rise of Pentecostal Spirituality and the Reshaping of Religion in the Twenty-first Century *(1994). His video* Jesus Christ Movie Star, *done for the BBC, was shown the first evening of the symposium.*

Cox's undergraduate degree is from the University of Pennsylvania, and he holds graduate degrees from Yale and Harvard, where he earned his Ph.D. Before becoming a professor at Harvard, he held positions at Temple University, Oberlin College, and Andover Newton Theological School. An ordained American Baptist minister, he is also an avid tenor saxophonist and plays regularly with a Boston band called The Embraceables.

This lecture flows out of his teaching for many years one of the most popular courses at Harvard, "Jesus and the Moral Life." In these pages, he describes the most striking qualities of the "twenty-somethings" who took the course (their suspicion of institutions, religious pluralism, and selective eclecticism) and shows how these qualities shape students' responses to Jesus. He then discusses the theological issues raised by this process and argues that, despite all, the question of the religious significance of Jesus remains.

For fifteen years I have taught a course at Harvard College on Jesus. Designed mainly for undergraduates, it begins with a careful review of the life of Jesus as it unfolds in the synoptic Gospels (Matthew, Mark, and Luke). It then moves on to two principal foci. The first is the effort currently being made toward the *historical reconstruction* of Jesus in the work of people such as Marcus Borg,

Dominic Crossan, and John Meier. The other focus might be called the *cultural resymbolization* of Jesus in current theologies, poetry, literature, and the popular arts. This second focus includes the appearance of indigenized interpretations of Christ among Asian, African, and Latin American Christians; the ways Jesus is understood in non-Christian religions such as Judaism, Islam, Hinduism, and Buddhism; and, finally, the persistent reappearance of Christ figures in contemporary films, music, novels, and even MTV.

The whole thing began in 1982 when a college administrator asked me to design a course that could be offered in the "moral reasoning" division of the newly devised core curriculum. The next fall I began teaching "Jesus and the Moral Life," at first in the basement auditorium of the Fogg Art Museum. To the astonishment of the people on the college administration who thought Harvard students were not too interested in religion, and of outside critics who thought of Harvard as a den of agnosticism, from the outset the course drew enormous numbers of students. Usually from four hundred to eight hundred enrolled. One year registration topped one thousand, and I had to move the lectures to Sanders Theater, where visiting orchestras and rock groups perform.

Although I would like to attribute the enormous interest in the course to my own eloquence, honesty compels me to say that the real reason probably lies elsewhere. Although Harvard students, like their counterparts elsewhere, had begun to evidence a growing interest in religion during the 1980s, one that continues unabated today, they had been given little opportunity to pursue this inquisitiveness at our school. In checking old catalogs, I noticed that no course specifically on Jesus had been taught at Harvard College since Professor George Santayana offered one just before he left Harvard for good in 1912. I was merely filling a very wide and continuous gap.

Like any course, this one has evolved over the years as new scholarship and new interpretations of Jesus continue to appear. Also, any teacher is constantly looking for new ways to present material so that it makes some connection with the changing student mentality; so while I was teaching, I was also carefully monitoring term papers, listening attentively to the questions students asked in class, leading discussion sections, and studying the evaluations students wrote at the end. I probably learned as much about them as they learned from me, and since the nearly four thousand students who have taken this course are now the twenty-somethings or the Generation X of so much recent analysis and speculation, I think I know at least a little about their minds and spirits.

I especially include the word *spirit* here because it quickly became evident to me that most of the students had not enrolled in the course merely to fulfill a moral reasoning requirement (there were forty other courses they could have taken to do that) or just to satisfy their idle curiosity. They were looking for something else, something more existential. I know this because after a few years, in addition to the exams and book reports, I also began requiring a paper at the end of the semester in which each student was invited to answer, entirely in his or her own terms, the question Jesus put to his disciples at Caesarea Phillipi: "Who do you say that I am?" (Mark 8.27). I assured them that they could be as orthodox or heretical, as appreciative or critical, as they chose, and that, although the paper was required, it would not be given a grade. I also announced that I would personally read and respond to as many of the papers as I could. Later on I also permitted those students who wished to, to submit a self-made video, poem, musical composition, or some other expression as long as it constituted their own response to Jesus' question.

As a result of what I have learned (and continue to learn) in this course, the purpose of this presentation is to record some observations about Jesus and Generation X. My data, therefore, do not consist of a clutch of dusty new manuscript finds from Nag Hammadi or the latest results of the Jesus Seminar polling. Instead, I rely on the stacks of term papers, tapes, songs, and poetry I have received from my students in the past decade. I want to address such questions as:

Who is Generation X?

What attracts (and repels) the members of this generation about Jesus?

Why do they feel and think the way they do about religion and spirituality?

How can the message of and about Jesus be most effectively communicated to them?

What can those of us who are not part of this generation learn from it about life, about Jesus, and maybe about ourselves?

Who is Generation X? The label itself suggests an anomalous conglomerate, a demographic blip with no distinct identity. These young men and women are certainly not Gertrude Stein's "lost generation" of the 1920s. They are not interested in fighting either bulls in Madrid or fascists in Barcelona. They are not the activist/hippie/dropout cohort of the 1960s. They are not even the narcissistic "me generation" of the 1980s. They are something different. Indeed, there is something indefinable about these twenty-somethings (some of whom are now early thirty-somethings). They are neither rebels nor conformists, neither libertines nor ascetics, and–perhaps most germane for our purposes–neither believers nor nonbelievers. They are something sui generis.

Perhaps the first thing to register about Generation Xers is that they are certainly not indifferent to religion. A 1994 Gallup poll reported that fully 86 percent of Generation X say that religion is "important" and 43 percent that it is "very important" to them. In these respects they do not differ markedly from the findings about the American population as a whole. Yet there is something else going on, for 83 percent of the Generation Xers questioned said they thought religion was losing influence in our society, while somewhat fewer (69 percent) of the general population think it is. As the baffled Harvard administration—and I myself—discovered from the experience of my course, this is *not* a generation that is bored or blasé about religion. But this generation is interested in religion, as I was to find out, in a quite different way.

Nevertheless, statistics cannot tell us much. Music does. One of the features I introduced in my course was that as the students entered the lecture hall, I would always have music playing. I played parts of a wide variety of selections during the ten minutes before the class actually began: hymns; Gregorian chant; the sacred music of Bach, Mozart, and contemporary composers; Mahalia Jackson; gospel choirs. After a while, students began requesting their favorites, then bringing in their own tapes. Now and then among these would be songs by rock groups that focused on Jesus. I was grateful for this introduction into a musical idiom with which I was not familiar.

But as I listened to it, I found I was learning something important about my students. For one thing, they are painfully aware of their lostness and confusion, and they know their dilemma has something important to do with the fact that they have a hard time believing anything. They see their situation in spiritual terms, a kind of latter-day "dark night of the soul." I learned this when a student brought in a tape by a group called the Goo Goo Dolls that to her seemed very germane to a course on Jesus:

> don't it make you sad to know that life is
> more than who we are
> we grew up way too fast
> and now there's nothing to believe
> and reruns all become our history

Indeed, for Generation X the admixture of confessing a sense of confusion with a wistful longing for something else is a central quality of much of the music. Take this lyric, for example, from the rock artist Sting:

> You could say I lost my faith
> In science and progress.
> You could say I lost my belief
> In the holy church.

As this song shows, the most striking quality about the young people of Generation X is that, although they may have lost faith in traditional religion, they have also lost faith in the adversaries of traditional religion. They have lost faith both in holy church and in science and progress. It is hard to imagine a member of Generation X losing his or her faith "like a sudden ascending whirl of dust particles" after reading Charles Darwin or Robert Ingersoll, as did the Reverend Clarence Wilmot in 1910 in John Updike's new novel *In the Beauty of the Lilies*.[1] Also, the fact that they have lost faith in traditional religion does not mean they have lost interest or even deep concern. They are willing to rely on science for the limited things it has proved it can do, but their heads are already crammed with images of dead fish and seagulls immobilized by oil spills, lists of endangered species, and the rancorous debate over global warming. They are grimly aware, as their parents sometimes were not, that science cannot answer their most pressing questions. They remain enormously intrigued with the traditional religions, especially with their mystical expressions, but not with conventional churches. They want to pick and choose and are less willing to accept religions either as full-blown systems of truth or as authoritative institutions.

But there is another equally impressive quality about Generation Xers. They are fully willing to admit that they have lost their sense of direction, even willing to sing about it. The lyrics of their songs contain neither the caustic polemics of the Grateful Dead nor the loopy fantasies of the Beatles. Their amorphous indeterminacy has its positive side. They appear ready to move on and are on the lookout for a more promising map of reality. Furthermore, as I also found out, although they have their doubts about doctrines and rituals, ministers and theologians, they retain a continuing fascination for Jesus. Sometimes Christ appears in a disguised form, but often his appearance is quite explicit, as in these lines from a rock tune entitled "I Still Haven't Found What I'm Looking For," which was sung by the wildly popular group U2:

> I believe in the kingdom come
> when all the colors will bleed into one . . .
> you broke the thorns
> and loosed the chains
> carry the cross of my shame
> you know I believe it
> but I still haven't found what I'm looking for . . .

Strangely attracted to the figure of Jesus, but still looking for something indefinable, Generation Xers see Jesus as beyond or before churches and different from the doctrines they have heard about him. Let us examine a couple of the most salient qualities of Generation X and note how they correlate with its "take" on Jesus.

1. Generation Xers are famously suspicious of all institutions, including governmental, educational, and religious ones. But they are looking for a Jesus they can trust. I think this explains some of the enormous popularity of the recent books about the "new quest" for the historical Jesus. Whatever Dominic Crossan and Marcus Borg and John Meier and the others think they are doing, I am convinced that what the young (and not-so-young) people who read them are looking for is a deinstitutionalized Jesus, one who does not come bearing any institution's imprimatur.

The problem, of course, is that if they take the current quest for the historical Jesus with any degree of intellectual seriousness, they often soon become more confused than they were before they started. No wonder. A few years ago in a widely influential article, Jesuit biblical scholar Daniel J. Harrington suggested that there were at least seven plausible contending portraits of Jesus in scholarly circulation.[2] One was E. P. Sanders's picture in *Jesus and Judaism* (1985) of an eschatological prophet bent on reforming the temple and Jewish national life. Another was the revolutionary Jesus of S.G.F. Brandon's *Jesus and the Zealots* (1967). In 1978 the recently deceased historian Morton Smith published *Jesus the Magician*, in which he claimed to discern behind the gospel stories—especially the exorcisms and the sojourn in Egypt—a popular wonder-worker who disturbed the religious establishment. Harvey Falk in *Jesus the Pharisee* (1985) situated Jesus within the School of Hillel during its struggle with the School of Shammai (two Pharisaic "schools" of interpretation) for control of the Jewish community in Palestine. Geza Vermes portrayed Jesus as a Galilean charismatic in *Jesus the Jew* (1973), and Bruce D. Chilton in *The Galilean Rabbi and His Bible* (1984) saw Jesus as a teacher of Torah.

Since these books appeared, a new generation of scholars has further multiplied the options. There has probably never been a period in which so many scholars—stimulated by new manuscript finds, the refinement of archaeological procedures, and new analytic methods—have been so preoccupied with the debate about who Jesus really was and have churned out so many options. Indeed, one of my students, puzzling over this cast of characters, told me it seemed to him like an old-fashioned police lineup in which a random gaggle of men is positioned against a height marker under bright lights while someone tries to identify the real culprit.

But where does all of this leave Generation X? Still baffled. Paradoxically, perhaps the most positive result of the "new search," its cumulative failure to answer the existential question about Jesus, is also its greatest success. Students—and the rest of us—discover that, despite all the splendid efforts of those committed to the new quest for the historical Jesus, the *existential* question about Jesus remains just as pressing as ever. Thus, any lingering misplaced confidence that science (in this case the "science" of history informed by the various archaeological, text-critical, anthropological, and associated disciplines) can answer our deepest spiritual questions is frustrated again, and we are back where we began: "But who do *you* say that I am?"

Well, not quite where we began. One of the most attractive features of the scholars engaged in this renewed quest is that they realize their best efforts fall short of answering the most important questions. I particularly appreciate Dominic Crossan's report that after he had finished his massive and brilliant work, he asked Jesus whether he had done enough. The Master answered, "No, Dominic, you have not." The fact is, of course, that for Generation X and for the rest of us, the question of who Jesus *was* is only half—and maybe not even half—of the story. The question of who Jesus *is* remains the big one. For this reason, I have devoted most of my course not to the historical retrieval of Jesus but to contemporary appropriations of him.

2. Generation X is the first to come of age in an America characterized by radical religious pluralism. I became graphically aware of this a few years ago when a student in my course—a typically hardworking premed student—sought me out during my office hours to inquire about courses on the other religions of the world. When I asked him what had prompted him to want to take a course that would pull him away from physiology and quantitative analysis, he said, "Well, my roommate is a Muslim, my girlfriend is a Buddhist, and my lab partner is a Hindu. I'm beginning to think it's time for me to find out where they're coming from."

As a consequence of this awareness of the religious heterogeneity of the world, and a discomfort with the traditional exclusivist claims of Christianity, students are fascinated by the section of the course that deals with the understanding of Jesus in non-Christian religions. They often seem relieved when they find out that Jesus continues to be religiously and morally significant for millions of people today who are not Christians. They are surprised to learn that Mohandas Gandhi, who remained a Hindu his whole life and explicitly refused to allow himself to be called "Christian," claimed to have been influenced by Jesus more than by any other single figure and by the Sermon on the Mount in particular. When Gandhi's biographer Louis Fischer visited the mahatma in 1942 in his simple cottage at the ashram, Fischer found only one picture on the wall. It was a picture of Jesus, with the words "He is our Peace" (from the Epistle to the Ephesians) underneath. This should not be surprising. As Indian scholar M. M. Thomas pointed out several years ago, Jesus was an important ethical and symbolic figure for many of the makers of the modern Hindu renaissance.

Meanwhile, many Buddhists celebrate Jesus as a consummate bodhisattva, one who refuses to abandon this world of suffering and illusion until all sentient creatures can accompany him. A recent large painting by a Buddhist artist from Sri Lanka depicts Jesus sitting in the lotus position, surrounded by the ugly demons of ego, but with his right hand touching the earth, as the Buddha's did at his moment of enlightenment. For the more philosophically inclined Buddhists, such as Masao Abe of the Kyoto School,[3] the idea that God "emptied himself," as Saint Paul writes, suggests that the Buddhist idea of God as emptiness or even nothingness may not be as foreign to Christianity as it first appears.

Among Jewish thinkers, there has also been an explosion of writing about Jesus in recent decades. The works of David Flusser, Pinchas Lapide, and Geza Vermes are probably best known.[4] But there is much more. In fact, by now a survey of this literature by Protestant scholar D. A. Hagner,[5] which was first published in 1984, is already out of date. Why this enormous new interest? Rabbi Alan Mittleman explains it this way:[6] Beginning with Moses Mendelssohn and his contemporaries, Jewish writers were already departing from the caricatures of Jesus that their medieval predecessors had favored and were discovering in him instead "a like-minded Jew." Jesus, Mittleman says, has been in a sense "returning to his ancestral home." This homecoming is an important part of the modern discovery by Jews of their own history, an aspect of the current Jewish search for "essence and definition."

This is obviously true, but let it be noted that a Jewish artist, namely, Marc Chagall, was decades ahead of Jewish scholars in attempting to reclaim Jesus for Judaism. I always project a slide of Chagall's *White Crucifixion* sometime during the course. It depicts a bearded, crucified Jew wearing a Jewish prayer shawl and surrounded by drawings of the expulsions, pogroms, and murders that have pursued the Jewish people for centuries. Jesus is seen as a part of this history of suffering. Year after year students tell me that if they forget everything else, they will never forget that image.

As time went by, however, I found that I was devoting more time in the section of the course on Jesus in non-Christian religions to Islam. There are several reasons. One is that Islam appears in the media far more than any other non-Christian religion and is usually associated with terrorists and fanatics. Also, the Muslim students at Harvard seem unusually well informed about their faith and quite willing to talk about it. Islam is, next to Christianity, the largest religion in the world, and it is my personal conviction that the dialogue between Christians and Muslims is becoming the most important interfaith frontier for the next century. Indeed, in some quarters the polemic is heating up in an ominous way. There is a virtual civil war between Muslims and Christians in the Sudan. In addition, the dialogue here in America has sometimes fallen into the wrong hands. Recently, a Christian student showed me a videotape of a debate between Jimmy Swaggart and one Ahmad Deedat. It brimmed with polemic and caricature, not the kind of dialogue I want to see happen. Consequently, I have made a special effort to understand current Muslim views of Jesus, relying frequently on my students to bring me summaries and translations of works in Arabic, a language I cannot read. In doing this work, I have made some surprising discoveries.

First, it is clear to me that whether Christian historical scholars are aware of it or not, the recent work they have done on Jesus has made a considerable impact on Muslim scholars. It is not hard to see why. Historically, Muslims have always contended that the Christian Gospels are corrupted versions of earlier and more accurate accounts. This contention supports the orthodox Muslim conviction that Jesus was never crucified, that a disciple took his place, or that Judas was crucified instead. Now as these alert Muslim scholars (who can read English more often than we can read Arabic) peruse current historical Jesus studies, which are marked by a deep skepticism about the historicity of whole portions of the Gospels, it is natural for the Muslims to say, "See, this is just what we've been telling you all along. The Gospels were written many years later by people who weren't even there and who *invented* Jesus' claim to be God. Look, your own people say so!"

Nor do Muslim critics restrict their reading to historical Jesus studies. Jamal Baduri, after reading John Hick's *The Myth of God Incarnate*,[7] wrote that the book confirmed that Christians were at last coming to see what Muslims have always held: that Jesus was not God in the flesh but a prophet and that the atonement, which has been a scandal to Muslims for centuries, is a fiction. The Muslim scholars' conclusion, however, which would not be pleasing to most members of the Jesus Seminar, is that the account of Jesus in the Koran is more trustworthy.

How all this will eventually affect the Christian-Muslim dialogue remains to be seen. Ironically, the portrait of Jesus that Muslims seem to favor—the miracle worker and ascetic mystic—is often the one that Christian historians find least attractive. However, some Christian biblical scholars have recently suggested that, given what we now know about the variety of views of Jesus that were alive and well during the first five centuries of Christianity, the Muslim view is not all that different and no more or less justified.

Once again, it seems to me that the best hope for a breakthrough in the Muslim-Christian contention about Jesus may not come from the historical critical scholars but from those Christians and Muslims who try to express the contemporary significance of Jesus in novels, poetry, and plays. Naguib Mahfouz is the Nobel prize–winning Egyptian novelist who has evoked both praise and condemnation from his fellow Muslims. His novel *Children of Gebelawi* tells the story of a reclusive old man named al Jabalawi who rules over a section of Cairo.[8] Since he rarely shows himself in public, those he authorizes to make decisions in his name often abuse his authority for their own purposes. It is clear to most readers and critics that al Jabalawi is God and that those who speak in his name are the prophets, Satan, and, more recently, scientists. There is also a figure in the novel named Rifa'ah who is obviously meant to represent Jesus. He is a gentle and loving man who is killed by his hateful enemies. The prophets do not succeed in their purposes, and finally a scientist stealthily enters al Jabalawi's palace to examine his credentials and his deed to the property. In a scuffle that follows, the old man is killed. The prophets have failed, the gentle mediator has been killed, and science has killed God.

Mahfouz received stinging criticism from conservative Muslims both for suggesting that the prophets have failed and that God is dead and for making a figure who obviously symbolizes Jesus the most attractive character in the book. But Mahfouz is hardly alone. Although for centuries Muslims wrote almost nothing about Jesus, they now seem to be making up for lost time. In an article recently published in *The Muslim World,* Hugh P. Goddard has catalogued literally dozens of articles, books, plays, and novels about Jesus written by Egyptian Muslims alone in recent years.[9] These authors seem to favor biographies, interpretations of Jesus as a teacher of wisdom, comparisons between Christ and the Prophet, and stories and plays in which a Muslim young man falls in love with a Coptic Christian woman, or vice versa, and catastrophe is averted when they come to see (at least in the minds of the writers) that there is no real contradiction between the two faiths.

What attracts Generation Xers to this flowering of non-Christian interpretations of Jesus? Is it that they can retain their belief in him, however they may parse that belief, without appearing to claim some spirituality superior to that of their Jewish, Muslim, and Buddhist classmates? I think that is part, though only part, of the answer. The fact that non-Christians see something of immense value in Jesus helps make Jesus the truly universal figure students somehow feel he must be. Therefore, they are happy to discover that some Christian scholars, instead of merely dismissing non-Christian interpretations of Jesus as unwarranted intrusions, have begun to see them as valuable insights that can be selectively integrated into a Christian's own understanding of Jesus. This is important because Generation X is the first to come of age in an era when religious pluralism is not somewhere across the globe but at the desk next to yours in the lab and across the hall in the dorm.

Maybe another explanation for this unprecedented openness to "outside" voices on what used to be considered the most "inside" of all topics–Christology[10]–is that so many new constructions and reformulations of the meaning of Jesus have appeared within the Christian community itself. With Christians themselves talking about Jesus as the liberator or the goddess-within, why lock the doors against avatars and bodhisattvas? At the meetings of the section of the American Academy of Religion that deals with Christology, one hears very few discussions nowadays about the Chalcedonian formula,[11] but papers abound on the importance of feminism, liberation theology, interfaith dialogue, and religious pluralism in understanding the significance of Jesus. The lesson for me in all of this is that one can no longer first work out one's doctrine of Christ without reference to the religious heterogeneity of the world and then, as a subsequent step, enter into the interfaith dialogue. Rather, the dialogue must help shape the Christology from the outset.

The exuberant eclecticism of Generation X may sound novel at first, but that is hardly the case. After all, from the beginning, Christians have drawn freely on the philosophical categories and religious images of the cultures around them to express who they thought this man Jesus was. We borrowed the idea of the Logos from the Hellenistic environment of the early church. We took the images of a sacrificial lamb from Jewish temple worship and the idea of a dying and rising savior from ancient mystery religions. Some historians have contended that Christianity is at its most vigorous when it can boldly utilize the cultural imagery of its time and place and at its weakest when it rigidly rejects this material and clings defensively to previously defined formulations. If so, then we are presently in a vigorous period indeed, and what some fearful defenders recoil from as syncretism is in fact a venturesome willingness to plunge in and take risks. If previous generations took this leap, why should Generation X not be allowed to jump in as well?

3. Generation X believes in picking and choosing, not in swallowing the whole package. This quality, of course, enrages some theologians and religious leaders, who inveigh against "cafeteria-style" religion. But selective appropriation (which also entails selective leaving out) has gone on throughout the his-

tory of Christianity and every other religion. In the case of Generation X, selective appropriation manifests itself in the fondness many of them show for Stephen Mitchell's *The Gospel According to Jesus.*[12] Mitchell, like many members of Generation X, is a *mischling*. He was raised Jewish, attended a private Christian school as a boy, and later underwent horrendously difficult training to become a Zen adept. He is also (unlike, alas, an increasing number of Generation Xers) a gifted linguist and has already published renditions of other religious texts. But the book is not a new translation of the Gospels. Rather, it is a highly selective rereading and interpretation of those parts of them that engage Mitchell's own very demanding and finely honed spiritual sensibilities. Like Thomas Jefferson, who once used a pair of scissors to snip out the portions of the Gospels that did not appeal to his deist leanings, Mitchell has culled the synoptic writings and given us brisk and accurate renderings of several portions, paired with his fascinating reflections on them and some well-suited comparisons to philosophers, Zen masters, Hasids, visionaries, and poets.

This may sound like a risky approach, and it is. But it seems to reach many Generation Xers at the core of their spiritual sensibility. For this reason, Mitchell's approach provides us with an invaluable insight into them, if not into Jesus himself. Jesus, or at least Mitchell's attractive portrait of him, seems to fire the interest of believers and nonbelievers alike. His treatments of the account of the woman taken in adultery, the parable of the prodigal son, and the healing of the Syrophoenician woman are particularly engaging. Students resonate with Mitchell's work because it is not exclusivist and it relates the gospel stories immediately to contemporary life experience.

But I have to admit that I have my doubts about this Jeffersonian approach to the texts. I do not suggest this comparison offhandedly: Mitchell himself compares his snip-and-paste method to that of Jefferson, the sage of Monticello, in the book's introduction. Can we really deal with the New Testament on the basis of such unapologetically subjective criteria–take what you like and leave the rest? On the one hand, I suppose there is no reason that we cannot. In fact, people have been doing so for centuries, often with considerably less candor than Mitchell. After all, the canonization process itself, by which the leaders of the early church put some Gospels in the New Testament and consigned others to the dustbin (or more accurately, to desert caves where quite a few have shown up in recent years) was a highly selective one.[13] And as Elaine Pagels has argued in *The Gnostic Gospels*, the people who made that selection were hardly evenhanded.[14] They were all celibate men who, in effect, scissored out embarrassing references to Jesus' relationship with Mary Magdalene and texts that suggested that God might be female or that one could find him or her without the mediation of a hierarchy. Jefferson was not the first to take the shears to the Scriptures.

The process, in fact, goes on all the time. Ever since the canon was closed, every theologian has had a "canon within the canon," working some of the teachings of Jesus to death while ignoring others. How many times have I heard opponents of liberation theology spout the verse about the poor being always with us or about leaving things of this world to Caesar? But they seem to ignore Jesus' constant condemnations of the rich and his promise of the first fruits of the Kingdom of God to the poor, the sick, and the prisoners. So maybe Mitchell is simply being more up front about a subjectivity that is always operative in these matters.

But I am still uneasy. As it happens, I almost always resonate with Stephen Mitchell's choices of what to include, though I am sorry he did nothing at all with the resurrection stories. This decision puzzled me since his is no ultrarationalistic edition. For example, he offers a wonderful reading of the Annunciation—the story of the angel Gabriel informing Mary that she is to have a child—and throws in a marvelous description of his own experience with angels during his 100-day Zen meditation ordeal. But even though Mitchell and I are attracted to the same passages, I could not help wondering as I read his collage of excerpts (for that is what it is) what Stephen King's scrapbook of gospel stories would look like. Or Madonna's. Or Rush Limbaugh's.

If we are to avoid the danger of the "a-thing-is-what-I-say-it-is" morass, then it is important for people with Mitchell's daunting capabilities to wrestle precisely with the episodes in Jesus' life they find most intransigent and unattractive. What do we do with his cursing of the innocent fig tree, his ordering his disciples to equip themselves with a sword (a sort of embarrassment to pacifists), and other instances of abrasive behavior and speech? Was he serious when he said that even to look at a woman with a lustful eye was as bad as adultery? Or was he engaging in hyperbole? Or demonstrating vividly that when it comes to sins of the flesh, we are all pretty much in the same boat, so there is no room to gloat, no excuse—as the Buddhists would say—for "moral aggression"? These are all intriguing questions. They leap out at you when you read the Gospels. I would love to hear Mitchell's ideas on them. But since he discusses only the passages he takes a shine to, we are deprived of that exchange. And that, in my view, is too bad.

As the never-ending task of interpreting and reinterpreting Jesus moves into the third millennium, the two waves I have touched on will surely continue as well. The historical reconstruction of Jesus will sharpen more and more precise analytic instruments and theoretical constructs. Only the most naive investigator could believe that we have seen the last of the "new" quests. The cultural resymbolization of Jesus will undoubtedly continue and, I think, expand. But a very critical question remains: *What is the relationship between the historical reconstruction of Jesus and the imaginative resymbolization of Jesus?* What is the proper interplay between historical studies, on the one hand, and poetry, iconography, and cinema, on the other, for the spiritual life of twenty-first-century Generation Xs to come? Do the historical records and the canonical Scriptures set any limits on the freewheeling play of the religious imagination? Do the new imaginative portraits suggest anything about what historical research might be most appropriate? In short, do these two trajectories have anything to do with each other?

I think they do. One might be struck at first by the variety of historical Jesuses that Harrington catalogs, but a second look reveals that they all have one very important thing in common: They are all recognizably Jewish. The Jesus they describe is a participant in one of the many Jewish subcultures of first-century Palestine. The God that Jesus talks about and whose will he tries to make known is not the deity of some generalized theism but the God of Abraham, made known through the covenant with the Jewish people as one who has active compassion for the outsider and who promises justice and healing to all nations. This Jewish parameter, though one may disagree on its exact boundaries, provides the playing field within which new images of Jesus must be worked out, unless they surrender all claims of being connected to the historical figure whose name they bear.

Also, however, since we all know that historians do not set out on their tasks with no intuitive inspiration or cultural presuppositions, how can we evaluate the impact that the prevailing cultural-theological climate has on their findings? I love the Jesus whom Dominic Crossan has recovered. But is it really a pure accident that his Jesus strongly resembles the Jesus of contemporary liberation theology, which I also like? The question is a very large one. It will fuel the new christological debate for some time to come, and it is hard to forecast what answers will be forthcoming.

This brings me to the most startling thing I discovered about myself in teaching these many years about Jesus. I found that as a person who holds to the central religious–call it existential–significance of Jesus, the old creedal formulas began to become oddly important. This came as a surprise to me because I was raised in a noncreedal denomination and heard about Nicea and Chalcedon only when I went to seminary. I had always been puzzled and a little put off by the creeds. But what I have come to see is that what they were trying to say, in their clunky Greek metaphysical categories, is that Jesus was a *real* historical figure, not a phantom, and that his continuing moral and spiritual meaning–his power to reveal God to us (his "divinity," if you will)–is integrally linked with his historicity. For me, this means that the Jewishness of Jesus and his identification with the outcasts and impoverished of his day, which led to his fatal clash with the imperial authority, are not optional elements in a future Christology. They have theological significance *because* they are historical.

But the significance of Jesus for people such as the students in my course (and for me) is not *merely* historical. That would be antiquarianism: interesting, perhaps even intensely interesting, but not existentially crucial. Maybe this stubborn recognition that Jesus must be both fully historical and yet somehow much more is what sparked those curious resurrection stories–so fugitive and incongruous–with which the four Gospels all come to their strangely postmodern endings. This is why I am so sorry that Stephen Mitchell, who was not afraid to take on the angel at the Annunciation, backed away from the one who confronted the women at the tomb and asked them, "Why seek ye the living among the dead?" Perhaps, like Jacob, Mitchell should have wrestled with that one as well, even if it took him all night. I think his Zen master would have approved, and I think the likable, searching, inquisitive young people of Generation X, in their fetching disquietude and distress, should do that wrestling, too. There is no way, in the end, to escape the question that Jesus himself puts to every succeeding generation, including Generation X: "Who do you say that I am?"

Questions and Responses from the Symposium

Q: What would you say in response to the question you asked your students to write on: "Who do you say that I am?"

A: I knew this question was going to come sooner or later. I'd like to hear all of the participants in this conference—speakers and audience alike—respond. My answer would be very much like the answer given by Peter to the question when it was first posed: "You are the Christ, the Son of the living God." That allows me a lot of space because yesterday I was given a big license by Karen Torjesen to redefine divinity in a very refreshing, new, and expansive way.

My response to your question is always in process. I have no final answer to it. But it's a question that I will never cease to try to respond to, not just verbally but in the way I lead my life. Remember what happened after Peter's response: Jesus told him what it was going to involve, namely, confronting the corrupt power structure in Jerusalem. Peter balked and said, "Oh, no, that's not what this is about." The two steps are both very important: both the affirmation and the existential step, which has to be taken.

Q: You said that Generation X was looking for a Jesus that they can trust, and I think that partially means that we don't believe in heroes anymore. I was wondering what kind of flaws the students come up with in Jesus or what you come up with—what kind of failings you see in the historical Jesus.

A: Paradoxically, the discovery that Jesus had moments in which he lost his temper and cursed the fig tree or did other things that seemed questionable, I sometimes find are very attractive to my students. They humanize a figure who for many of them has been too elevated, too much in a stained-glass window. That he had some of what you have called "flaws" is often a helpful point of entry into understanding what he's about.

And I think the first part of your question—that we don't believe in heroes any more—is very significant. It causes me to doubt, sometimes, the whole enterprise of my course, maybe this symposium, and the whole historical project that it's based on. We are in a period in which hero worship is perhaps legitimately fading, and our confidence in the "great man," whether it's the great political man or the great musician man or the great religious or spiritual man (I use "man" here very deliberately), is declining.

Dom Crossan has said that if he were making a movie on Jesus, he would show a very realistic picture of the crucifixion and then have the camera pan out across a wide field and show dozens, maybe hundreds, of other crucifixions going on because thousands of people were crucified in Jesus' time. He was part of a movement that was there before him and that continues. There's something that has begun to disturb me a little bit about the singularization of the figure of Jesus, which does border a little bit too much on this kind of heroizing. And I think we have to be careful about that, and that suggests a new kind of quest that moves beyond heroization.

Q: I wanted to comment on your request for a dialogue. What is the problem with uncertainty? Why is it a danger for confidence? Religions in general may be characterized as inventions to corner certainties. Maybe the intra- and interfaith dialogue could be most effective by exploring and even exalting the uncertain middle ground, wherein might lie more effective ways to answer the question on how to live—more effective, that is, than asserting and buttressing arbitrary truths.

A: If I were to speculate on the future of our discussions about Jesus, his significance, and his historicity, one word that would come to my mind would be *pluriform* or *heterogeneous* or *multiple*. I do not see a firm consensus emerging either in the historical reconstruction or the cultural resymbolization or the spiritual retrievals of Jesus. I think we're going to see multiplications of these, and I think your position is entirely right. Why should we want to have something that all parties agree on? I am refreshed by the wonderfully interesting studies of the early centuries of Christianity, by which a monolithic unitary view of the early church has now been completely demolished. Early Christianity was pluralistic; there were a lot more options, a lot more Christologies, a lot more forms of church life, devotion, and spirituality, than we have generally thought. Maybe we're moving into a period now that is paradoxically more like that than the fifteen centuries of Christendom have been, with their rigidly structured doctrinal systems and ecclesial institutions. I welcome that. You call that uncertainty, that's fine. I think it's a bracing climate.

Q: Christianity so often ignores and even excludes the divine as revealed by other leaders and other religions. I suspect Generation X would trust Christianity more if the search for the divine would examine or at least be open to other paths as well.

A: I agree entirely. We now live in a period in which the recognition of the presence of the spirit of God in other religious traditions has to be part of our own spiritual mentality and our faith. I think this is a providential gift of God, a step toward recognizing a much wider and more fathomless mystery than we often allow. We have the opportunity for this conversation now because of the way we've been pushed together in this small world, elbow to elbow with people from different religious traditions. And I'm very encouraged that what is centrally important to me as a Christian, namely, Jesus, is not necessarily a barrier but can be an opening to talking with people in other traditions.

Q: Your statement that Jesus' Jewishness must be central to the search for Christ leads to this question. Our Christianity has resulted in a persistent annihilation of millions of Jews. Is this relevant to the search for Jesus?

A: The anti-Semitism and anti-Judaism that have been present in Christianity are probably the single most catastrophic, embarrassing, and humiliating aspects of Christian
history that those of us who are Christians have to deal with. They have made their
contribution to various kinds of pogroms leading up to and including the Holocaust.
That's terrible, terrible news for all of us. Jesus himself, as a Jew, would have been
rounded up by the SS and sent to Auschwitz. That's where he would have been.
Not outside looking in, not maintaining his Aryan purity—he would have been inside
and incinerated. Once that sinks in, then our recognition of the dismal, catastrophic
record of Christianity in this regard, which has been transformed, I hope, at least in
many of our minds, by the Holocaust and the recognition of its impact, allows for an
understanding of Jesus and of Jews as our brothers and sisters who share the same
covenant in a way that has not been possible before.

Q: If Jesus were to return to earth today, how would he react to what we call Christianity, particularly to its diversity?
A: I think he would be very puzzled by Christianity. He didn't know the term; it was
only invented later. To some extent, the term *Christianity*, as a way of talking about
that which Jesus introduced into history and wants us to be a part of, is only partially helpful. In some ways it's even misleading. So we have to be careful not to
identify Christianity with Jesus.

I think he would love the diversity. He reveled in diversity and meeting different kinds
of people (including people he wasn't supposed to meet as a respectable rabbi) and
rubbing shoulders and conversing with people who were on the margins and edges.

Q: Religious institutions often claim the authority of God so that the selection of certain texts and doctrines is the "work of the Holy Spirit." That seems to be at odds
with the openness to pluralism you commend. What are the implications for the immediate future of the institutional churches and Generation X?
A: Caution, bordering on suspicion of the institutionally or doctrinally prepackaged
version of Jesus, is justified. I think that the claims that religious institutions have
made to speak for God, or to give us the last word on who Jesus is or what he
means, are arrogant and unacceptable. We simply have to question that. And I think
that as the diversity breaks out and opens up, there's going to be more intransigent
circling of the wagons on the part of religious institutions and hierarchies and leaders.

Q: I believe that the Jesus of history and the Jesus of faith, the pre- and post-Easter
Jesus, are one divine revelation. Seeking to understand Jesus Christ by attempting to
unearth the historical Jesus is like trying to understand a tree by digging up its roots.
The result is that you will get to know the roots, but you may also kill the tree. Do
you think it is possible that some root diggers fail to see the tree for the roots?
A: I think the metaphor, when carried to that extent, is a little unfortunate. What most
historical Jesus scholars are doing is, in fact, helpful because it clears away a lot of
the rubbish and garbage and false interpretations that have been laid over Jesus and
provides a refreshing beginning for understanding who he was.

If there is a problem, it's if people are misled into thinking that this is going to give them the answer to the question I have posed–Who do you think that I am?–it's not going to provide the answer. Theologically, I agree with you. The whole process– the seed, the root, the trunk, the leaves, and, I would go on to say, the birds that land in the tree–is a disclosure of God. It is a revelation. So I don't question the historical enterprise; I only question some of the false expectations that have been attached to it.

Q: Why are many in Generation X turning to alternative religions or fundamentalist Christian groups for spiritual guidance?

A: The environment in which Generation X lives is full of alternative religions, and not all of them bear the name religion. Some of them bear the name of the vision of a free-market world or the global expansion of capitalism or the flat tax. There are a lot of religions around nowadays claiming our allegiance. About fundamentalism: Fundamentalism (and not just Christian fundamentalism, but other kinds as well) takes so much energy. Constantly to fight against the reality that's breaking in on you becomes exhausting. I don't believe it can last long in the life of most individuals. Experiences, encounters, and ideas come along that simply don't fit the grid, and finally your energy for resisting begins to fray, and you have to begin to look for something else.

Q: My father is a priest and has just been diagnosed with HIV and is symptomatic. I cannot see beyond tomorrow. His impending death has made me question all my beliefs. What can the historical Jesus show me about trying to deal with this tragedy?

A: I'm not sure that I'm in a position to respond to your question. What leaped into my mind, of course, is the stories of how Jesus touched the sick, even the people who had leprosy, which in his day, I am told, was thought to be a little like AIDS in our time–not just as a sickness, but seen by some people as a curse and proof that you have fallen into divine disfavor. Jesus not only spent time with these people; he also touched them, ate with them, and made himself part of their lives. I think the most important thing for you to do is simply to be present with your father, as close as you can be, as open as you can be. Be with him. And have confidence that something is going to happen that will enable you to do that. More than that, I think, would be intrusive of me to say.

7

Jesus and the World's Religions

HUSTON SMITH

Huston Smith is perhaps the best-known religious scholar in North America. He became famous more than three decades ago through his public television series The Religions of Man. *His book with the same title is the best-selling book in the history of American academic religious publishing (revised edition in 1990 under the title* The World's Religions*). Other important books include* Forgotten Truth *(1976),* Beyond the Post-Modern Mind *(1989),* Huston Smith Essays on World Religions *(1995), and (with David Griffin)* Primordial Truth and Postmodern Theology *(1989).*

He is also known for other television series and films. His films on Hinduism, Tibetan Buddhism, and Sufism have all won awards at international film festivals. His movie Requiem for a Nation *brought the world's attention to Tibetan Buddhist monks who can individually sing several notes at once. In 1996 national public television featured Smith in a five part series,* The Wisdom of Faith, *hosted by Bill Moyers.*

Smith has taught at Washington University (St. Louis), Massachusetts Institute of Technology, Syracuse University (where he was Thomas J. Watson Professor of Religion until he retired), and the University of California, Berkeley. As both a historian of religions and a philosopher, he is known for his empathetic interpretation of the great religions and for his critique of the intellectual assumptions of modernity. In his lecture, Smith describes how he, after spending more than fifty years studying the religions of the world, sees Jesus.

Previous speakers at this symposium have focused on Jesus in his Mediterranean context and the Christian civilization that issued from his life. My job is to push back our horizons so that we can see Jesus in world historical terms. Gestalt psychologists have shown us that things look different when their backgrounds are changed; peripheral vision affects focal vision. So what Jesus do we see when we place him in the context of religious history in its entirety? There is an easy answer to that question, and there is a difficult one.

What Other Religions Say About Jesus

The easy answer comes from riffling through the other religions and lifting out what they say about Jesus. That doesn't take long because with the exception of Christianity's cousins, Judaism and Islam, the other religions do not mention him at all. I am speaking of religions in their great, formative periods. Later, Neo-Vedantists in Hinduism will include Jesus in their roster of avatars (divine incarnations), and in Islam the quasi-heretical Ahmadiyyah movement will claim that Jesus escaped from the cross and lived out his later years in Kashmir. But these are late accretions that have no solid place in their respective traditions.

As for the Abrahamic religions, the Jewish view of Jesus is well known, but Jesus' place in Islam is not common knowledge. As for his mother, Mary, the Koran mentions her twice as many times as does the New Testament, always reverently, and there is one Sufi order I know of that is dedicated to her. As for Jesus, Islam would not be a distinct religion if it endorsed the Christian doctrines of the Incarnation and the Trinity. It also denies that Jesus died on the cross, holding that Allah rescued him from that fate. But despite those differences, the Koran affirms Jesus' virgin birth. Jesus' soul and Adam's are the only two that God created directly, which means that today there are probably more Muslims than Christians who accept the doctrine of the virgin birth at face value. The Koran also endorses Jesus' second coming. It credits him as a greater wonder-worker than Muhammad, and it ranks his sanctity above Muhammad's. Thus, while Muhammad is the Seal of the Prophets, being the last in that line, Jesus (in Islam) is both the Seal of Sanctity and the Seal of the Ages. (Two meanings of "seal" are at work in these three contentions. In the first and third the word connotes closure, as when one seals an envelope; whereas in the second it connotes endorsement, as when we speak of a seal of approval.)

There are more sayings attributed to Jesus in Arabic than in any other language, many of them presumably apocryphal. My favorite comes from Kabir: "Said Jesus, blessed be his name, 'This world is a bridge; pass over, but build no house upon it.'" Muslims never mention Jesus without adding, "May peace be upon him." Muhammad is the only other human being to whom that honor is accorded.

That's about it for what the other religions say about Jesus, so the easy part of my task is accomplished. Now for the difficult part. The commission that Marcus Borg laid on me in inviting me to this conference did not stop with an easy reading. "What we really want to hear from you, Huston," he said, "is what Jesus means to a Christian who has spent his entire life dunking himself– not just professionally but personally and experientially–in the world's great religions." That's a different mandate, frighteningly different, actually. It requires that I speak personally, so I shall begin at the beginning.

My Odyssey

Born of Methodist missionary parents in China, I grew up with the typical Protestant understanding of Jesus of that era. When I came to America, however, modernity hit me between the eyes and changed my Christology drastically. At the Divinity School of the University of Chicago, I fell among naturalistic theists who looked to science to inventory the world and fitted religion into its findings. This reduced Jesus to the best that the evolutionary process has produced thus far. His ethical teachings remained normative for me, and his character exemplary, but there was nothing supernatural about him or his genesis. Shirley Jackson Case was a towering presence in New Testament studies at the University of Chicago, and his 1929 *Experience with the Supernatural in Early Christian Times* impressed me particularly.[1] It was written to show that Christianity arose in a superstitious age in which miracles were the order of the day and emperors routinely claimed to be born of virgins in order to elevate themselves in the eyes of their subjects. The writers of the New Testament were children of their times, so they naturally portrayed Jesus in a credulous light. That depiction needs to be stripped of its supernatural overlay, we were taught—"demythologizing" was coming into vogue—if Christianity is to be credible to modern ears.

I can remember as if it were yesterday the night that this entire naturalistic outlook crashed before me like a house of cards. There were no voices, no ethereal rays of celestial light. Only my mind was working, but with an intensity, focus, and excitement I do not recall theretofore having experienced. With no help from my theological mentors, I discovered the mystics.

What those mystics taught me, or rather showed me, that night was another world, and I have never wavered from the conviction that it is the true world, compared with which the world we normally experience is but a world of shadows. That true world is not elsewhere, any more than the quantum world, while different, is elsewhere; as Alfred Lord Tennyson noted, it is "closer [to us] than breathing, and nearer than hands and feet" (*The Higher Pantheism,* stanza 6). It is other only in being radically different from the world we normally experience and superior to it in every way.

It was this conversion to mysticism that led me to the study of the world's religions. I wasn't schooled in that subject; my professional training was in philosophy. But the philosophy and religion I was schooled in—this was fifty years ago—did not hold the mystics in high regard. I still remember the derisive quip of Reinhold Niebuhr, the most famous American Protestant theologian of the time: Mysticism begins in mist, centers in "I," and ends in schism. Catholics were more respectful, but even they censured Meister Eckhart, just as the Jews excommunicated (Baruch) Benedict de Spinoza. I had heard rumors, however, that other peoples honored their mystics. What would Hinduism be without the Upanishads or Krishna's stupendous epiphany in the eleventh chapter of the Bhagavad-Gita? What would Buddhism be without the Buddha's enlightenment under the Bo tree? What would Islam be without the Sufis or China without the twenty-fifth chapter of the Tao Te Ching, which I quote to give you the flavor of what I was hearing from Asia:

> There is a being, wonderful, perfect;
> It existed before heaven and earth.
> How quiet it is!
> How spiritual it is!
> It stands alone and it does not change;
> It moves, but does not on that account suffer.
> All life comes from it, yet it does not demand to be Lord.
> I do not know its name, so I call it Tao, the Way,
> And I rejoice in its power.

Eulogies like these fed my soul. For three years I divided my teaching between modern philosophy and world religions, and in those years things sorted themselves out. I loved my world religions courses. Their roomy outlooks allowed me to live and breathe and soar and roam. Modern philosophy, in contrast—and yes, modern theology, too—felt like a cage. Mirabai, that wonderful medieval Indian saint and mystic, gave me words for the contrast I felt between the two worlds, traditional and modern. "I have felt the sway of elephant's shoulders," she wrote, "and you expect me to mount this jackass! Try to be serious."[2]

An Excursus

Before proceeding, I feel the need to make a small detour. George Will tells us that the magic word of modernity is *society*, and as that is the case, I feel the need to say something about social issues before continuing with the ontological ones that primarily concern me. If my conversion to the traditional worldview entailed espousing traditional social patterns—master/slave hierarchies, gender relations, and the like—I could not expect your continued attention to what I am saying, so let me say categorically that it did not. I never fell into thinking that the past as a whole was better than the present. In our concern for the rights of minorities and the oppressed, I think we have actually gained ground. With the exception of isolated cases such as Tibet, political colonialism is over; and while cultural colonialism is another matter, I cannot think of any country that could get away today with exhibiting an African American behind bars, caged alongside the great apes, as the Bronx Zoo did in the 1920s. The "fairness revolution" is having an impact. I wonder if Dominic Crossan's remarkable *Jesus: A Revolutionary Biography* could have been written in any century previous to ours.[3]

Having identified myself with this conference politically in the broad sense of that word, let me indulge in a moment of whimsy and claim inclusion in the company of the distinguished biblical scholars I find myself among. There was a brief moment when I, too, plied that trade. It was in the late 1940s when (as some of you will remember) a claque of clerics (headed by Father Coughlin for the Catholics and Gerald L.K. Smith for the Protestants) filled the radio airwaves with allegedly proof-texted sermons directed against Negroes, Jews, Catholics (if the preacher was Protestant), and the United Nations, which they identified as the Antichrist. Their torturing of biblical texts for their purposes galled me into composing a song, which I titled "Bible Libel" and sang at a political rally in Denver with Pete Seeger backing me up on his banjo. I'll share a snippet from it to give you the idea. [At the symposium, Smith actually sang this to the audience.] After targeting a number of their exegetical monstrosities, I continued,

> They make the Bible say the white race is supreme,
> but the Bible doesn't harp on any such theme.
> Refrain:
> There's Bible Libel going around,
> Gonna tell it to the Lord 'til the heavens resound,
> Gonna sing and shout 'til that Judgment Day
> When the Lord tells some preachers they've got hell to pay.

Put Pete Seeger's banjo behind that, and it's not bad.

Having now justified my inclusion in this conference on both political and hermeneutical grounds, I can proceed to my proper assignment. What Jesus do I see against the backdrop of the world's religions? I begin with an anecdote that almost tells the entire story.

An Anecdote

The first "foreign" religion that I studied seriously was Hinduism, at the Vedanta Society of St. Louis. During those years, the Christmas Eve pageant at our Methodist church was scheduled before supper to include children, and it was invariably fulfilling, as the beauty of the Christmas story, "Silent Night" in the candlelit sanctuary, and the manger scene reminded us of how much our family meant to us. But after supper, when our children had been tucked into bed, I would regularly slip off to the local Vedanta Society, where at 8:00 P.M. every Christmas Eve Swami Satprakashananda would give a talk to the handful assembled. His title never varied; every year it was "Jesus Christ, the Light of the World." And it was there, far more than in my own church, that I experienced Christ's incarnation. That the Swami regarded Jesus as one of a number of incarnations was altogether secondary to the fact that he believed–believed absolutely–that God literally became man that first Christmas night.

As I say, that anecdote virtually tells the story of what Jesus, restored to Jesus Christ, now means to me when I view him through the wide-angle lens of history as a whole. But obviously I can't leave matters with that, for innumerable questions bristle for the modern mind. So as space permits, I shall try to articulate what Satprakashananda's talks conveyed. The main thing was the angle from which he approached Jesus, the angle of the traditional worldview, so I need to say a little more about that perspective before proceeding to Jesus.

The Traditional Worldview

A useful place to begin is by noting that it is a *world* view, first for including everything, and second, for affecting everything it includes in the way the comprehensive composition of a painting affects its every detail.[4] These two features of worldviews are not well recognized today, as this anecdote from a theologian I know indicates.

Two summers ago he directed a tour, "In the Footsteps of the Reformation," that pilgrimaged to the historic sites of Protestant beginnings. Its members were a select group of informed Protestants. They were keenly interested in, and knew a lot about, Wittenburg and Gutenberg, Martin Luther's Ninety-five Theses and John Calvin's plan of salvation. My friend was surprised, therefore, to find that they missed the main point. They were not aware that Luther had a worldview, a theological system that encompassed everything–all human life and the universe as well. They thought in terms of isolated claims–justification by faith, the priesthood of all believers, and the like. They considered those claims important and gave them wholehearted assent. But they did not have what Calvin called "the Christian world and life view"; indeed, they were hardly aware that such a thing existed, much less that it might be important, if not decisive, for faith. My informant sensed a change here. Whereas earlier in this century Christians of many denominations vigorously opposed Darwinism because of its naturalistic and atheistic worldview, the situation today is different. It is not so much that most Christians have been persuaded that the naturalistic account of evolution is true and can be reconciled with the truths of Christianity. The two have been compartmentalized so that not only do they not conflict; they also don't seem even to impinge on each other. For many Christians, Christianity no longer includes a worldview.

I hear in this anecdote a reflection of the state of modern theology generally. To a large extent it accepts the naturalistic world of the modern university and then adds God to the equation; this process produces a world that is half religious and half secular. For my part, I find it impossible even to strive for spiritual wholeness in an incoherent worldview, for as Franz Kafka shrewdly noted, "In your struggle with the world, bet on the world." If the world doesn't cohere, our lives can't cohere either.

The traditional worldview does cohere, and because my fifteen years at MIT showed me that modernity has discovered nothing that disturbs this worldview's metaphysical outlines (cosmologically the case is otherwise), I apprentice myself to its Christian version for my understanding of Jesus. In that version, everything centers in Absolute, Infinite Being, which is perfect for exemplifying every virtue we know—truth, beauty, goodness; being, awareness, and bliss; tenderness, love, and compassion—to an unimaginably superlative degree, while fusing them, causing each to absorb the virtues of the others. God knows lovingly and loves knowingly, and pari passu with the other virtues. Everything other than God exists because it is required by God's infinity and compassion, but what is other-than-God cannot be as real as God because two Gods are impossible. The world stands to God's total reality as a postcard of Everest stands to Mount Everest itself, or, in Plato's image, as the shadow of a flower stands to the flower casting that shadow. As less real than God, the world has no claims on God save those that God has lovingly endowed it with.

As for our minds, being situated in this half-real, half-unreal world, they are positioned to the way things actually are in something of the way a dog's mind is positioned toward Albert Einstein's. It follows that we will never understand who Jesus really was or what God accomplished through him. Even so, being theomorphic creatures created in God's image, we can know because God knows, though our knowledge is approximate. From a distance, we cannot see the boulders, trees, and ravines of the Himalayas, but we can discern the outlines of its range and take in its majesty. Plato took account of our distance from the way things really are by calling our descriptions "likely tales," so within the contours of the traditional worldview just sketched I proceed to my likely tale of who Jesus was and what God accomplished in him.

Jesus, Traditionally Conceived

We begin with God, who created the world and human beings within it. As with other beings, she created the human species perfect in its kind, and this perfection included freedom, which at some point people misused. This led to confusion, chaos, and strife until God, seeing that people were probably not going to work their way out of the mess they had made of things, concluded that they needed a helping hand. God needed a human agent to work through and spotted Abraham as promising material. God may have approached other candidates, but it was Abraham who rose to the overture. He managed a special attentiveness to God's will, which he transmitted to his descendants. There were ups and downs along the way, but by the time the Torah was canonized, an understanding of God and human existence in God's presence was in place for the Mediterranean world. God's workings elsewhere in the world constitute a separate story.

A problem remained, however. This saving discernment that the Jews had won was too important to remain theirs alone. It needed to be broadcast to the world but was embedded in the history of the Jews and their sense of their peoplehood to an extent that extrication of this discernment from these factors was difficult. An ethnic religion needed to give birth to a universal religion without losing its own distinctive identity, which continued to have an important mission. How was this severance to be accomplished?

By God's becoming incarnate, this time in a person rather than a people. For God simply to have plunked down in a human ovum would have circumvented the freedom with which God had dignified human beings, so again (as with Abraham) God extended an overture, perhaps to others before Jesus. But Jesus responded. When God offered himself to Jesus at his baptism, Jesus opened himself to that offer unconditionally, which reduced his humanity to a shell, a sheath in which God was contained. Thereafter, Jesus was God to the extent that God can be contained in a human frame. He was unconditionally accepting, forgiving, healing, and loving.

I find that it helps me here to think of divinity as a substance, a thing, that Jesus allowed to fill him completely, in the way water fills a cup. That "thing"– God, or pure Spirit–is invisible, but that doesn't counter its power, for science now relates power to materiality inversely. The well-founded law that the shorter a wavelength is, the larger is the energy that is compressed into it produces the conclusion that a thimbleful of vacuum contains more energy than would be released by all the atomic bomb fuel in the universe. The divine power that Jesus *became* by allowing divinity to consume his person completely attracted and transformed his followers to the point that it launched one of the world's great historical religions, and that power seems even to have influenced natural laws at points, perhaps in something of the way immaterial thoughts and emotions can affect the physiological processes that relate to immune systems. Given nonlocality, a more recently established finding in physics, Christians right down to today can tap into Jesus' divine substance and become members of his extended body, the church.

If the claims of the previous paragraph strain credulity, they at least escape theology's greatest danger, which is ordinariness. The reason that science has become the operative religion of our time is due less to the miracles its technology accomplishes than to the awesomeness of its noetic foundations–the way in which, with increasing regularity, its investigations lead to paradoxes that defy comprehension. Einstein said that if quantum mechanics is true, the world is crazy. Well, quantum mechanics *is* true, so the world is crazy–crazy from our everyday standpoint. When scientists drive that point home by adding, as David Finkelstein said, that "we haven't the capacity to imagine anything crazy enough to stand a chance of being right," I want theologians to get in on the act in their claims for Jesus, for not to do so subordinates Christianity to science in the mind of our times. If I am right in this, the entire move toward demythologizing–demystifying–the Bible was misbegotten from the start. In saying such a thing, I am obviously flaunting my amateur standing as an exegete, but in situations like this it seems best to convert ignorance into an asset and circumvent the niceties that vex the specialists to try to get one's own handle on the subject. True, that reduces my claims to opinions and my entire account to the status of a personal confession, but that was all that I was asked for from the start.

I do want, however, to deny the (possible) charge that my likely tale places me in the camp of fundamentalists and biblicists, for their positions are as modern as the exegetical principles they were simplistically designed to offset. One of the forgotten glories of Christianity is its profound hermeneutical strain. Approached from one angle, that hermeneutic calls for distinguishing four levels in interpreting a text: the literal, the ethical, the allegorical, and the anagogic, the latter being the power of a text to elevate the human spirit. From a complementary angle, Christian hermeneutics teaches that truth should be approached through Scripture, tradition, reason, and personal experience, the four working together. Fundamentalists do not understand this rich Christian hermeneutical tradition, if they are even aware that it exists.

Nevertheless, fundamentalism would not have arisen had it not been provoked by secular excesses that, again by my amateur assessment, overlook the fact that truth is the whole. It is not true that the earliest accounts of Jesus are the most reliable; even the latest can present Jesus in a more reflective manner. Vivid witness to lived Christian truth can be found in apparently secondary writings. No part is complete in isolation; like a living organ in the body, each part is connected to all the others. Each gospel points to the others. Paul presupposes them, and the book of Acts is their continuation. They develop elements already present in germ, as Mahayana Buddhists argue (against their Theravada objectors) that their later and distinctive Scriptures do.[5]

I do not see my position as discounting biblical scholarship in principle; serious research can continue to enrich our faith in the person of Jesus. Everything depends on the worldview that controls the "facts" it brings to light and to which it gives meaning. Within the traditional worldview, which undergirds faith in biblical accounts, research applies itself to showing how the strands of tradition (whose elements were formed by the faith of the first Christians) come together, penetrate each other, and acquire distinct forms. This research throws a brilliant light on earlier traditions until finally, not omitting the workings of the Holy Spirit, a representative and normative picture of the whole Christ-event emerges. That the composite picture feels its way around the central phenomenon in a great variety of perspectives is a major strength, for human beings must be prevented from trying to grasp that phenomenon directly. That attempt would equate the letter with the body of the incarnate Word of God, instead of seeing the texts as only pointers to that Word.

Epilogue

In the course of delivering this paper at the symposium itself, I threw in an aside that I have reserved for this concluding section because a graduate student in the audience picked up on it in a way that enables me to sharpen my entire thesis. In the course of telling my likely tale about Jesus, I remarked that if someone were to object to it on grounds of some scientific or historical fact, in my pugnacious moods I would charge the objector with being a "fact fundamentalist." This prompted October Adamson-Woods—she has permitted me to use her name—to write me an important letter, which I quote in part.

Dear Professor Smith,

It was certainly a peak of my graduate school experience to meet you and hear your presentation at the Jesus at 2000 symposium. [I pass over the specific points in my lecture that she found praiseworthy, but I include this opening sentence to indicate the entirely constructive character of her letter as a whole.]

Now to the crux of my letter. I wanted to ask you, and there wasn't time, why you are so harsh with those of us who cannot say the Nicene Creed [which I had suggested might be taken to epitomize the traditional understanding of Jesus]. I fault it for two things: it literally isn't true and I think the words we use and say are terribly, terribly important, and second, since I can't wear a sign saying, "I'm taking this metaphorically," when the majority of my faith community thinks I'm taking it literally, I believe I'm projecting a lie about myself and my belief. It IS a matter of ethics for me. I left the auditorium in tears when I heard you call people in my position, "fact fundamentalists."

Here is my reply. I do not disagree on the importance of the words we use or on the honest, and hence ethical, use of them. The difference turns on what we take to be ultimately the case or (in the words of the letter writer) on what we believe to be true, literally true, and fundamentally true. Those three formulations come to the same thing.

Her letter doesn't tell us what "literally isn't true" in the creeds, but it seems safe to surmise that "born of a virgin" and "on the third day he arose from the dead" would qualify. If it is indeed claims like these that she has in mind, her objections to them show us that her literal, fundamental truth resides elsewhere, presumably in scientific facts that show that events such as resurrection and human life without a biological father are impossible. If this is her position, it is not harsh to characterize her as a scientific (and presumably in other cases historical) fact fundamentalist, provided I avoid capitalizing fundamentalist, which would turn the word into a pejorative. The phrase simply provides a precise indication of where (1) truth, (2) literal truth, and (3) what is fundamentally and nonnegotiably true—again, the three come to the same thing—reside for her. As an honestly held, considered position, it deserves respect.

It is not, however, the position to which my schooling in the formative periods of the world's religions has brought me. In that outlook (as I have indicated) the spatio-temporal-material world in which scientific and historical facts reside derives from another world that is vastly more momentous and real. To grant scientific and historical facts jurisdiction over that original world–God would not be an inappropriate synonym–would be equivalent to asserting that the peaks of Kanchenjunga and Mount Everest cannot be more than two inches apart because our postcard of the Himalayan range *shows* that they are only that far apart. I do not know if Jesus was born of a virgin, but in confessing that I do not know that he was *not* so born, I show that I do not allow putative scientific and historical assertions the last word on what God can be and do. Like everyone who has a considered position, I, too, am a fundamentalist in taking something–in my case, God's ultimacy–to be fundamental, but no more than the letter writer am I a (capitalized) Fundamentalist, for no more than she do I take the Bible's literal words as my court of last appeal. Where she and I appear to differ is in what we do take as our final courts of appeal. If I read her correctly, her court is scientific and historical facts, whereas mine is the world's deep, mysterious, theological structure, which relativizes scientific and theological facts in the way that Einstein's theories of relativity relativize the Euclidian space of everyday human experience.

As for metaphor, the fact that our minds are less equal to God's than dogs' minds are to Einstein's entails that all human attempts to describe the ultimate nature of things are metaphorical in being unable to map reality isomorphically. Differences in the degree to which they succeed in doing so are important, however. I believe that taken together, the articles of the Christian creeds come closer to articulating the literal truth as to who Jesus was than do depictions that are controlled by putative facts about this half-real, half-unreal world of maya that constitutes our earthly abode.

Questions and Responses from the Symposium

Q: If Jesus was a mystic, in what ways did he manifest that in his life and in his teachings? How can we in the church follow Jesus and his mystical way?

A: I think of mysticism as first and foremost a vision of the nature of reality grounded in one's own mystical experience. The force of Jesus' vision of God was all consuming, and it seems to me that his actions and his words flowed from that source. That's the way his mysticism manifested itself. And it's an example for all of us.

Q: By studying Hinduism, I was able to clarify my thoughts about Jesus and the incarnation. Would you briefly comment on the tension between seeing Jesus as one of a long line of avatars and the tendency of some Christians to see Jesus as the only begotten son or child of God?

A: This raises the very important and troubling issue about the relationship between the religions. Although I referred to an enormous amount that they have in common, they are not carbon copies of each other. Moreover, one is not really committed to a religion unless one senses an absolute in it and in the other senses a different absolute.

I think it's going to take us perhaps two or three centuries, now that we're fully into multiculturalism, to work this out, just as it took the early church several centuries to crystallize its conception of Jesus. The fact that each revelation was for a particular community and was intended for that community means that each one has a superlative in it. It's not true that only the Abrahamic religions say that they are the best or that Christ is the only way; one finds counterparts to that in Buddhism as well. For the time being, I think that we simply need to live out the imperatives in our respective traditions.

Q: Are you aware of increasing harmony these days between science and religion in a fundamental sense? Do you think there is a convergence?
A: Is there a growing rapprochement between science and religion? It's a very complex matter. I cited a couple of points about the unseen as evidence of convergence. But there is a lot of talk about convergence, particularly in New Age mentality, that I think is very mushy and plows over remaining differences.

There remains a major point. I think the major problem has become almost a disciplinary problem. Whereas science initially had to struggle to break through the authority of the church to gain its own freedom, now the shoe is on the other foot. Theology is having to struggle against an excessive, I won't say science, but scientism. And every discipline (I'm never more of a Marxist than when I think about the conflicts between departments in a university) takes its stand and seeks to colonize the other. I'm concerned about this. This isn't true of all scientists; some leading scientists are aware that there are things they don't know and actually cannot know by their method and thus acknowledge that their methodology is partial and limited. On the whole, I think the so-called harmony between science and religion is an unstable détente at present.

Q: You said that one of humankind's advances involved progress in racial relationships. Has humankind achieved any other advances over the life as enjoyed by primitive or Stone Age societies? Do we laugh more? Do we have more free time? Are we more creative? Are we more or less subject to myths? Do we understand reality better? How far have we progressed as we approach the coming millennium?
A: Let me respond with a story. I had the opportunity of interviewing Reinhold Niebuhr once, the great American theologian and social ethicist from the middle part of this century. I was a young man and eager for progress, but he was dubious about it. I pressed him at every point: "Hasn't there been progress?" And all I could get from him was, "In certain areas, yes." Well, "plumbing" was an easy one, but I wanted to know, "Have there been any net gains?" Niebuhr adamantly refused to say that there had been, and so I asked, "Doesn't that cut the nerve of social action?" He responded with an example I still remember.

For medical doctors to behave responsibly day after day in doing their duties, must they believe that they are eliminating disease from the human race? It was a rhetorical question, and it persuaded me. Now, I confess that I have a tin ear for taking the pulse of different periods in history. It always seems like a series of trade-offs. With Dickens, it was the best of times and the worst of times. Or with the French, the more things change, the more they stay the same. That's what I believe. But I didn't want to leave the impression that I thought that the traditional period as such was better than ours.

Q: We've talked about the relationship between religion and science. What about between religion and technology? Isn't modern technology what's really transforming our world?

A: Well, it's a mixed picture. Technology has doubled the life span in the "have" nations in the last century, and there are many other virtues we could list. I had prostate cancer four years ago, and had it not been for technology, I would not be here. I'm very happy to be here! So I'm not going to bad-mouth technology. But more and more over the horizon, we're seeing the problems. Moreover, it takes about thirty-five years before the problems attending a major technological breakthrough show up. When DDT came on, nobody could have predicted how it would affect the eggs of certain birds, and when nuclear energy came on, the dangers were partly unknown and partly shoved under the rug. All we can say is it's here. There's no turning back the clock. It provides a challenge that let's hope we can live up to.

Q: Jesus' message of enlightenment, spirituality, and self-awareness are the same in spirit as the teachings of Lao Tzu, Buddha, Confucius, and Gandhi. Do you think that the fact that Jesus was the only one of this group to be executed adds something to his appeal or to the meaning of Christianity?

A: I think that every religion is an organic whole. It is a gestalt, a configuration of components, and it is that configuration of components that is distinctive for each tradition, that gives it its power. Every religion changes throughout history, and I think that there is danger in losing the gestalt, which could be compared to a great painting or an organism. Each part derives its meaning from its relation to the whole, and this brings me to the death of Jesus as part of the Christian gestalt. Yes, I think Jesus' crucifixion has contributed to the power of Christianity through the centuries.

8

The Historical Study of Jesus
and Christian Origins

MARCUS J. BORG

Some readers of this book are already familiar with the historical study of Jesus and Christian origins. Commonly known as the "historical-critical" method, it has developed within the academic discipline of biblical scholarship over the last two hundred years. Other readers may be students in their first or second religious studies course, and still others may be among the "newly curious," whether part of a church study group or readers in the general culture. This chapter is intended for those to whom the historical-critical approach to the study of Jesus and Christian origins is new.

Because both Christians and non-Christians (and persons who aren't quite sure where they belong) will be readers of this book, I want to begin with some comments about my own religious commitment and its connection to the historical-critical study of Jesus that I am about to describe. I am a Christian, deeply involved in the life of the church and strongly committed to living my life of relationship with the sacred within the framework of the Christian tradition. I am a "mainline" Christian. By that I mean that I am a member of one of what are commonly known as mainline Christian denominations in North America. These include most Protestant denominations that have been around for a while, as well as the Roman Catholic Church. In my own case, I was a Lutheran until about age thirty and am now an Episcopalian, a process that began at about age forty.

I am a nonexclusivistic and nonliteralistic Christian. By nonexclusivistic, I mean that I believe that God (or the sacred) is known in religious traditions other than Christianity. I did not grow up with this belief. Like many of my Christian contemporaries, I learned that Jesus, the Bible, and Christianity are the only way of salvation. For several reasons (including my studying other religions and meeting persons of those traditions), I no longer believe that. Instead, I see Christianity as one of the ways humans have responded to God.

By nonliteralistic, I refer to a way of hearing and reading the Bible. I do not think the Bible is literally the "words" of God, as if it were a divine product unlike any other piece of literature. Moreover, I do not read the Bible literalistically. I do not think the Bible must be literally true in order to be true; we should not confuse "truth" with "literal truth" or "historical fact." This way of seeing the Bible and Christianity is affirmed by many mainline Christians. Indeed, nonexclusivity and nonliteralism are among the characteristics that most distinguish mainline Christians from fundamentalist and most conservative-evangelical Christians.

I mention that I am a Christian in part to inform the reader about my own religious stance, but also to emphasize that I have no difficulty reconciling this way of seeing the Gospels and Jesus with being a Christian. At the same time, the approach I describe in this chapter is the approach followed by most mainstream scholars, whether Christian or non-Christian. Thus, this approach to the study of Jesus does not depend upon distinctively Christian beliefs, even though I as a Christian affirm it. I have no difficulty combining this approach with what I see as orthodox mainstream Christianity over the centuries, even though doing so leads to a revisioning of some widely held popular Christian beliefs.

In the rest of this chapter, I treat four matters. In a historical introduction, I describe the revolution in our understanding of the Bible and the Gospels that has occurred in the last few hundred years. I then provide a sketch of gospel origins as understood by contemporary scholarship. Following this, I use four case studies to illustrate modern methods of study and the factors affecting the development of the Gospels. Finally, I conclude with some comments about how scholars move "back to Jesus."

Historical Introduction

The story of the modern historical-critical study of Jesus and Christian origins is best told as part of a larger story. That larger story concerns the historical-critical study of the Bible as a whole. It involves a transformation in our understanding of the Bible. The change began some three centuries ago in the Enlightenment, that development in Western intellectual history that has decisively shaped and essentially defines modern culture to this day. To tell the story of this transformation, I must begin before the Enlightenment.

The Bible Prior to the Enlightenment

Before the Enlightenment, the Bible was seen as the sacred foundation of Western culture. It was the world of Christendom, that blending of Christianity and European culture that lasted roughly one thousand years. Within this world, it was taken for granted that the Bible as God's Word described the way things were. Sacred authority was the basis of truth. That authority was the Bible, and the church was its authoritative interpreter. How did one know such and such to be true? Because the Bible said so.

The Bible's stories of creation, the flood, and the ancestors were seen as the early history of the earth. The Bible's stories of God's redemptive acts (climaxing, above all, in the life, death, and resurrection of Jesus, the Son of God) were seen as divine disclosures of the way of salvation. The Bible's laws were seen as God's laws. And just as the Bible's stories of the beginning of the world explained its origin, so, too, the Bible's picture of the last judgment portrayed the world's future destiny.

Importantly, the intertwining of Christianity and culture in Christendom meant that it was not just a particular group of people (Christians or the church) who saw the Bible this way. Rather, culture and church saw the Bible the same way. There was little or no conflict between the two. Science, religion, and philosophy agreed, forming a harmonious understanding of what was true.

Natural Literalism

In this period of history, both educated and noneducated people heard and read the Bible in a state of "natural literalism."[1] In this state of mind, the language of the Bible is understood in its literal sense; distinctions between literal and nonliteral, factual and nonfactual, historical and symbolic, are not made. No reason for making the distinction (except for obvious metaphors) has yet emerged. From the vantage point of natural literalism, a number of things seem obviously to be true about the Bible. They do not even require belief; rather, they are taken for granted as self-evident.

1. *The Bible is a divine product.* Such is the "natural" or "immediate" meaning of traditional Christian language about the Bible. It is "the Word of God" and "inspired by the Holy Spirit." For natural literalism, the Bible is thus not a human product but comes from God in a way no other book does.

2. *The Bible is therefore true and authoritative.* For natural literalism, the nature and authority of the Bible are directly related: Because the Bible is a divine product, it is guaranteed to be true and must be taken seriously as the ultimate revelation of what to believe and how to live.

3. *The Bible is literally true.* In a state of natural literalism, it is taken for granted that whatever the Bible says happened *really* happened: Adam and Eve were the first two people, there really was a Garden of Eden, the story of Noah and the flood is historically factual, Jesus was born of a virgin, Jesus said and did all of the things reported about him, and so forth. Believing all of this to be literally and factually true takes no effort; for natural literalism, there is no reason to think otherwise.

True, not every passage need be interpreted literally. Sometimes biblical language is obviously metaphorical, as when mountains shout with joy and hills flow with wine. Natural literalists can recognize and appreciate metaphor. Moreover, theologians and Bible scholars before the Enlightenment could find the spiritual or allegorical meaning of a text to be more important than the literal meaning, and they could even deny the literal meaning of some texts. For example, while commenting on the story of Jesus' temptation (Matt. 4.1–11 = Luke 4.1–13), the early-third-century theologian Origen said that no mountain existed from which Satan could show Jesus all the kingdoms of the earth; therefore, Origen concluded, something else must be meant.

Similarly, Martin Luther in the 1500s denied the literal meaning of this scene from the Garden of Eden: "Adam and Eve heard the sound of the LORD God walking in the garden in the cool of the day, and hid themselves (because they were afraid) from the presence of the LORD God among the trees of the garden" (Gen. 3.8). God never walked in any garden, Luther said. Instead, Adam and Eve must have heard the wind; and because of the fall into sin, nature (which previously had seemed benevolent) became a source of fear. Yet despite examples like this, the pre-Enlightenment view of Scripture generally took it for granted that the events reported in the Bible had really happened.

4. *The Bible (and therefore Christianity) is uniquely and exclusively true.* Finally, natural literalism takes for granted that the Bible is the exclusive revelation of God and that Jesus and Christianity are the only way of salvation. Such is the plain meaning of Jesus' words in John's gospel: "I am the way, the truth, and the life; no one comes to God but by me" (John 14.6). In the Bible, saving knowledge of God is found as nowhere else.

This way of seeing the Bible, dominant in Western and Christian culture for over one thousand years, is familiar to this day. Although it began to be challenged some three hundred years ago by a small circle of intellectuals, it remained virtually omnipresent within both culture and church until about a century ago. Most of our ancestors three or four generations ago were natural literalists.

Moreover, natural literalism is familiar to many of us who grew up in the church because it is the image of the Bible we formed as children. We took it for granted that the Bible came from God and that what it said was factually true. As children, it never occurred to us to ask about the story of Noah and the ark or about the virgin birth, "Now, are these stories literally or symbolically true?" Rather, we took their literal truth for granted. Why would we have thought otherwise? Indeed, *taken for granted* is the key phrase for understanding natural literalism's approach to the Bible: In this state, the distinction between literal and nonliteral has not yet arisen. There is no reason for it to do so: To use a somewhat technical phrase, there is no *cognitive dissonance* (conflict between two kinds of knowledge and/or experience) between a literal reading of the Bible and what is thought to be true on other grounds.[2]

The Collapse of Natural Literalism

This whole way of looking at the Bible came undone in the Enlightenment. Beginning in the seventeenth and eighteenth centuries, the Enlightenment revolutionized our sense of what constitutes "knowledge" and "truth." The story of Galileo's experiments with falling bodies exemplifies this revolution. Prior to Galileo, it was taken for granted that heavier objects fall faster than lighter objects. Why? Because traditional authority said so (in this case, the ancient Greek philosopher Aristotle). Galileo decided to experiment and found that objects fall at the same rate regardless of their weight. His experiment symbolizes the birth of the scientific method, which is at the heart of the Enlightenment: Truth is to be established not by appeal to authority but by investigation. The modern period, with its emphasis on empirical ways of knowing, had been born.

Enlightenment ways of knowing were soon extended from the natural sciences to the study of history and literature, including the study of the Bible. This is not the place to describe in detail the early and continuing history of modern biblical criticism.[3] Rather, I want to highlight the central reasons that over time led to a very different view of the Bible.

The careful investigation of biblical texts disclosed their intimate connections to the ancient communities in which they had been written. Not only were the texts seen to be relevant to the times in which they had been written; that was only to be expected. In addition, scholarly study showed that the texts themselves were profoundly shaped by the ancient world in which they emerged and by the beliefs of the people who wrote them. Some of these beliefs seem clearly from our point of view (and with good reasons) to be wrong. They tell us what people in these ancient communities believed.

For example, in the opening chapters of Genesis, we find an ancient view of the cosmos borrowed from Babylonian thought: The earth (thought of as flat) is covered by the dome of the sky (the "firmament"); rain is the result of the waters above the sky falling through the "windows" of the firmament. Or in the New Testament, many passages clearly indicate that the authors expected the second coming of Jesus and the last judgment (what is sometimes loosely called "the end of the world") *soon*.[4]

Moreover, the careful comparison of texts in the Bible indicated that we often have different versions of the same story, with the differences best explained as the result of multiple traditions and human authors at work. To cite two examples from the Old Testament: There are two different stories of creation (Gen. 1.1–2.4a and Gen. 2.4b–3.24) and two different accounts of the crossing of the sea at the time of the exodus from Egypt (Exod. 14.21–29). In the New Testament, there are often two or three different versions of a story about (or a saying of) Jesus. Furthermore, the biblical authors sometimes disagree with each other. A classic example: The author of Job challenges the claim of the book of Proverbs that God has set things up in such a way that the righteous will prosper and the wicked will suffer. Not so, the author of Job says. There seems to be more than one voice speaking in the biblical tradition.

The investigation of the Bible suggested that it is not a divine product, at least not in any direct sense. Moreover, for reasons in addition to those just mentioned, the notion that God specifically guided the writing of this collection of documents (and no other collection of documents) became doubtful. In part, this was because of the Enlightenment's skepticism about supernatural intervention: Does God intervene directly in the world so that some things have natural causes and others are directly caused by God? The doubt also flowed from a rational and theological difficulty—namely, the difficulty of supposing that God would choose to be revealed in only one religious tradition, with dire consequences for everybody outside of that tradition. Does it make sense that the creator of the whole universe would be known in only one religious tradition (which fortunately just happens to be our own)? And is such a notion theologically consistent with the notion of a gracious God?

Thus, a new view of the Bible emerged in the scholarship of the last two centuries. This view can be summed up in a single sentence with equally important negative and positive statements: The Bible is not a divine product; rather, it is the human product of two ancient communities. The Hebrew Bible is the product of ancient Israel;[5] the New Testament is the product of the early Christian movement. As the product of two ancient communities, the Bible expresses their way of seeing things. The stories of creation in the book of Genesis are ancient Israel's stories of creation, not God's stories of creation; the laws of the Hebrew Bible are ancient Israel's laws, not the laws of God for all times and places; the claim of some authors in the New Testament that Jesus is the only way of salvation tells us what they thought, not what God has said or requires. Therefore, in studying the Bible historically, we are put in touch not with "what God says" but with what these ancient people thought and believed about God, the world, and their lives.

The denial that the Bible is a divine product is sufficiently startling to some people that a few clarifying words may be helpful. This claim need not involve a denial of either the reality of God or the activity of the Spirit in people's lives. It is completely possible to affirm both the reality of God and the activity of the Spirit without also affirming that the Bible is the unique and direct revelation of God. This position is not atheistic.

Moreover, it is possible to hold this position and still regard the Bible highly as the Word of God. The Bible as God's Word suggests that it is a means whereby God becomes known to us (both through study of what those ancient people said about God and through devotional use of the Bible as a way of "listening" for God in the present). One can affirm that the Bible is the Word of God (with *Word* capitalized and singular) without seeing it as the words of God (lowercased and plural).

Although this way of looking at the Bible is now common among scholars and mainline Christians, it caused great disturbance and resistance when it first began to emerge some three hundred years ago. In 1697 an eighteen-year-old Scottish student named Thomas Aikenhead was hanged in Edinburgh for claiming that the Pentateuch was written not by Moses but by someone else eight hundred years later. In England in the early 1700s, Thomas Woolston, a professor at Cambridge, was put in prison for one year for claiming that the miracles of Jesus had not happened. Near the end of the 1700s, in *The Age of Reason* Thomas Paine of Revolutionary War fame denied the truthfulness of much of the Bible; his publishers in England were heavily fined and put in prison. In the 1800s in both England and the United States, the new way of looking at the Bible led to heresy trials and threats of heresy trials. In some Christian circles, the battle over the Bible continues to this day.

The story of the historical-critical study of Jesus and Christian origins is part of this larger story. Prior to the Enlightenment, it was taken for granted that the Gospels, as part of a Bible inspired by God, were historically factual. If one wanted to know what Jesus was like, one simply needed to compile together everything the Gospels said about him. But a new view of the Gospels (and thus of Jesus) began to emerge in the 1700s and 1800s. Of the thousands of books written about Jesus and the Gospels during this time, I single out three as landmarks.

REIMARUS

The birth of the quest for the historical Jesus is usually traced back to a German scholar named Hermann Samuel Reimarus (1694–1768).[6] In the last years of his life, Reimarus wrote a manuscript that was published ten years after his death (and anonymously) as *The Intention of Jesus and His Disciples.* In it, Reimarus argued that Jesus' own intention (and message) during his lifetime differed sharply from the intention (and message) of his followers after his death. Jesus' message was about the coming of the Kingdom of God, which, according to Reimarus, would involve liberation from Rome. For Jesus' efforts, he was crucified as a political rebel by order of the Roman governor. That should have been the end of things.

But Jesus' followers were unwilling to go back to their previous lives of hard work, and so they turned the message *of* Jesus into a message *about* Jesus and made him into the central figure of a new religion of which they became the leaders. They even, according to Reimarus, stole Jesus' body from the tomb in order to fake a resurrection. Their message–about a risen Jesus who would come again as the judge of the living and the dead–is what is found in the Gospels and the rest of the New Testament. Although many of Reimarus's claims are not taken seriously by scholars (including the notion that the disciples stole Jesus' body), his central claim has become one of the foundations of modern scholarship: namely, the distinction between Jesus as a figure of history and Jesus as portrayed in the Gospels.[7]

STRAUSS

Because Reimarus's book was published after his death, Reimarus himself was spared the uproar that the book caused. Not so David Friedrich Strauss (1808–1874), whose two-volume *The Life of Jesus Critically Examined* appeared in 1835 when Strauss was only twenty-seven. Strauss used the notion of myth (or symbolic narrative) in his analysis of gospel texts about the miraculous.[8] He rejected both of the understandings of the miracle stories that were common among scholars in his day. Traditionalists argued that the stories of the miraculous were historically accurate reports of supernatural interventions. Rationalists saw them as accounts of natural events that were wrongly thought to have had supernatural causes. For example, the bread and sea miracles were seen as involving mistaken perception of events that had natural explanations: The feeding of the five thousand happened because people in the crowd shared food they had brought with them; the story of Jesus' walking on the water really involved Jesus walking on a barely submerged set of stones, which the disciples failed to perceive.

Instead, Strauss persuasively suggested a third alternative: The miracle stories are symbolic narratives (or myths) that make use of language and themes drawn from the Hebrew Bible in order to speak the religious truth about Jesus. Thus, the miracle stories didn't happen. But neither are they mistaken or false accounts of something the disciples thought happened or invented for the sake of exaggerating their portrait of Jesus. Rather, the miracle stories are religiously true, even though not factually true.

The reaction to Strauss was intense. He was seen by one reviewer as a "Judas," and his book was called "the Iscariotism of our times." He was fired from his teaching position at the University of Tübingen in Germany. Offered a teaching position in Zurich, he accepted it; but before he could give his first lecture, forty thousand people signed a protest petition, and the job offer was withdrawn. He never held another teaching position. Yet as with Reimarus, Strauss's major claim has become central to the historical study of Jesus and Christian origins: Some of the stories in the Gospels are better understood as symbolic narratives rather than as historically factual reports.

SCHWEITZER

Albert Schweitzer (1875–1965) is best known as a medical missionary and humanitarian who spent most of his adult life in Africa and eventually won a Nobel Prize. But as a young man (indeed, by the time he was thirty), he wrote two books about Jesus, one of which became famous: *The Quest of the Historical Jesus* (1906).[9] In it, he brilliantly reported the history of the modern study of Jesus from Reimarus to his own time. Schweitzer then developed his own understanding of Jesus by making central two major themes in the Gospels:

the coming of the Kingdom of God and the coming of the Son of Man. Both were to be understood eschatologically–that is, as "end-time" events (the word *eschatology* comes from the Greek word *eschaton,* which means the end). At the heart of Jesus' message and actions was his expectation that God would very soon supernaturally intervene, establish the Kingdom of God promised in the Hebrew Bible, and install Jesus as the Son of Man who would rule over the Kingdom of God.

About this, Jesus was wrong, of course; the end did not come. But Jesus' expectation of the imminent end was the animating conviction of his ministry. Schweitzer called this way of seeing Jesus "thorough-going eschatology," and it is commonly called "apocalyptic eschatology" or "imminent eschatology" by scholars today.

Schweitzer's work was enormously influential. Indeed, his *Quest of the Historical Jesus* has been called one of the most important books of the twentieth century and the single most important book of New Testament scholarship in modern times.[10] He argued that both Jesus and the early Christian movement were dominated by imminent eschatological expectation; that is, they expected the end-time events of last judgment, resurrection of the dead, and the coming of the Kingdom of God in their time. His argument that Jesus is to be seen within the framework of apocalyptic eschatology became one of the "assured results" widely accepted by New Testament scholars for much of this century. Only recently are there signs that his dominance has waned.[11]

To bring this brief history of scholarship to a close, I list the central conclusions that emerged.

1. Like the Bible as a whole, the Gospels are human, not divine, products. They therefore are to be studied in the same way as other ancient documents.
2. The Gospels are the products of early Christian communities. Of course, individual authors were involved, but they wrote from within a community and for a community.
3. Although the Gospels contain some historical material, their primary purpose is not historical reporting. The authors of the gospels were neither journalists nor historians who sought simply to report "what happened." Rather, they were evangelists (from the Greek word for gospel) whose purpose was to proclaim the "good news." To make the point slightly differently, the Gospels are not biographies, and their concern is not historical factuality; rather, they seek to express what Jesus had become in the life and thought of early Christian communities.
4. The gospel traditions develop. They grow. The Gospels of the New Testament were written some forty to seventy years after the death of Jesus, and during those decades the traditions about Jesus continued to develop.

5. The Gospels contain both history and symbol. That is, they preserve to some degree traditions going back to Jesus, even as they also include symbolic narratives that use the language of myth and metaphor to speak about the meaning of Jesus in the life of the communities for which the Gospels were written.

6. Some of the material in the Gospels (and elsewhere in the New Testament) expresses an apocalyptic eschatology; there are apocalyptic voices in early Christianity. These voices must be accounted for, either as continuing the voice of Jesus or as arising after his death with the expectation of a second coming.

A Contemporary Sketch of Gospel Origins

Among non-Christian writers in the first century, Jesus is mentioned only by the Jewish historian Josephus. Born in the Jewish homeland around the year 37 C.E., he died in Rome around the year 100. In his history of the Jewish people, written around the year 90, Josephus briefly mentions Jesus when describing Pontius Pilate's tenure as the Roman governor of Judea. Because this is the earliest non-Christian reference to Jesus (and the only one from the first century), I quote it in full:

> At this time there appeared Jesus, a wise man. For he was a doer of startling deeds, a teacher of people who receive the truth with pleasure. And he gained a following both among many Jews and among many of Greek origin. And when Pilate, because of an accusation made by the leading men among us, condemned him to the cross, those who had loved him previously did not cease to do so. And up until this very day the tribe of Christians (named after him) has not died out.[12]

It is an interesting description: Jesus was a wisdom teacher and a wonder-worker who attracted a following; he caused alarm among both Jewish and Roman authorities, who collaborated in his execution; but "those who loved him" continued to do so, and his movement was still around in Josephus's day.

For more information, we are completely dependent on Christian sources. Most important are the Gospels of the early Christian movement. Four of these are in the New Testament and were written in the last third of the first century. A fifth gospel, the recently discovered Gospel of Thomas, is from the early second century, though it may well contain some material that is considerably earlier.

The Synoptic Gospels and John

Among the gospels of the New Testament, scholars make a sharp distinction between what are called *the synoptic Gospels* (Matthew, Mark, and Luke) and the gospel of John.[13] The first three are called the synoptic Gospels (or simply the synoptics) because they are similar enough to be seen together, as the root of the word *synoptic* suggests. The gospel of John, in contrast, is very different.

The distinction between the synoptics and John is foundational to the historical study of Jesus and Christian origins. The best way to see this distinction is to read through the gospel of Mark (exemplary of the synoptic Gospels) and then through the gospel of John, noting the following:

1. How does Jesus speak of himself in each gospel?
2. What is Jesus' message most centrally about in each gospel?
3. What is Jesus' style of teaching in each gospel? Short sayings? Parables? Long speeches?
4. What happens in each gospel? What events/stories are reported and in what sequence? How much overlap and how much difference are there?

Although it is best to see the differences by reading the Gospels oneself, I provide a summary in order to take this sketch a step further. One of the greatest differences is Jesus' self-proclamation. In John, Jesus speaks frequently of his own extraordinary status. In the great "I am" statements (found only in John), Jesus speaks of himself in the most exalted language. These include:

> "I am the light of the world" (8.12, 9.5).
> "I am the bread of life" (6.35).
> "I am the resurrection and the life" (11.25).
> "I am the way, the truth and the life" (14.6).

Also in John, Jesus speaks of himself as one with God and as the revelation of God: "I and the Father are one" (10.30), "Whoever has seen me has seen the Father" (14.9), and "No one comes to God except through me" (14.6).

In Mark, there is none of this. Jesus never refers to himself with any of these exalted images and phrases. On only two occasions does he apparently accept an exalted status for himself. Both times, it happens in private, and then in response to what somebody else has said. In Mark 8.27–30, Peter says to Jesus, "You are the Christ" (which means *Messiah,* a Jewish term that means literally the anointed one and that by the first century meant something like God's anointed deliverer). The Jesus of Mark says nothing in response, though apparently he accepts the statement.

The second (and last) time something like this happens in Mark is very near the end of Jesus' life. In Mark's story of Jesus' trial, his interrogator asks, "Are you the Messiah, the Son of the Blessed One?" Jesus responds, "I am," and then speaks of "the Son of Man coming with the clouds of heaven" (Mark 14.61–62). It is important to highlight that both of these occasions occur in private. That is, Jesus' exalted status is *not* part of Jesus' public teaching in Mark. It is not part of his message. The contrast to John is stark, where Jesus regularly proclaims his identity.

There are other sharp differences between the synoptics (as represented by Mark) and John. In the synoptics, Jesus performs many exorcisms; in John, none. In the synoptics, Jesus most commonly teaches by using short sayings (called aphorisms by scholars) and memorable short stories (the parables); in John, Jesus often teaches in long, complex discourses. In Mark, Jesus drives the money changers out of the temple in Jerusalem in the final week of his life (indeed, it is the cause of his arrest); in John, Jesus does so at the very beginning of his public activity (at the end of Chapter 2). In John, Jesus' message is to a large extent about himself; in Mark, Jesus' message is not about himself but about the Kingdom of God.

Cumulatively, these differences have persuaded scholars that a foundational choice must be made: The historical Jesus was either more like the Jesus of the synoptics or more like the Jesus of John. The differences are so great that the synoptic and Johannine portraits of Jesus cannot be harmonized into a single whole. For mainline scholars, the choice is the synoptics.

Importantly, this does not mean that John's gospel should be cast aside as worthless. Rather, it is "the spiritual gospel," as the early church theologian Clement of Alexandria said around the year 200. Using exceptionally rich and evocative images, John's gospel tells us what the post-Easter Jesus had become in the life of the Christian community out of which this gospel came and for which it was written. For these followers, Jesus was the light of the world, the bread of life, the way that had led them from death to life; for them, he was one with God, and in seeing him, they saw God. John's gospel is thus a powerful and profound testimony to what Jesus had become in their experience.

The Origin of the Synoptics

The amount of overlapping material in the synoptic Gospels is striking:

1. 90 percent of Mark appears also in Matthew (roughly 600 of Mark's 661 verses).
2. Sixty-seven percent of Mark appears also in Luke (roughly 450 of Mark's 661 verses).
3. About 200 verses not found in Mark at all appear in both Matthew and Luke.

However, some material is found only in Matthew (including Matthew's birth stories and a few parables), some material is found only in Luke (including Luke's birth stories and many parables), and a very small amount of material is found only in Mark.

The overlapping material is the key to understanding the origins of the synoptic Gospels. How does one explain categories (1) and (2)–the amount of material shared in common by all three? The most commonly accepted solution is that the authors of Matthew and Luke each had a copy of Mark in front of them when they wrote. To be obvious, 90 percent of Mark appears in Matthew because Matthew used 90 percent of Mark; and 67 percent of Mark appears in Luke because Luke used that much of Mark. From this it follows, of course, that Mark is the earliest of the synoptic Gospels (a view commonly referred to as "the priority of Mark").

How does one account for category (3), the 200 verses shared by Matthew and Luke but not found in Mark? The situation is somewhat analogous to a professor receiving term papers from two students that share many sentences and sometimes whole paragraphs (often with exactly the same words). I would not imagine that they had simply discussed their papers with each other. The possibilities are threefold: Student A copied from student B, student B copied from student A, or both used and copied from the same source.[14]

To apply the analogy, it seems very unlikely that either the author of Matthew or the author of Luke knew the other's gospel. It follows, therefore, that there must have been an early Christian document that included these 200 verses and that both Matthew and Luke used; scholars call this document "Q" or "the Q Gospel." Because we do not have such a document, the claim that there must have been one is known as "the Q hypothesis." But it seems a strong hypothesis, and most scholars accept it.[15]

Summary of Gospel Origins

Thus, for most scholars, the earliest documents among the Gospels are Mark and Q.[16] To fill out and complete this sketch of the origin of the written Gospels, I provide the following summary.[17]

1. The Q Gospel is the earliest written source of the Gospels. It may be as early as the 50s of the first century. The 200 verses that make up Q are primarily sayings of Jesus. To make the point negatively, there are basically no narratives about Jesus in Q—no miracle stories (though healings and exorcisms are referred to in sayings) and no stories about Jesus' birth, journey to Jerusalem, or death and resurrection. Q thus seems to have been an early collection of the teachings of Jesus or the sayings of the master.

2. Mark is next. Written around the year 70, it is the earliest surviving gospel, as well as the shortest of the New Testament Gospels.[18] It is largely a narrative gospel; that is, it consists mostly of stories about Jesus, with relatively little of his teachings.[19] Mark also provides the basic pattern of Jesus' public activity followed by Matthew and Luke: a time of teaching and healing in Galilee, followed by a fatal trip to Jerusalem, all fitting into a one-year period of time. Mark emphasizes the coming of the Kingdom of God, the miracles of Jesus, and the path of discipleship as following Jesus on the path of death and resurrection. Mark seems to have an apocalyptic eschatology (see, for exam-

ple, Mark 13.24–30 and 9.1), perhaps heightened by the destruction of Jerusalem and the temple in the year 70.

3. Matthew and Luke follow within a decade or two (and probably by the year 90). It is not clear which is earlier. Both used Mark and Q as sources. Each added his own distinctive story of Jesus' birth, as well as distinctive resurrection stories.

4. Matthew basically followed Mark's narrative and to it added teachings from Q, as well as some material found only in Matthew. Matthew assembled Jesus' teachings into five major blocks of material (the most famous is the Sermon on the Mount in Matt. 5–7), perhaps echoing the five books of the Pentateuch (the first five books of the Hebrew Bible, also known within Judaism as the Torah) and thus presenting Jesus as one like Moses, even though greater than Moses. Matthew seems to continue Mark's apocalyptic eschatology.

5. Like Matthew, Luke (who also wrote the book of Acts) combined Mark and Q, though he used them somewhat differently. He also included many parables not found in other Gospels. For Luke, Jesus is a radical Spirit-anointed social prophet, as indicated in Jesus' "inaugural address" in Luke 4.16–19. A major theme of Luke's two-volume work is the incorporation of Gentiles into what began as a Jewish movement. Thus, the gospel (essentially describing Jesus' mission to Israel) begins in Galilee and moves to Jerusalem, the center of Judaism; the book of Acts (essentially describing the movement's expansion into the Gentile world) begins in Jerusalem and moves to Rome, the capital of the empire. Apocalyptic eschatology is less evident than in Mark and Matthew.

6. John is probably (but not certainly) written a few years after Matthew and Luke and most likely before the year 100. Although scholars early in this century thought it to be a quite Hellenistic gospel perhaps written in Asia Minor, scholars now locate it in a much more Jewish environment. As already noted, John's gospel is very distinctive and not very historical. It may be completely independent of the synoptic Gospels.[20]

7. The Gospel of Thomas, discovered in upper Egypt in 1945, was probably put into written form between 125 and 140. Like Q, Thomas is a sayings gospel. Its 114 sayings contain some sayings that are similar to those of the synoptics, as well as some that are very different. In the judgment of at least a slight majority of North American scholars, Thomas is independent of the other Gospels and may contain some material as early as anything in the synoptic Gospels.[21]

Case Studies: The Gospels as a Developing Tradition

Foundational to the modern historical-critical understanding of the Gospels is the claim that they are a developing tradition. Because this claim is so central, it is important (as well as interesting) to illustrate the claim by looking at specific examples. I begin with two relatively simple case studies and then add two more extended ones.[22]

The Entry into Jerusalem

The story of Jesus riding into Jerusalem on what Christians call Palm Sunday is found in all four Gospels (Matt. 21.1–9, Mark 11.1–10, Luke 19.28–38, John 12.12–15). Of particular interest for our purpose are the accounts found in Mark and Matthew. According to Mark (the earlier account), Jesus as he neared Jerusalem sent two of his disciples ahead to fetch a colt: "Go into the village opposite you, and immediately as you enter it you will find a colt tied, on which no one has ever sat; untie it and bring it" (Mark 11.2). They did so, brought it back to him, threw garments on it, and then Jesus sat on the colt and rode it into the city.

As Matthew copied this account from Mark, he changed it in two ways. First, Matthew added an animal—the disciples are told to fetch two animals, an ass and a colt: "Go into the village opposite you, and immediately you will find *an ass tied, and a colt with her*; untie *them* and bring *them* to me" (Matt. 21.2). The two animals remain throughout Matthew's narrative: The disciples fetched both and "brought *the ass and the colt*, and put their garments *on them* and Jesus sat *on them*" (Matt. 21.7). Thus, according to Matthew, Jesus entered Jerusalem riding on two animals—an almost comic picture if one tries to visualize it, especially since the animals are presumably of different heights.[23]

Why did Matthew do this? Why did he add a second animal to the story? The explanation is found in the second major change Matthew made as he copied Mark. Namely, Matthew added a quotation from the Hebrew Bible, specifically from Zechariah 9.9. In Matthew's words: "This took place to fulfill what was spoken by the prophet, saying, 'Tell the daughter of Zion, Behold your king is coming to you, humble, and *mounted on an ass, and on a colt*, the foal of an ass'" (Matt. 21.4–5).

Note that Mark did not refer to this passage at all. What seems to have happened is that Mark's story of the entry led Matthew to think of a passage from the Hebrew Bible. He looked it up, found two animals in it, and so changed Mark's one animal to two animals. In short, Matthew modified a story from Mark in order to make it better fit what he regarded as a prophecy.[24]

These changes illustrate several points, a couple of which have already been made. First, the changes indicate a human author at work who felt free to modify the story he received, thus illustrating the claim that the Gospels are human products, not divine products. Second, the changes illustrate the claim that the Gospels are a developing tradition (here, Matthew develops Mark). Third, the addition of a passage from the Hebrew Bible regarded as prophecy illustrates a general pattern in Matthew's gospel. Matthew frequently does this, regularly introducing each with a formula used thirteen times: "This took place to fulfill what was spoken by the prophet."[25] Fourth (and related to the third), Matthew's alteration of Mark's story illustrates the difference between "history remembered" and "prophecy historicized" and the meaning of the latter.[26] Are the two animals in Matthew's story history remembered? Obviously not. Clearly, the second animal is there not because Matthew had better historical information on the basis of which to correct Mark (history remembered) but because the second animal comes from Matthew's understanding of Zechariah. It is an instance of prophecy historicized–that is, a passage from the Hebrew Bible regarded as prophecy is generating details in the gospel narrative. "Prophecy" is "historicized" and reported as an event in the gospel.[27] Moreover, historicized prophecy is not only a characteristic of Matthew but also a factor shaping the development of the gospel tradition and the New Testament as a whole.

Jesus Walking on the Water

Stories of Jesus' power over the sea–stilling a storm and walking on the water–are in all four Gospels.[28] The story of his walking on the water appears in Mark 6.45–52, Matthew 14.22–33, and, in a quite different version, John 6.16–21. As Mark tells it, the story is a model of brief and compelling narration. The story is set at night, on the sea; the disciples are in a boat, alone (Jesus is not with them), with the wind against them, in distress. They see what they think is a ghost and are terrified, but then they hear the voice of Jesus, "Take heart, it is I; have no fear." He has come to them "walking on the sea"; and when he gets into the boat, the wind stops and the storm is over. Mark then ends the story with the disciples astonished and puzzled: "And he got into the boat with them and the wind ceased. And they were utterly astounded, for they did not understand about the loaves, but their hearts were hardened" (Mark 6.51b–52).

When Matthew copied this story from Mark, he made two major changes. First, he added the story of Peter's briefly successful attempt to walk on the water himself (Matt. 14.28–31). Second–and this is what we focus on–he changed the ending of the story. Namely, he replaced Mark's ending with "And when *they* [Matthew changes Mark's 'he' to 'they' because there are now two people out on the water, Jesus *and* Peter] got into the boat, the wind ceased. *And those in the boat worshiped him, saying, 'Truly you are the Son of God'*" (Matt. 14.32–33). Matthew changed the disciples' puzzlement and lack of understanding into an act of Christian adoration and acclamation. Jesus is *worshiped*; and he is hailed as the Son of God.

Why did Matthew do this? Presumably because he found the way Mark told the story unsatisfactory. Perhaps Matthew was as puzzled by Mark's ending as the disciples in Mark's story were puzzled about what had happened. Whatever the motive, the change Matthew made illustrates once again that the Gospels were written by human authors who felt free to revise the traditions they received and that the Gospels are a developing tradition. In addition, this example illustrates a further factor at work shaping the tradition as it develops: the emerging christological images and beliefs of the Christian movement. In this text, Matthew adds the christological title *Son of God* to a text that did not have it. Recall that in Mark, Son of God is not used by either Jesus or any of his followers during his lifetime. Language about Jesus as the Son of God (and probably all exalted titles) seems to be a post-Easter development. Matthew here projects a post-Easter perception of Jesus (as the Son of God) back into his lifetime. Matthew also projects a post-Easter practice back into Jesus' lifetime, namely, the worship of Jesus.[29] Thus, the general principle illustrated by this text is that as the gospel tradition develops, it tends to add christological titles.[30]

The Lord's Prayer

Our third case study is the Lord's Prayer, one of the most familiar portions of the Bible.[31] Many people know it by heart. Not as familiar is the fact that there are three different versions of it in early Christian documents. An examination of the three versions illustrates much about the Gospels as a developing tradition.

Two are in Matthew and Luke:

Matthew 6.9b–13	**Luke 11.2b–4**
Our Father who art in heaven	Father,
hallowed be thy name.	hallowed be thy name.
Thy kingdom come,	Thy kingdom come
thy will be done	
on earth as it is in heaven	
Give us this day our	Give us each day our
daily bread	daily bread
And forgive us our debts	And forgive us our sins
as we also have forgiven	for we ourselves forgive
our debtors.	everyone who is indebted
	to us.
And lead us not into	And lead us not into
temptation,[32]	temptation.
but deliver us from evil.	

A third version is found in an early Christian document from around the year 100 C.E. called *Didache* (pronounced dih-dah-kay), or *Teaching*:[33]

Our Father who art in heaven,
hallowed be thy name.
Thy kingdom come,
thy will be done,
as in heaven so also upon the earth.
Give us today our daily bread

And forgive us our debt
as we forgive our debtors.
And lead us not into trial,
but deliver us from the evil one.
For thine is the power and the glory forever. (*Did.* 8.2b–3)

Matthew's version is most familiar because of its widespread use in Christian worship services.[34] But even in Matthew, something seems to be missing (at least to Protestant ears): His prayer ends abruptly with "but deliver us from evil." Where is the familiar closing doxology "For thine is the kingdom and the power and the glory forever"? Matthew doesn't have it; it is closest to what we find in *Didache*, which in other respects is very close to Matthew's form of the prayer. Thus, our familiar version is Matthew plus the doxology from *Didache*.

Luke's version is considerably shorter. Instead of Matthew's "Our Father who art in heaven," Luke has simply "Father." Both then have what is called "the first petition": "Hallowed be thy name." They also both have the second petition–"Thy Kingdom come"–though Luke lacks Matthew's "Thy will be done, on earth as it is in heaven." There are slight differences in wording in the third petition (concerning daily bread) and the fourth petition (concerning forgiveness). Both then have the fifth petition (save us from the trial or ordeal), but Luke lacks Matthew's sixth petition ("Deliver us from evil").

What are we to make of these differences? Did Jesus teach three different forms of the Lord's Prayer, each of which was accurately remembered? That is, are the differences because of history remembered, to employ that useful phrase again? Or are other factors at work?

Initial help is provided when we recognize that the *similarities* between the prayer in Matthew and Luke indicate that it is Q material (recall that the Q Gospel is material shared by Matthew and Luke but not found in Mark). Given that it is Q, two main possibilities exist for explaining the *differences* between Matthew and Q: Luke has shortened an originally longer prayer more like Matthew's version; or Matthew has lengthened a shorter version more like the one found in Luke.

Of these two possibilities, the second is more likely for two reasons. First, it is difficult to imagine a motive for Luke shortening an originally longer version of the prayer.[35] Second, it is easy to imagine a motive for Matthew's longer version. Namely, the extra material in Matthew makes sense as an expansion designed to adapt the prayer for use in the corporate worship of the community (for "liturgical" use). The more formal and solemn opening line "Our Father who art in heaven" not only is easy to imagine in a prayer used in worship, but it also echoes a Jewish liturgical prayer of the time. Moreover, it forms a nicely balanced couplet with the next line, "Hallowed be thy name." Similarly, Matthew's expansion of "Thy Kingdom come" with "Thy will be done, on earth as it is heaven" creates another rhythmic and nicely balanced couplet. Finally, at the end of Matthew's prayer, the same effect is accomplished by Matthew's addition of "But deliver us from evil" to "And lead us not into temptation." Thus, the Q form of the Lord's Prayer is likely to have been closer to Luke's version. If we restrict ourselves to the overlapping material, the Q prayer included the following:

1. An introductory address to God (as simply "Father")
2. A petition for the hallowing of God's name
3. A petition for the coming of the kingdom
4. A petition for daily bread
5. A petition for forgiveness (of debts or sins?)[36]
6. A petition for preservation from trial or ordeal

Suppose one wanted to ask about what lies behind the Q form of the prayer. Does the prayer go back to Jesus himself? Many scholars suspect that the sixth item is a post-Easter addition (whether by Q or earlier) on the grounds that persecution of the new movement did not begin until after the death of Jesus. If this assumption is correct, what is left as possibly going back to the historical Jesus is "Father" plus four petitions.

What can one say about whether or not this much of the Lord's Prayer does? A relevant factor is whether we can imagine Jesus teaching his followers *a prayer to be memorized.* Does this fit what else we think we can glimpse of Jesus? An answer is at best an educated hunch. Or if Jesus didn't teach his followers a prayer to be memorized, might the content of the prayer nevertheless reflect concerns that go back to Jesus? Was he known to pray for these things? Or might he have encouraged his followers to pray for these things, even though he never set them out as a list in a compact prayer that followers were to use? Or did his followers know that these were all central concerns of Jesus and thus after his death create a prayer so that they could collectively pray for what mattered to Jesus? Note that if any of these suggestions are correct, then the prayer itself does not go back to Jesus, but its content nevertheless reflects his convictions and teaching.

To bring this case study of the Lord's Prayer to a close, what does it illustrate? It illustrates once again that the Gospels are a developing tradition. We have three versions of the Lord's Prayer in early Christianity (four, if we count the reconstructed Q version). The three (or four) renditions are best understood as versions of the prayer as it developed in three (or four) early Christian communities. Moreover, a major factor affecting the development of the prayer is the corporate life of the community, seen especially in Matthew's adaptation of the prayer for use in community worship.[37] Finally, this analysis also illustrates the process of seeking to push back into earlier layers of the developing tradition and the kinds of questions that arise as one considers "How much, or in what ways, may early layers of the tradition go back to Jesus?"

The Passion Stories

Our final case study concerns the stories of Jesus' death, the "passion stories." They are found, of course, in all four Gospels.[38] As we begin, it is important to note that the manner of Jesus' execution–crucifixion–indicates both the authority by which and the offense for which he was executed. In the Jewish homeland of the first century, crucifixion was a Roman form of execution, and it was used for only two categories of people: political rebels and chronically defiant slaves.[39] Since Jesus was not a slave, it follows that he was executed as a political rebel against Rome.

In this analysis of the passion stories (done illustratively and not comprehensively), we treat the synoptic accounts. Mark 14.43–15.47 is the earliest and forms the basic pattern for Matthew and Luke. Jesus, betrayed by Judas, is arrested in the Garden of Gethsemane by an armed "crowd" sent by the Jewish authorities. Then there are two "trials," the first Jewish and the second Roman.[40] At the Jewish trial, the issue is a religious offense: Jesus is convicted of "blasphemy" because of his affirmative answer to the question "Are you the Messiah, the Son of the Blessed?" At the Roman trial before Pilate, the governor of Judea, the issue is political: whether Jesus is "the king of the Jews" and thus guilty of insurrection or treason against Caesar. Pilate is not convinced of Jesus' guilt, tries to find a way to release him, but finally gives in to the crowd (which had been incited by the chief priests). Jesus is then crucified, and his last words (and only words) from the cross are, "My God, my God, why hast thou forsaken me?" He is then buried by a member of the Jewish council, Joseph of Arimathea.

To Mark's narrative, Matthew and Luke each make some additions. Luke adds an account of the charges brought by the Jewish authorities to Pilate (23.2), an appearance of Jesus before Herod Antipas (23.6–16), the weeping women of Jerusalem (23.27–31), and the story of the repentant "brigand" (23.39–43).[41] He omits the final saying of Jesus from Mark ("My God, my God, why hast thou forsaken me?") and adds three "last words" spoken by Jesus from the cross: "Father forgive them, for they know not what they do" (23.34); "Today you will be with me in paradise" (to the brigand; 23.43); and "Father, into thy hands I commit my Spirit" (23.46).

Matthew adds a story about the suicide of Judas (27.3–10) and two scenes to the story of Jesus before Pilate (more about these soon). At the moment of Jesus' death, Matthew adds a curious story about the resurrection of many saints who come out of their tombs, enter Jerusalem, and appear to many (27.52–53). Finally, Matthew adds the story of guards being placed at Jesus' tomb (27.62–66).

These changes illustrate once again the general claim that the gospel tradition develops. They also enable us to see a further factor affecting the development: Namely, Matthew's two additional scenes before Pilate have the effect of heightening Jewish responsibility for the death of Jesus. During the trial, Pilate's wife sends a message to Pilate that reports a dream attesting to Jesus' innocence (27.19): "While Pilate was sitting on the judgment seat, his wife sent word to him, 'Have nothing to do with that righteous man, for I have suffered much over him today in a dream.'" Then after the crowd has demanded that Pilate order Jesus to be crucified, Matthew adds the scene of Pilate washing his hands of Jesus' blood (27.24–25): "Pilate took water and washed his hands before the [Jewish] crowd, saying, 'I am innocent of this man's blood, see to it yourselves.' And all the people answered, 'His blood be upon us and our children.'"

The effect created by Mark has been heightened. According to Mark, the highest Roman authority in the Jewish homeland was reluctant to have Jesus crucified but finally gave in to the Jewish authorities. According to Matthew, the Roman governor not only perceived Jesus to be innocent but also performed a public ritual act absolving himself of responsibility, which "all the people" (who are Jewish) then take upon themselves and their children.

In short, Matthew's changes reflect a progressive shifting of responsibility for the execution of Jesus from Roman authority to the Jewish authorities *and* to the Jewish people as a whole.[42] If we ask why Matthew has done this, there may be more than one answer. One reason flows out of the setting in which Matthew's community lived and in which the gospel was written. At the time Matthew was written, late in the first century, there was increasingly bitter conflict between two groups of Jews: Christian Jews (Jews who had become part of the early Christian movement) and non-Christian Jews. This conflict was projected back into the gospel itself.

A second reason grows out of the situation that the early Christian movement faced throughout the Roman Empire. Christians were followers of a person who had been crucified as a political rebel by Rome. Why should they not be regarded as politically dangerous? Christians could not deny that Jesus had been crucified by order of Roman authority; but they could say that Roman authority had actually found him innocent and wanted to let him go.

This realization makes one wonder whether the process of shifting responsibility from Roman authority to Jewish authority was already under way before Mark was written. Perhaps Mark's portrayal of Pilate's reluctance and a Jewish trial at which the issue was not political insurrection but the religious offense of blasphemy is part of the early Christian movement's attempt to explain that it was not an anti-Roman political movement, despite the crucifixion of its founder as a political rebel.[43] Thus, one factor affecting the development of the passion stories is early Christian apologetic (the effort to defend the movement against untrue or damaging charges).

Before we leave these stories, I want to mention one more factor: the use of the Hebrew Bible and symbolism drawn from the Jewish tradition in the telling of the story of Jesus' death. I focus on the earliest synoptic version, Mark. Mark echoes the Hebrew Bible at many points. The wine mixed with myrrh offered to Jesus in Mark 15.23 echoes Psalm 69.21, as does the sponge filled with vinegar in Mark 15.36. Echoes of Psalm 22 show up several times: the wagging of heads in Mark 15.29 and the mocking in Mark 15.31 (Ps. 22.7), the soldiers dividing Jesus' garments among themselves in Mark 15.24 (Ps. 22.18), and Jesus' last words in Mark (quoted from Ps. 22.1). When Mark 15.33 tells us that "when the sixth hour [noon] had come, there was darkness over the whole land until the ninth hour," he echoes Hebrew Bible passages that associate the darkening of the sky with calamity and judgment.[44]

Finally, Mark 15.38 reports that at the moment of Jesus' death, "the curtain of the temple was torn in two, from top to bottom." Here the allusion is not to a particular passage from the Hebrew Bible but to a Jewish institution, the temple in Jerusalem. The most sacred and innermost part of the temple was "the holy of holies," symbolizing the place where God's presence was most concentrated. It was so sacred that it could be entered by only one person (the Jewish high priest) and on only one day of the year (the Day of Atonement); and it was separated from the rest of the temple by a curtain. When Mark reports that the curtain was torn in two at the moment of Jesus' death, Mark is saying that the death of Jesus opens up access to the presence of God.[45]

Thus, an existing "symbolic tradition" (the Hebrew Bible and Jewish tradition) affects the telling of the story of Jesus' death. Some details in the story seem to be symbolic, not historical. In the former category are the three-hour darkness over the land and the tearing of the temple curtain. In other examples where the Hebrew Bible is echoed, we are faced with the choice described in our case study of Matthew's addition of a second animal to the story of Jesus' entry into Jerusalem. Are the details in the passion story history remembered or prophecy historicized? In particular cases, it is difficult to know. For example, was there "mocking" of Jesus while he was on the cross? It is not intrinsically unlikely; indeed, it might be regarded as likely. But is mocking mentioned because it was remembered, or does it come from Christian use of Psalm 22? But however difficult the judgment is in particular cases, it seems clear that the development of even our earliest canonical passion story has been affected by Christian use of the Hebrew Bible.[46] Here, as elsewhere, symbolism and history are combined. The former articulates the significance of the latter.

Thus far our case studies have illustrated the developing gospel traditions by focusing primarily on development within the written traditions, with occasional comments about what may lie behind them. In my final section, I turn directly to that question: What lies behind our earliest written sources?

Back to Jesus

The heading of this section leads me to make an important clarifying remark. I do not presume that *only* that which goes back to Jesus matters. Both the pre-Easter Jesus and the post-Easter Jesus matter. They matter to the historian who seeks to give a coherent and comprehensive account of Jesus and Christian origins. And they matter to me as a Christian. The gospel portraits of Jesus–the "canonical Jesus"–matter for Christian life and understanding.

Moreover, I agree with Huston Smith's statement in Chapter 7: "It is not true that the earliest accounts of Jesus are the most reliable; even the latest can present Jesus in a more reflective manner. Vivid witness to lived Christian truth can be found in apparently secondary writings." And I am in accord with Dom Crossan's statement in Chapter 3: "I have no presumption that what is primary is always better than what is secondary, that what is original is better than what is derivative." Nevertheless, suppose one wants to get as close to the pre-Easter Jesus as one can, whether for historical or theological reasons. What is involved in moving from the written gospel traditions back to Jesus himself?

Here a division of the first century into thirds is helpful.[47] The canonical Gospels were all written in the last third of that century (between ca. 70 and 100 C.E.). Jesus' life and public activity occurred in the first third (ca. 4 B.C.E. to 30 C.E.). In between, in the second third of the first century, was the time of oral tradition.

The Oral Tradition

In the beginning were the words. More exactly, oral tradition carried the teachings of Jesus and the stories about Jesus in that middle third of the first century.[48] They circulated in oral form within early Christian communities. We can get a glimpse of how this worked by reflecting on Jesus' own activity as an oral teacher speaking to a preliterate audience in a preprint world.[49] The two most common teaching forms used by Jesus were the short saying (collectively referred to in shorthand as aphorisms) and the short story (parables).

The aphorisms were memorable "one-liners."[50] They include sayings like "Leave the dead to bury the dead," "No one can serve two masters," "You can't gather grapes from a bramble bush," "The eye is the lamp of the body." As an oral teacher, Jesus would have said each short saying more than once, perhaps scores or hundreds of times. No oral and itinerant teacher uses a great one-liner only once. Moreover, he may have used them differently on various occasions: sometimes as a provocative one-liner left hanging in the air, sometimes as the "oral text" of an extended teaching, whether at the beginning or end or in the middle. Furthermore, he may not have said exactly the same words each time he used them. Thus, from the beginning there might very well have been a variety of versions of the same saying. What is constant, however, is the "gist" of the saying or the "core" of the saying.[51] And the gist is what is remembered.

Just as the aphorisms were memorable sayings, so the parables of Jesus were memorable short stories.[52] Like the aphorisms, each parable would have been told many times by Jesus as an oral itinerant teacher. Moreover, it is likely that they were told at varying lengths, depending upon the occasion. To use his longest parable as an example, the parable of the prodigal son (Luke 15.11–32) can be read out loud in about three minutes. Yet it is easy to imagine a skillful storyteller like Jesus elaborating the story by expanding one or more of the three acts (the prodigal's adventures and eventual plight in a far-off country, his father's joyful welcome of his return, the older brother's reaction). Thus, with the parables as with the aphorisms, more than one version is likely to have existed from the beginning. And again like the aphorisms, what is remembered is the gist, which in this case might also be called plot summaries.

With the stories about things Jesus did, a similar process occurred, with one difference: He said his aphorisms and parables many times, but he did each *particular* thing only once. To clarify, I think he healed many times, but he could have done each *particular* healing only once. Yet the process of remembering would have been the same: What was remembered was a plot summary of what had happened. Thus, for roughly one-third of a century, the teachings of Jesus and the stories about Jesus circulated within the community as oral tradition. Moreover, during this period the community's traditions about Jesus were already developing and growing; we should not assume that development occurred only after they were put into written form.

Given all of these factors, how are the Gospels to be used as sources for constructing an image of the historical Jesus? To return to the voice metaphor that I used earlier, the Gospels are literally the voices of their authors. Behind them are the anonymous voices of the community talking about Jesus. And embedded within their voices is the voice of Jesus, as well as the deeds of Jesus (for some of the stories were about deeds).

Constructing an image of Jesus–which is what the quest for the historical Jesus is about–involves two crucial steps. The first step is discerning what is likely to go back to Jesus. The second step is setting this material in the historical context of the first-century Jewish homeland.

Step 1: Discerning What Is Early

The process of discerning what is early is neither a science nor an art but is more of a craft. It is not purely objective, and it involves more than one factor or principle. Perhaps the single most important principle is *multiple independent attestation in early traditions.* Put very simply, if a saying or story appears at least twice in traditions that are early and independent of each other, that is a very good reason for thinking that the gist of it goes back to Jesus. For most scholars, the two earliest independent layers of the tradition are Q and Mark; some scholars would add an early layer of Thomas. Thus, if something shows up in both Q and Mark, it may be regarded as very early tradition.

This test can be applied not only to specific sayings or stories but also to motifs, or themes. A motif would be "sayings about seeing and blindness" or "sayings about children and the Kingdom of God." If such sayings are found in more than one independent source, then one may be confident that the theme goes back to Jesus, even if one is less confident about the wording of a particular saying expressing that theme. So also with stories of healings and exorcisms. No one story is attested by more than one independent source (almost all of our *stories* about the adult Jesus–as distinct from his sayings–have only one attestation within the synoptics, namely, Mark). Yet cumulatively the theme of healings and exorcisms has impressive attestation, especially since there are sayings in Q (in addition to the stories in Mark) referring to healings and exorcisms.

A second principle flows out of reflection about the period of oral transmission: We can seriously entertain the notion that a tradition might go back to Jesus if we can imagine it being preserved orally. To some extent, this principle functions negatively: *If we cannot imagine a tradition being preserved orally, then we cannot think that it goes back to Jesus.* The most obvious examples are the extended discourses attributed to Jesus in John's gospel. One cannot imagine Jesus' complex and quite abstract "farewell address" in John 14–17 being preserved orally. One would have to imagine one or more disciples memorizing it as it was spoken and then preserving it through the decades.[53] What one can imagine being remembered is the gist of a saying, parable, or story.[54]

A third principle also functions negatively. To put it abstractly at first: *One must discount the demonstrable tendencies of the developing traditions.* That is, whenever a saying or story reflects a known tendency of the developing tradition, the historian must suspect that saying's historicity. To use examples from this chapter of demonstrable tendencies of the developing traditions:

1. To add christological titles to texts that did not originally have them; one must be suspicious of even the earliest texts that do this.
2. To adapt material for use in Christian worship; traditions that reflect such adaptation are suspect.
3. To add quotations from the Hebrew Bible; passages that depend upon the Hebrew Bible text are suspect.[55]
4. To seek to exonerate Rome of responsibility for the death of Jesus; whether any of the details in the "trials" of Jesus are historical is difficult to determine.

A fourth principle is *consistency with the generative impulse, or "originative impulse," of the tradition.*[56] This principle can be used only after a core of material has been established by other means as likely to be historical. If a saying or story is consistent with the picture of Jesus that is emerging from well-attested material, then it may be considered likely to have been historical. This principle is most useful when one is making a judgment about a story or teaching that is attested only once. A classic example is the parable of the prodigal son; though found in only one relatively late source (Luke), almost all scholars regard it as going back to Jesus. Why? Because it is consistent with what has already been discerned as the generative, or originative, impulse or distinctive voice within the tradition.

STEP 2: SETTING THE MATERIAL IN CONTEXT

Context is utterly central for historical reconstruction. Words spoken and actions done derive their meaning from context. They mean little (or are ambiguous) apart from context. To say the obvious, the same gesture often means two very different things in two different cultures. Or a word or an image that has a positive meaning in one culture may have a negative meaning in another culture. To do a wordplay using the etymology of context, the prefix *con* means "with"; thus con-text is what goes with a text.

For the historical Jesus (as distinct from the canonical Jesus, the Jesus we meet on the surface level of the Gospels), that context was not a literary one, but a cultural one, a social world. The context in which early Jesus material is to be set is the social world of the Jewish homeland in the first third of the first century.

One of the major features of the contemporary renaissance in Jesus scholarship (as both a cause and a consequence) is a dramatically increased understanding of his social world. The reasons for this are several. We have more data because of manuscript discoveries and archaeological excavation. We have more detailed analyses of both new and existing data because of the greater number of scholars involved in the field. And we have the advantage of interdisciplinary models and insights that enable us to understand the patterns and dynamics of Jesus' social world in ways impossible for an earlier generation of scholars.

This chapter is not the place to describe the social world of the Jewish homeland in the time of Jesus.[57] Rather, I content myself with underlining its crucial importance for discerning the *meaning* of traditions that are believed on historical grounds to go back to Jesus. They derive their meaning from that context, and they must make sense in that context (rather than some later context) if they are to be attributed to Jesus.

Conclusion

This two-step process for constructing an image of the historical Jesus–determining what traditions are actually early and then setting them in their historical context–also applies to the study of Christian origins after the time of Jesus (just as it applies generally to all historical study). That is, later layers of the tradition also matter. In the New Testament, these later layers tell us about the narratival Jesus and the canonical Jesus. These later layers tell us about the development of early Christian experience, thought, and practice.

About texts from the gospel of John, for example, one would ask, "What did this mean as part of John's gospel in the late-first-century historical context of his community?" Or to use an example from Chapter 5 of this book, what did it mean to call Jesus "teacher" (both *paidagogos* and *didaskalos*) in the second- and third-century Hellenistic world of the early church? Or what did it mean to speak of Jesus as "being of one substance" with God in the fourth-century world of early Constantinian Christianity?

The historical study of Jesus and Christian origins intrinsically involves understanding the developing traditions in the contexts in which they emerged. Of course, the meaning of these texts is not exhausted by their historical meanings. The texts of the Gospels and the Bible as a whole have become "religious classics," texts that have a surplus of meanings beyond their original particular meaning.[58]

But if one's interest is a historical understanding of Jesus and Christian origins, then the two-step process just described is the method to be followed. The reward of this kind of study is the illuminating power of setting text in context: We understand more clearly the meanings that our ancestors expressed in these traditions. Ultimately, this process can provide us with glimpses of the pre-Easter Jesus, even as it also provides us with glimpses of what the post-Easter Jesus became in the lives of early Christians.

Study Questions

These questions are designed to guide readers through what is most important in each chapter. Although especially suitable for classroom use, these questions may be helpful for general readers as well. Because some chapters deal with large questions and others with more detailed matters, the number of questions varies considerably from chapter to chapter.

Chapter One (Borg)

1. What is the reason for commemorating 2,000 years of Jesus in 1996 rather than 2000?

2. What does Borg mean when he says that every perspective is a limited one? And what is the significance of recognizing that this is so?

3. How does Borg describe his own perspective?

4. What does it mean to say that the Gospels are a developing tradition?

5. How does the work of the Jesus Seminar illustrate the foregoing claim?

6. According to mainline scholars, what can we know about the birth of Jesus? Why can't we know more?

7. How does Borg see the stories of Jesus' birth?

Chapter Two (Borg)

1. Foundational to this chapter is the distinction between the pre-Easter Jesus and the post-Easter Jesus. How does Borg define each?

2. Summarize Borg's two descriptions of the pre-Easter Jesus. Then ask yourself, Are you surprised by anything that's *not* in his description?

3. The central theme of this chapter is the process whereby the pre-Easter Jesus (a Galilean Jewish peasant) becomes the post-Easter Jesus of Christian tradition (the only begotten Son of God and second person of the Trinity). Borg describes this process as moving from foundational experience through metaphorical and conceptual development to formulation into doctrine. According to Borg, what was the foundational experience?

4. What metaphors for Jesus are found in the New Testament?

5. What meanings did the metaphor *Son of God* have in the Jewish tradition?

6. What was the process whereby *Son of God* as a designation for Jesus moved from metaphor to concept/doctrine? What meanings did the phrase come to have in Christian tradition?

7. What did "Wisdom/Sophia of God" mean in a Jewish context? When you think of this metaphor applied to Jesus, what does it suggest to you? Or what do you puzzle about?

8. According to Borg, how is the Christian doctrine of the Trinity related to early Christian experience?

9. What is the distinction between resuscitation and resurrection, and why does the distinction matter as one thinks about Easter?

10. According to Borg, what is the central meaning of Easter?

11. How does the Emmaus road story illustrate the meaning of Easter?

12. Using Borg's distinctions, how would you answer the question "Was Jesus divine?"

13. As you think about Borg's claim that we get from Galilean Jew to the face of God through a process of foundational experience and metaphorical development, do you find this view illuminating? Or puzzling? Or both? In what way(s)?

Chapter Three (Crossan)

1. Crossan's essay is valuable for two main reasons. First, it summarizes his understanding of Jesus (the first two-thirds of his essay). Second, it provides a case study of a particular interaction in early Christianity—namely, the dialogue and tension between radical itinerant followers of Jesus and settled householder followers of Jesus (the final third). The first third of the essay describes Crossan's method. Much of it concerns the society (social world) in which Jesus lived. Define/describe the following:

The economic characteristics of an agrarian empire and of a commercialized
    agrarian empire
Traditional Jewish understandings of landownership
The Jewish covenant's theme of social justice
Unrest in first-century Jewish Palestine
The effects of the building of two cities in first-century Galilee (Sepphoris and
    Tiberias); what Crossan thinks the ceramics (pottery) evidence suggests

2. Based on what Crossan says, how would you describe the central social-economic-political tensions in the social world of Jesus?

3. The other major theme in the first third is Crossan's understanding of the Gospels as developing traditions containing layers. What does Crossan illustrate with Witherington's approach? What are Crossan's own formal procedures for deciding what is early in the Gospels?

4. The second third of his essay is a compact summary of what Crossan thinks was most central to Jesus: his vision and program. His vision was the Kingdom of God. According to the first paragraph under "The Kingdom of God," what did this phrase mean for Jesus?

5. Much of the section "The Kingdom of God" involves a discussion of eschatology. How does Crossan define the following terms?

eschatology
apocalypse (or apocalyptic)
apocalyptic eschatology
sapiential eschatology

6. According to Crossan, which forms of eschatology did Jesus affirm?

7. The rest of "Vision and Program" treats Jesus' program of reciprocity in eating and healing. This section begins with a collection of early Christian texts that Crossan uses to describe the program of Jesus. What is the significance of each of the following for seeing the program of Jesus, and what does each disclose about his program?

eating
healing
itinerancy
gender
dress

8. What is the point of Crossan's discussion of the Twelve?

9. What does the phrase *a companionship of empowerment* mean as a summary of what was central to Jesus?

10. "Itinerant and Householder" concerns the relationship between two groups of early Christians near the end of the first century: itinerants (early Christians who deliberately became homeless and possessionless and practiced ethical radicalism—a "radical and absolute counterculturalism"), and householders (early Christians who continued to live in families and homes, worked for a living, and practiced a "relative and pragmatic counterculturalism"). What is ethical radicalism as we see it in the itinerants?

11. What does Crossan mean by the phrase *an eschatology realizable in the wisdom of social radicalism?* (Think about the meaning of the words.) Crossan finds this eschatology in sayings common to Q and Thomas (and therefore very early) and claims that the householders domesticated or toned down the radicalism of the itinerants.

12. According to the first two paragraphs of Crossan's section "The Itinerants Speak Out," what significant question did the householders face?

13. In the section "The Householders Talk Back," Crossan describes the resistance of householders to the ethical radicalism of the itinerants. He does so with a detailed case study of a late-first-century Christian document known as *Didache*. Arguing that this document reflects the viewpoint of Christian householders, Crossan examines how *Didache* "sees" Christian itinerant figures (teachers, apostles, and especially prophets) and what it teaches about how to deal with them. Briefly, what does *Didache* say about each?

14. In "Sayings," Crossan argues that a large body of teaching in *Didache* (Chapters 1 through 6, on "The Two Ways") is framed at the beginning and end with sayings that domesticate the ethical radicalism of the itinerants. These sayings are 1.5–7 and 6.2. What does each saying say? And do you see how they relativize and moderate the ethical radicalism of the itinerants?

15. At the end of "Itinerant and Householder," what is Crossan's point in the section "Kingdom"?

Chapter Four (Segal)

1. What question/issue was posed by the Enlightenment?

2. How does Segal define the criterion of dissimilarity?

3. According to Segal, what is the important but limited function of the criterion of dissimilarity?

4. What passes (or meets) this criterion?

5. Why does Segal think it is desirable to go beyond this criterion?

6. In "What Is Most Certain," Segal begins with some "virtually assured conclusions" about Jesus. What are they?

7. Segal then turns to three passages from the Hebrew Bible with which early Christians interpreted the resurrection of Jesus: Daniel 7.13–14, Psalm 110.1–4, and Psalm 8. What does each passage say, and how are these combined to refer to the resurrected Jesus?

8. Segal then argues that these passages show that the designation of Jesus as the "Son of Man" is early and important. Segal argues that, although Jesus may not have referred to himself as the Son of Man, the reference to Daniel 7 probably does go back to Jesus. Thus, Segal affirms that Jesus had an apocalyptic eschatology, that he was a millennialist, and that he was the leader of an apocalyptic movement. What do you understand these claims to mean?

9. What does Matthew 16.27–28 say, and what does Segal conclude about it?

10. What does Matthew 10.23 say, and what does Segal conclude about it?

11. Why does he think Mark 8.38 is significant?

12. In "Beyond What Is Most Certain," Segal turns to other things he thinks we can say about Jesus with a lesser degree of probability. According to Segal, what do scholars mean when they speak of Jesus as a Cynic sage or a magician? And why does Segal think these are not helpful categories?

13. What does Segal think about Jesus' relationship to the Dead Sea Scrolls community (Essenes) at Qumran, the Pharisees, and Jewish mysticism?

14. What do you understand Segal to be saying with his contrast between holy insecurity and fanaticism? What does each mean, which does he commend, and why?

Chapter Five (Torjesen)

1. Torjesen describes the development of early Christian images of Jesus during Christianity's formative centuries, from about one hundred years after Jesus into the 300s. What were the five images (in English and in Greek, when relevant) discussed by Torjesen?

2. A cosmology is a map of reality. According to Torjesen, what was the popular cosmology of the ancient world (and also of early Christians)? What do you think our popular modern cosmology is, and how is it different from this ancient one?

3. Wisdom and Sophia refer to the same notion/figure. Who/what is she in Jewish traditions? What are her roles?

4. Where in the New Testament is Jesus referred to as Sophia? In what roles?

5. What is the communal setting for Christ as Sophia? Why do you think Torjesen talks about new birth, spiritual persons, spiritual truths, spiritual gifts, and language in this section? What is the connection? In the next section, Torjesen describes the early Christian image of Christ as Victor. Note that this image defines Christ as Savior as Christ as Victor or triumphant hero.

6. What is the story of Perpetua about, and why does Torjesen tell it? What is its connection to the theme she is developing?

7. What pattern does Torjesen see in the story of Jesus' crucifixion and resurrection?

8. According to Torjesen, over what does Christ as Victor triumph? What is defeated by Christ as Victor?

9. What does Torjesen suggest as the communal setting for this image?

10. Torjesen begins "Jesus as Divine Teacher" by speaking of Roman ridicule of early Christians as an illiterate and superstitious lower-class group of people. Christians responded to this ridicule by portraying Jesus as Divine Teacher. What did the second-century Christian Justin (also known as Justin Martyr) argue?

11. What was the role of teacher in Roman society?

12. What is the difference between *paidagogos* and *didaskalos,* and how did early Christians apply these terms to Jesus?

13. What was the communal setting for this image?

14. Torjesen begins the exposition of her next image, Christ as Logos/Cosmic Reason, with a description of how ancient thinkers thought of cosmic reason. What do you understand this to be?

15. Given this understanding, what did early Christians mean when they said that Christ was/is Cosmic Reason/Logos?

16. The final image is Christ as World Ruler (*Pantocrator*). What role did the conversion of Constantine play in the development of this image?

17. How does this image portray Jesus?

18. What is its communal setting?

19. What is the effect/significance of having a multiplicity of images of Jesus? What does one "see" by thinking about this? What difference does it make if there are several images whose development can be traced?

Chapter Six (Cox)

1. In his first paragraph, Cox uses the phrases *the historical reconstruction of Jesus* and *the cultural resymbolization of Jesus* to describe the two focal points of the course he teaches to Generation X. What do you understand each phrase to mean?

2. According to Cox, how interested is Generation X in religion?

3. According to Cox, what does music disclose about Generation X and its attitude toward religion and/or Jesus?

4. According to Cox, why might some members of Generation X be interested in the current quest for the historical Jesus?

5. According to Cox, what is a major effect ("perhaps the most positive result") of the recent quest? What question remains?

6. What does Cox mean by radical religious pluralism?

7. What did you find interesting in his description of how Jesus is seen by Hindu, Buddhist, Jewish, and Muslim thinkers and writers? Why, according to Cox, does Generation X find this material interesting?

8. What does Cox mean by a "pick-and-choose" mentality? How does he use Generation X's response to Stephen Mitchell's image of Jesus to illustrate this?

9. What does Cox suggest might be a way of avoiding the dangers of pick-and-choose approaches?

10. In his concluding section (paragraph beginning with "I think they do"), Cox describes three matters that are important to him: the Jewishness of Jesus, the creedal formulas of the church, and the more-than-historical importance of the question "Who do you say that I am?" What significance does the Jewishness of Jesus have?

11. Why are the creedal formulas significant to Cox? What, in his view, do they affirm?

12. The perspectives Cox discerns in Generation X are late-twentieth-century perspectives—the perspectives of people coming of age as we approach 2000. What do you think of these perspectives? Do you think the perspectives of Generation X enable us to "see" anything about Jesus and Christian theology? Do you find these perspectives illuminating? (And if so, how?)

Chapter Seven (Smith)

1. How does Jesus look from the perspective of the world's religions? How does he look within the framework of the comparative study of religions?

2. What do you find interesting in Smith's section "What Other Religions Say About Jesus"?

3. What is the major question (Smith's "commission") that Smith treats in this chapter?

4. What did Smith discover in his own "odyssey"? What are the mystics like? Or what is mysticism?

5. What does Smith clarify in "Excursus"?

6. What does "An Anecdote" illustrate about what Smith thinks about Jesus?

7. What is the traditional worldview?

8. How does the traditional worldview differ from the naturalistic worldview of the modern university or modern world?

9. What do you suppose Plato meant by calling our descriptions of the way things are "likely tales"?

10. In the section "Jesus, Traditionally Conceived," Smith describes how Jesus looks within the framework of the traditional worldview. How does Jesus look within this framework? To put it slightly differently, how does Jesus look within the likely tale told by Christianity?

11. How does Smith's position differ from fundamentalists and biblicists (who are the same)? Or what does Smith find to be deficient in their approach?

12. Smith concludes his chapter with the story of a letter he received from a symposium participant. What is Smith's understanding of a fact fundamentalist (and how is this different from a biblical fundamentalist)? What is fundamental for Smith? What is Smith illustrating in this section—that is, why does he end his chapter this way?

Chapter Eight (Borg)

1. What does Borg say about his Christian orientation–the kind of Christianity he affirms? Why does he include this information in his discussion?

2. According to the section "Historical Introduction," how was the Bible seen in Western culture before the Enlightenment?

3. What is natural literalism, and how does it see the Bible? Is this view familiar to you at all?

4. How does the story of Galileo's experiment illustrate the revolution in what constitutes knowledge brought about by the Enlightenment?

5. What are the central reasons (three) that over time led to a very different view of the Bible?

6. What was (is) the new view of the Bible? And can it be reconciled with religious/Christian convictions and beliefs?

7. Why do you suppose this new view of the Bible initially encountered resistance?

8. Who were Reimarus, Strauss, and Schweitzer, and what did each contribute to the scholarly study of Jesus?

9. What are six central conclusions that have emerged from the scholarly study of the Gospels? Do you find anything unclear or puzzling about them?

10. Who was Josephus, and what did he say about Jesus?

11. What are the synoptic Gospels, and why are they differentiated from the gospel of John?

12. What is John's gospel?

13. What do scholars mean by "the priority of Mark"?

14. What is "Q," and why do scholars think it existed?

15. What is characteristic of Q, Mark, Matthew, Luke, John, and Thomas?

16. What is illustrated by the comparison of Mark's and Matthew's stories of the entry into Jerusalem?

17. What is illustrated by the comparison of Mark's and Matthew's stories of the walking on water?

18. What is illustrated by the comparison of different versions of the Lord's Prayer?

19. What is illustrated by the comparison of the passion stories?

20. What does an understanding of oral tradition (and the oral forms of Jesus' teaching, aphorisms and parables) contribute to an understanding of what is involved in going "back to Jesus"?

21. What factors/principles/guidelines "count" for discerning what is early in the developing gospel tradition?

22. What does "con-text" mean, and what is the relevant context for glimpsing the historical Jesus?

23. What do later layers of the tradition tell us?

24. To what extent do you think you understand what is involved in the historical study of Jesus and Christian origins? Is there a particular insight or awareness that is central to your understanding (perhaps an "ah ha" moment while reading or thinking about the chapter)? Is there anything about which you remain puzzled? Or about which you are newly puzzled?

Notes

Chapter One

1. See my essay "A Renaissance in Jesus Studies," in *Jesus in Contemporary Scholarship* (Valley Forge, Penn.: Trinity, 1994), pp. 3–17. For a survey of six contemporary portraits of Jesus (E. P. Sanders, Burton Mack, Elisabeth Schüssler Fiorenza, Richard Horsley, John Dominic Crossan, and me), see Chapter 2 in the same book, pp. 18–43. To these should be added John Meier's two-volume (with a third forthcoming) *A Marginal Jew: Rethinking the Historical Jesus* (New York: Doubleday, 1991, 1994); Stevan L. Davies, *Jesus the Healer: Possession, Trance, and the Origins of Christianity* (New York: Continuum, 1995); and two books scheduled to be published in late autumn of 1996: Robert Funk, *Honest to Jesus* (San Francisco: HarperSanFrancisco); and N. Thomas Wright, *Jesus and the Victory of God* (Minneapolis: Augsburg Fortress).

2. Three of them are by John Dominic Crossan (all published by HarperSanFrancisco): *The Historical Jesus: The Life of a Mediterranean Jewish Peasant* (1991); *Jesus: A Revolutionary Biography* (1994); and *Who Killed Jesus? Exposing the Roots of Anti-Semitism in the Gospel Story of the Death of Jesus* (1995). The other two are the Jesus Seminar's *The Five Gospels*, ed. Robert Funk and Roy Hoover (New York: Macmillan, 1993); and my own *Meeting Jesus Again for the First Time* (San Francisco: HarperSanFrancisco, 1994).

3. Luke Timothy Johnson, *The Real Jesus: The Misguided Quest for the Historical Jesus and the Truth of the Traditional Gospels* (San Francisco: HarperSanFrancisco, 1995), is the best-known mainline critique of contemporary Jesus scholarship. Conservative-evangelical critiques include Michael J. Wilkins and J. P. Moreland, eds., *Jesus Under Fire* (Grand Rapids, Mich.: Zondervan, 1995); Ben Witherington III, *The Jesus Quest: The Third Search for the Jew of Nazareth* (Downers Grove, Ill.: Intervarsity Press, 1995); and Gregory A. Boyd, *Cynic Sage or Son of God?* (Wheaton, Ill.: Bridgepoint Books, 1995).

4. E. H. Carr, *What Is History?* (Baltimore: Penguin, 1964).

5. In accord with increasingly widespread scholarly practice, this book uses B.C.E. and C.E. instead of the more familiar B.C. and A.D. B.C.E. and C.E. mean "before the common era" and "common era," respectively. The change reflects the growth of both religious pluralism and secularization in Western culture.

6. Readers who want to know more about this may wish to read Chapter 8 now, especially if this is an unfamiliar way of looking at the Gospels.

7. The Jesus Seminar has recently become the target of considerable criticism and attack. See Johnson, *The Real Jesus;* Wilkins and Moreland, eds., *Jesus Under Fire;* Witherington, *The Jesus Quest;* and Boyd, *Cynic Sage.* Criticism of any scholarly position is, of course, warranted. But both the tone and content of many of these criticisms seem un-

fair. As one who has been deeply involved with the seminar for the past ten years, I must say that I simply do not recognize the group of scholars portrayed by some of our critics.

8. Funk and Hoover, eds., *The Five Gospels.*

9. Passages in gray are best understood as belonging to a large, undecided category. For reasons, see my *Jesus in Contemporary Scholarship,* p. 163.

10. The most detailed treatment of the birth stories is by Raymond Brown, *The Birth of the Messiah,* exp. ed. (New York: Doubleday, 1993). For a chapter-length treatment, see John Dominic Crossan, "The Infancy and Youth of the Messiah," in *The Search for Jesus: Modern Scholarship Looks at the Gospels,* ed. Hershel Shanks, pp. 59–81 (Washington, D.C.: Biblical Archaeology Society, 1994).

Chapter Two

1. John Meier, *A Marginal Jew: Rethinking the Historical Jesus,* 2 vols. (New York: Doubleday, 1991, 1994). A third volume is forthcoming.

2. See, especially, my *Jesus: A New Vision* (1987), and *Meeting Jesus Again for the First Time* (1994), both published by HarperSanFrancisco.

3. For an excellent study of the way the stories of Jesus' death were formed and how they have contributed to anti-Semitism, see John Dominic Crossan, *Who Killed Jesus? Exposing the Roots of Anti-Semitism in the Gospel Story of the Death of Jesus* (San Francisco: HarperSanFrancisco, 1995). See also Raymond Brown's massive two-volume study, *The Death of the Messiah* (New York: Doubleday, 1994).

4. That there is a strong political dynamic in Jesus' message and activity is an emphasis of much contemporary Jesus scholarship. For an overview, see my *Jesus in Contemporary Scholarship* (Valley Forge, Penn.: Trinity, 1994), pp. 97–126. See also John Dominic Crossan, *The Historical Jesus: The Life of a Mediterranean Jewish Peasant* (San Francisco: HarperSanFrancisco, 1991); John Dominic Crossan, *Jesus: A Revolutionary Biography* (San Francisco: HarperSanFrancisco, 1994); and Richard Horsley, *Jesus and the Spiral of Violence* (San Francisco: HarperSanFrancisco, 1987). For a compact compelling summary of Jesus' challenge to the domination system, see Walter Wink, *Engaging the Powers* (Minneapolis: Fortress, 1992), pp. 109–137.

5. For further development, see Borg, *Meeting Jesus Again for the First Time,* chap. 5 and the literature referred to there.

6. Cited in ibid., p. 117 n. 50.

7. For further development of this whole section, see my "The Historian, the Christian, and Jesus," *Theology Today* 52 (1995):6–16.

8. William James, *The Varieties of Religious Experience.* Available in several editions, this remarkably valuable and enduring book was originally published in 1902.

9. Alan Segal, *Paul the Convert: The Apostolate and Apostasy of Saul the Pharisee* (New Haven: Yale University Press, 1990).

10. Volume 1 of Wright's projected five-volume New Testament theology is *The New Testament and the People of God* (Minneapolis: Fortress, 1992). Volume 2, *Jesus and the Victory of God,* is scheduled to be published in the fall of 1996 (Minneapolis: Augsburg Fortress). See also his popular-level *Who Was Jesus?* (London: SPCK, 1992).

11. Crossan, *Jesus,* p. 197.

Chapter Three

1. Albert Schweitzer, *The Quest of the Historical Jesus* (New York: Macmillan, 1968; originally published in 1906), pp. 4–5.

2. Gerhard E. Lenski, *Power and Privilege: A Theory of Social Stratification* (New York: McGraw-Hill, 1966); Gerhard E. Lenski and Jean Lenski, *Human Societies: An Introduction to Macrosociology,* 3d ed. (New York: McGraw-Hill, 1974); Gerhard E. Lenski and Jean Lenski, "Rethinking Macrosociological Theory," *American Sociological Review* 53 (1988):163–171; and John H. Kautsky, *The Politics of Aristocratic Empires* (Chapel Hill: University of North Carolina Press, 1982).

3. Lenski, *Power and Privilege,* p. 278.

4. Teodor Shanin, "Peasantry: Delineation of a Sociological Concept and a Field of Study," *European Journal of Sociology* 12 (1971):294–297; see also Teodor Shanin, ed., *Peasants and Peasant Society* (Baltimore: Penguin, 1971).

5. George M. Foster, "Introduction: What Is a Peasant?" in *Peasant Society: A Reader,* ed. Jack M. Potter, May N. Diaz, and George M. Foster (Boston: Little, Brown, 1967), pp. 4, 6, 9.

6. Marianne Sawicki, *Seeing the Lord: Resurrection and Early Christian Practice* (Minneapolis: Augsburg Fortress, 1994), p. 12 n. 6; and Marianne Sawicki, "Caste and Contact in the Galilee of Jesus: Research Beyond Positivism and Constructivism," in *Galilean Archaeology and the Historical Jesus: The Integration of Material and Textual Remains,* ed. J. Andrew Overman (forthcoming).

7. Susan Carol Rogers, "Female Forms of Power and the Myth of Male Dominance: A Model of Female/Male Interaction in Peasant Society," *American Ethnologist* 2 (1975):728–729, 746.

8. Susan Carol Rogers, "Woman's Place: A Critical Review of Anthropological Theory," *Comparative Studies in Society and History* 20 (1978):158–159. See also Susan Carol Rogers, *Shaping Modern Times in Rural France: The Transformation and Reproduction of an Aveyronnais Community* (Princeton: Princeton University Press, 1991).

9. David A. Fiensy, *The Social History of Palestine in the Herodian Period: The Land Is Mine* (Lewiston, N.Y.: Mellen, 1991).

10. Richard A. Horsley and John S. Hanson, *Bandits, Prophets, and Messiahs: Popular Movements in the Time of Jesus* (Minneapolis: Winston, 1985).

11. James F. Strange, "Some Implications of Archaeology for New Testament Studies," in *What Has Archaeology to Do with Faith,* ed. James H. Charlesworth and Walter P. Weaver (Philadelphia: Trinity, 1992), pp. 31, 53 n. 41.

12. Christopher Seeman, "The Urbanization of Herodian Galilee as an Historical Factor Contributing to the Emergence of the Jesus Movement" (M.A. thesis, Graduate Theological Union, 1993).

13. Susan E. Alcock, *Graecia Capta: The Landscapes of Roman Greece* (Cambridge: Cambridge University Press, 1993), p. 5.

14. Jonathan L. Reed, *Places in Early Christianity: Galilee, Archaeology, Urbanization, and Q* (Ann Arbor, Mich.: University Microfilms International, 1993), pp. 71–72, 96; Jonathan L. Reed, *The Population of Capernaum,* Occasional Paper 24 (Claremont, Calif.: Institute for Antiquity and Christianity, 1992); and Jonathan L. Reed, "Population Numbers, Urbanization, and Economics: Galilean Archaeology and the Historical Jesus," in *Society of Biblical Literature 1994 Seminar Papers,* ed. Eugene H. Lovering Jr., pp. 203–219 (Atlanta: Scholars Press, 1994).

15. John R. Patterson, "Settlement, City, and Elite in Samnium and Lycia," in *City and Country in the Ancient World*, ed. John Rich and Andrew Wallace-Hadrill (New York: Routledge, 1991), pp. 147, 148, 155.

16. David Adan-Bayewitz, *Common Pottery in Roman Galilee: A Study of Local Trade* (Ramat-Gan, Israel: Bar Ilan University Press, 1992), p. 219. See also David Adan-Bayewitz and Isadore Perlman, "The Local Trade of Sepphoris in the Roman Period," *Israel Exploration Journal* 40 (1990):153–172.

17. Dean E. Arnold, *Ceramic Theory and Cultural Process* (Cambridge: Cambridge University Press, 1985), pp. 168, 193.

18. Ben Witherington III, *The Jesus Quest: The Third Search for the Jew of Nazareth* (Downers Grove, Ill.: Intervarsity Press, 1995), p. 96, see also pp. 128, 131–132.

19. See John Dominic Crossan, *The Historical Jesus: The Life of a Mediterranean Jewish Peasant* (San Francisco: HarperSanFrancisco, 1991), pp. xxx–xxxiv.

20. John Dominic Crossan, *Jesus: A Revolutionary Biography* (San Francisco: HarperSanFrancisco, 1994); John Dominic Crossan, *The Essential Jesus: Original Sayings and Earliest Images* (San Francisco: HarperSanFrancisco, 1994); John Dominic Crossan, *Who Killed Jesus? Exposing the Roots of Anti-Semitism in the Gospel Story of the Death of Jesus* (San Francisco: HarperSanFrancisco, 1995); and John Dominic Crossan, with Richard Watts, *Who Is Jesus? Answers to Your Questions About the Historical Jesus* (New York: HarperPaperbacks, 1996).

21. Peter Farb and George Armelagos, *Consuming Passions: The Anthropology of Eating* (Boston: Houghton Mifflin, 1980).

22. Arthur Kleinman, *Patients and Healers in the Context of Culture: An Exploration of the Borderland Between Anthropology, Medicine, and Psychiatry* (Berkeley and Los Angeles: University of California Press, 1980); and Arthur Kleinman, *The Illness Narratives: Suffering, Healing, and the Human Condition* (New York: Basic Books, 1988).

23. John Davis, *The People of the Mediterranean: An Essay in Comparative Social Anthropology* (London: Routledge and Kegan Paul, 1977); and Richard P. Saller, *Personal Patronage Under the Early Empire* (Cambridge: Cambridge University Press, 1982).

24. Elisabeth Schüssler Fiorenza, *Jesus: Miriam's Child, Sophia's Prophet* (New York: Continuum, 1994), for example, p. 189.

25. Gerd Theissen, "Itinerant Radicalism: The Tradition of Jesus Sayings from the Perspective of the Sociology of Literature," *Radical Religion* 2 (1975):86, 88–89. For a more complete translation, see Gerd Theissen, "The Wandering Radicals: Light Shed by the Sociology of Literature on the Early Transmission of Jesus Sayings," in *Social Reality and the Early Christians: Theology, Ethics, and the World of the New Testament*, trans. Margaret Kohl, pp. 33–59 (Minneapolis: Fortress, 1992). See also Gerd Theissen, "Legitimation and Subsistence: An Essay on the Sociology of Early Christian Missionaries," in *The Social Setting of Pauline Christianity: Essays on Corinth*, trans. John H. Schütz (Philadelphia: Fortress, 1982), pp. 7, 17; and Gerd Theissen, *Sociology of Early Palestinian Christianity*, trans. John Bowden (Philadelphia: Fortress, 1978), p. 28.

26. Theissen, "The Wandering Radicals," p. 41.

27. James M. Robinson and Helmut Koester, *Trajectories Through Early Christianity* (Philadelphia: Fortress, 1971); Helmut Koester, "Apocryphal and Canonical Gospels," *Harvard Theological Review* 73 (1980):105–130; Helmut Koester, *Ancient Christian Gospels: Their History and Development* (London: SCM Press, 1990), pp. 86, 95, 150; John S. Kloppenborg, *The Formation of Q: Trajectories in Ancient Wisdom Collections* (Philadelphia: Fortress, 1987), pp. 22, 189, 242, 318; John S. Kloppenborg, "Symbolic

Eschatology and the Apocalypticism of Q," *Harvard Theological Review* 80 (1987): 287–306; Stephen J. Patterson, *The Gospel of Thomas and Jesus*, rev. ed. (Sonoma, Calif.: Polebridge, 1993), pp. 4, 214; Stephen J. Patterson, "Wisdom in Q and Thomas," in *In Search of Wisdom: Essays in Memory of John G. Gammie*, ed. Leo G. Perdue, Bernard Brandon Scott, and William Johnston Wiseman, pp. 187–221 (Louisville, Ky.: Westminster/John Knox Press, 1993).

28. Following Helmut Koester, *Synoptische Überlieferung bei den Apostolischen Vätern* (Berlin: Akademie, 1957), pp. 159–241, 260; and Bentley Layton, "The Sources, Date, and Transmission of Didache 1.3b–2.1," *Harvard Theological Review* 61 (1968):343–383. They explained well *how* an author could have read Matthew and Luke and came up with the insertion in *Did.* 1.3b–2.1 but not *why* anyone would do it and then omit any mention that it came from Jesus. What has changed my mind is reading authors who are primarily interested in studying *Didache* as a document in its own right and not just to see if it contains independent Jesus materials. For example: Jean-Paul Audet, *La Didache: Instructions des apôtres* (Paris: Gabalda, 1958); Willy Rordorf and André Tuilier, *La doctrine des douze apotres (Didache)* (Paris: Cerf, 1978); Willy Rordorf, "Le probleme de la transmission textuelle de *Didache* 1.3b–2.1," in *Überlieferungsgeschichtliche Untersuchungen*, ed. Franz Paschke, pp. 499–513 (Berlin: Akademie, 1981); Jonathan Draper, "The Jesus Tradition in the Didache," in *The Jesus Tradition Outside the Gospels*, ed. David Wenham, pp. 269–287 (Sheffield, England: JSOT Press, 1985); Aaron Milavec, "The Pastoral Genius of the Didache: An Analytical Translation and Commentary," in *Religious Writings and Religious Systems*, vol. 2, *Christianity*, ed. Jacob Neusner, Ernest S. Frerichs, and A. J. Levine, pp. 89–125 (Atlanta: Scholars Press, 1989); Kurt Niederwimmer, *Die Didache* (Göttingen: Vandenhoeck and Rupprecht, 1989); Ian H. Henderson, "*Didache* and Orality in Synoptic Comparison," *Journal of Biblical Literature* 111 (1992):283–306; Willy Rordorf, "Does the Didache Contain Jesus Tradition Independently of the Synoptic Gospels?" in *Jesus and the Oral Gospel Tradition*, ed. Henry Wansbrough, pp. 394–423 (Sheffield, England: Sheffield Academic Press, 1992).

Chapter Four

1. See Norman Perrin, *Rediscovering the Teaching of Jesus* (New York: Harper and Row, 1967), pp. 15–49, for a detailed and full exposition of the criterion; and John Gager, *Kingdom and Community: The Social World of Early Christianity* (Englewood Cliffs, N.J.: Prentice-Hall, 1975), esp. pp. 2–18.

2. Strictly speaking, this last phrase does not pass the criterion, but the Gospels are impossible to understand without the early and very widespread notion that Jesus was raised after his death. This is not the place to make inquiry as to what precisely this may have meant for the early church. But see my *Writing the Hereafter* (New York: Anchor Doubleday, forthcoming).

3. That the early Christian movement believed this seems clearly true; this claim does not involve the criterion of dissimilarity at all because it pertains entirely to the church's post-Easter beliefs.

4. Paul, however, is something of a puzzle in this respect. On account of his ecstatic experience, he identifies Jesus as risen savior and messiah but not, apparently, as the Son of Man of Daniel. Or at least Paul is silent about that particular identification,

though he reflects the other aspects of the notion. There is no question, however, that for Paul, Jesus is Lord enthroned as messiah and victor in heaven and is to be identified as the name of God.

5. See my books *Rebecca's Children: Judaism and Christianity in the Roman World* (Cambridge, Mass.: Harvard University Press, 1986), esp. chap. 3; and *Paul the Convert: The Apostolate and Apostasy of Saul the Pharisee* (New Haven: Yale University Press, 1990), pp. 158–159.

6. The Parables of Enoch, 1 Enoch 37–71, is the significant exception. But because it is not attested at Qumran or anywhere else before its Christian appearance in the canon of the Ethiopian church, we must bracket the date of 1 Enoch 37–71 as uncertain and probably post-Christian.

7. A minority of scholars see the self-referential *Son of Man* as Jesus' primary usage of the term because it could hypothetically be used in Aramaic in a reflexive way and was then misunderstood by later church tradents as a reference to Daniel 7.13. There are two problems with this solution. First, the term is never actually shown to be reflexive in the same way as *hahu gavra*. Second, this solution discounts the great importance that Daniel 7 has on independent grounds in the New Testament. It strains credibility to think that the entire importance of Daniel 7.13 is due to a misunderstanding in translation from Aramaic to Greek.

8. Burton Mack, *The Lost Gospel: The Book of Q and Christian Origins* (San Francisco: HarperSanFrancisco, 1993).

9. See John Dominic Crossan, *The Historical Jesus: The Life of a Mediterranean Jewish Peasant* (San Francisco: HarperSanFrancisco, 1991), esp. pp. 303–353. Morton Smith also uses magician as a central category for speaking of Jesus in *Jesus the Magician* (New York: Harper and Row, 1978). Smith uses the word in the sense of a miracle worker, not in the modern sense of an entertainer.

10. See Abraham Malherbe, *Moral Exhortation: A Greco-Roman Sourcebook* (Philadelphia: Westminster, 1985); and Abraham Malherbe, *Paul and the Thessalonians: The Philosophic Tradition of Pastoral Care* (Philadelphia: Fortress, 1987).

11. See Jonathan Klawans's work on purity in Judaism: "Notions of Gentile Impurity in Ancient Judaism," *AJS Review* 20 (1995):285–312; "The Impurity of Immorality in Ancient Judaism," *Journal of Jewish Studies* (forthcoming); and his dissertation, in progress at Columbia University.

12. Mark 9.2–8 and parallels.

13. See Marcus Borg, *Jesus: A New Vision* (San Francisco: HarperSanFrancisco, 1987), esp. pp. 39–75.

14. Here the connection is made with the use of Psalm 45.6–7.

Chapter Five

1. For descriptions of this cosmology, see Alan Scott, *Origen and the Life of the Stars* (Oxford: Clarendon Press, 1991), pp. 63–103; and Robert Hauck, *The More Divine Prophecy* (Atlanta: Scholars Press, 1989).

2. Recent works on the implications of the Sophia tradition for reinterpreting Christology include Elisabeth Schüssler Fiorenza, *Jesus: Miriam's Child, Sophia's Prophet* (New York: Continuum, 1994); and Elizabeth A. Johnson, *She Who Is* (New York:

Crossroad, 1992). See also Gail Corrington, *Her Image of Salvation* (Louisville, Ky.: Westminster/John Knox, 1992); Bernhard Lang, *Frau Weisheit* (Düsseldorf: Patmos Verlag, 1975); Robert Wilken, ed., *Aspects of Wisdom in Judaism and Early Christianity* (Notre Dame, Ind.: University of Notre Dame Press, 1975); and Burton Mack, *Logos and Sophia: Analysis of the Wisdom Theology in Hellenistic Judaism* (Göttingen: Van den Hoek and Rupprecht, 1974).

3. Both passages come from the earliest layer of the gospel traditions, the Q document. See Fiorenza, *Jesus*, p. 140.

4. Elizabeth A. Johnson, "Jesus: The Wisdom of God," *Ephemerides Theologiae Louvanienses* 61, no. 4 (December 1985):264.

5. For the historical background of wisdom in the Ancient Near East, see Leo G. Perdue, *Wisdom and Cult* (Missoula, Mont.: Scholars Press, 1977).

6. Wisdom of Solomon 10.1–21, 11.4.

7. Sophia is also a central figure in a constellation of early Christianities. See Deirdre J. Good, *Reconstructing the Tradition of Sophia in Gnostic Literature* (Atlanta: Scholars Press, 1987).

8. Johnson, "Jesus," p. 278.

9. Ibid., p. 284.

10. Ibid., pp. 284–286.

11. See Luise Schotroff, *Der Glaubende und die feindliche Welt* (Neukirchen: Neukirchener Verlag, 1970); and Birger Pearson, *The Pneumatikos-Psychikos Terminology in I Corinthians* (Missoula, Mont.: Society of Biblical Literature, 1973).

12. 1 Corinthians 2.6–9.

13. 1 Corinthians 2.16; 2.13.

14. In Greek, to judge (*anakrinein*) means to examine closely such as a magistrate examines or to interrogate in a judicial setting. Both contexts are political rather than instructional and underline the kind of authority claimed by the person who possesses wisdom.

15. Antoinette Clark Wire, *The Corinthian Women Prophets* (Minneapolis: Fortress, 1990), pp. 135–158.

16. 1 Corinthians 2.6–16.

17. Wire, *The Corinthian Women Prophets*, pp. 138–144.

18. In Paul's letter to the Corinthians, he seeks to connect the knowledge of the crucified Christ (a confession of faith) with knowledge of the timeless realm of the divine (wisdom).

19. The text is found in *The Acts of the Christian Martyrs*, trans. Herbert Musuro (Oxford: Clarendon Press, 1972), pp. 108–131. See also Maureen Tilley, "The Ascetic Body and (Un)Making of the Word of the Martyr," *Journal of the American Academy of Religion* 59, no. 3 (1991):467–479; Elizabeth Castelli, "'I Will Make Mary Male': Pieties of the Body and Gender Transformation of Christian Women in Late Antiquity," in *Body Guards*, ed. Julia Epstein and Kristina Straub, pp. 35–42 (New York: Routledge, 1991).

20. In an earlier vision, her martyrdom was dramatized as a ladder surrounded by instruments of torture and guarded by a dangerous dragon, symbolizing the devil. Perpetua ascends the ladder by first stepping on the head of the dragon, signifying her defeat of the devil.

21. In Perpetua's dream of climbing the ladder, she had to climb past each one of these dangerous tools of torture on her way to martyrdom.

22. The theme of Christ as liberator draws on the theme of victory over death, Hades, and the devil, familiar from Jewish literature: Wisdom of Solomon 17.9, 42.11; and Testament of Daniel 5.11.

23. Gustaf Aulen, *Christus Victor* (London: SPCK, 1951), p. 20; and Alois Grillmeier, *Christ in Christian Tradition* (Atlanta: John Knox, 1975), pp. 72ff.

24. Epiphanius, *Against Heresies* 3.18.7.

25. See M. C. Toynbee, *Death and Burial in the Roman World* (Ithaca: Cornell University Press, 1941); and Alfred C. Rush, *Death and Burial in Christian Antiquity* (Washington, D.C.: Catholic University Press, 1971).

26. For the ideals of moral formation and their relationship to the elites, see Werner Jaeger, *Paideia: The Ideals of Greek Culture* (New York: Oxford University Press, 1939); and Donald C. Earl, *The Moral and Political Tradition of Rome* (Ithaca: Cornell University Press, 1967).

27. Justin, *Apology* 10, trans. C. Richardson, in *Early Christian Fathers* (New York: Macmillan, 1970), p. 247.

28. Justin, *Apology* 14.

29. There were other philosopher teachers in antiquity who were recognized as divine. The divinity of Apollonios and of Porphyry was attested by some form of miraculous birth; other philosophers such as Plotinus and the Christian Origen were called godlike. Miracle-working powers were attributed to those philosophers who were classed as sons of god on the basis of divine origin. By the second century it was not unusual for the philosopher to be considered a divine man. See Patricia Cox, *Biography in Late Antiquity: A Quest for the Holy Man* (Berkeley and Los Angeles: University of California Press, 1983), pp. 17–44.

30. Richard Valantasis, *Spiritual Guides of the Third Century* (Minneapolis: Fortress, 1991), shows how teachers functioned as mediators of the divine. Friedrich Normann, *Christos Didaskalos* (Münster Westfalen: Aschendorffsche Verlagsbuchhandlung, 1966), traces the development of Jesus as a divine teacher from the four Gospels to Clement of Alexandria.

31. Valantasis, *Spiritual Guides*, p. 25.

32. Origen, *Commentary on the Song of Songs*, Prologue, trans. R. P. Lawson (London: Longmans, Green, 1957), pp. 29–30.

33. See Henri Marrou, *A History of Education in Antiquity* (New York: Sheed and Ward, 1956), p 206.

34. This is the same wisdom that in the Corinthian church was immediately accessible to the new convert; by the end of the second century, this higher wisdom was reached only through a long developmental process.

35. Normann, *Christos Didaskalos*, pp. 1–66.

36. Ibid., p. 179.

37. Jaroslav Pelikan, *Jesus Through the Centuries* (New Haven: Yale University Press, 1985), pp. 57–70, elaborates this portrait.

38. See, for example, Origen, *On First Principles*. For a survey of the varieties of philosophical systems, see Robert Berchman, *From Philo to Origen: Middle Platonism in Transition* (Chico, Calif.: Scholars Press, 1984).

39. See also Pelikan, *Jesus*, pp. 34–45.

40. See Francis Dvornik, *Early Christian and Byzantine Political Philosophy* (Washington, D.C.: Dumbarton Oaks Center for Byzantine Studies, 1966), pp. 205–277; and

Sabine MacCormack, *Art and Ceremony in Late Antiquity* (Berkeley and Los Angeles: University of California Press, 1981), pp. 1–92.

Chapter Six

I wish to thank three of my students–Thomas Beaudoin, Kate Moschandreas, and Whit Bodman–for the invaluable help they gave me in the preparation of this paper.

1. John Updike, *In the Beauty of the Lilies* (New York: Knopf, 1996).
2. Daniel J. Harrington, "The Jewishness of Jesus," *Bible Review* 3, no. 1 (Spring 1987):33–41. See also E. P. Sanders, *Jesus and Judaism* (Philadelphia: Fortress, 1985); S.G.F. Brandon, *Jesus and the Zealots* (Manchester, England: Manchester University Press, 1967); Morton Smith, *Jesus the Magician* (New York: Harper and Row, 1978); Harvey Falk, *Jesus the Pharisee* (New York: Paulist Press, 1985); Geza Vermes, *Jesus the Jew* (New York: Macmillan, 1973); and Bruce D. Chilton, *The Galilean Rabbi and His Bible* (Wilmington, Del.: Glazier, 1984).
3. Christopher Ives, ed., *Divine Emptiness and Historical Fullness: A Buddhist-Jewish-Christian Conversation with Masao Abe* (Valley Forge, Penn.: Trinity, 1995).
4. David Flusser, *Jesus* (New York: Herder and Herder, 1969); and David Flusser, *Judaism and the Origins of Christianity* (New York: Adama Books, 1987). Pinchas E. Lapide, "What Did Jesus Ask? The Sermon on the Mount: A Jewish Reading," *Christianity and Crisis* 42 (May 24, 1982). Geza Vermes has published three books about Jesus: *Jesus the Jew; Jesus and the World of Judaism* (Philadelphia: Fortress, 1984); and *The Religion of Jesus the Jew* (Minneapolis: Fortress, 1993).
5. D. A. Hagner, *The Jewish Reclamation of Jesus: An Analysis and Critique of Modern Jewish Study of Jesus* (Grand Rapids, Mich.: Academie Books, 1984).
6. In Leonard Swidler, ed., *Breaking Down the Wall Between Americans and East Germans: Jews and Christians Through Dialogue* (Lanham, Md.: University Press of America, 1987), pp. 161–175.
7. John Hicks, ed., *The Myth of God Incarnate* (Philadelphia: Westminster, 1977).
8. Naguib Mahfouz, *Children of Gebelawi* (London: Heinemann, 1981).
9. Hugh P. Goddard, "An Annotated Bibliography of Works About Christianity by Egyptian Muslim Scholars (1940–1980)," *Muslim World* 80 (July-October 1990):251–277.
10. Christology is that branch of Christian theology that treats the "person" and "work" of Jesus Christ–the relationship of Jesus to God, the significance of Jesus' life and death, and so forth.
11. The Chalcedonian Creed of 451 C.E., which speaks of the two natures of Christ (human and divine), is second only to the Nicene Creed of 325 C.E. in importance.
12. Stephen Mitchell, *The Gospel According to Jesus* (New York: HarperPerennial, 1991).
13. Canon (from a word that means measuring stick or standard) refers to those books that made it into the Bible. The process of canonization in the case of the New Testament took several hundred years; the first Christian "list" to include exactly the twenty-seven books that now make up the New Testament is from the second half of the fourth century.
14. Elaine Pagels, *The Gnostic Gospels* (New York: Random House, 1979).

Chapter Seven

1. Shirley Jackson Case, *Experience with the Supernatural in Early Christian Times* (New York: Century, 1929).

2. Quoted from Robert Bly, *Mirabai Versions* (Red Ozier Press, 1980), in Stephen Mitchell, *The Enlightened Heart* (HarperSanFrancisco, 1989), p. 77.

3. John Dominic Crossan, *Jesus: A Revolutionary Biography* (San Francisco: Harper-SanFrancisco, 1994).

4. Here there is space for only the barest essentials of the traditional worldview. My *Forgotten Truth* (San Francisco: HarperSanFrancisco, 1992), is a book-length account of the position.

5. This cross-cultural comparison needs to be explained. The concept of grace barely figures in the original, Theravada Buddhism, which contents itself with the Buddha's admonition to "work out your own salvation with diligence." When Mahayana Buddhism arose several centuries later, it all but reversed this relation between grace and self-effort; availing oneself of the merit that bodhisattvas have accumulated over many lifetimes and want to transmit to others became an important Mahayana motif. This seeming inversion led Theravadins to argue that the Mahayana texts that introduce the doctrine of salvation through "other power" or grace are spurious inventions.

To that charge, the Mahayanists developed two rejoinders. First, they argue that the Buddha taught not only through his words but also through his example–the example of a life that was totally dedicated to transmitting to his followers (for their salvation) what he had himself acquired through intense self-effort. Second, the Mahayanists contend that the Buddha considered certain of his teachings to be too subtle to be openly proclaimed; had he bandied them about indiscriminately, they would have been misunderstood and perverted. He therefore reserved them for an inner coterie of his disciples, who passed them on orally until the exoteric teachings of Buddhism had produced a climate wherein they could be rightly assessed. By these routes the Mahayanists claim that their distinctive doctrines are fully orthodox because they derive as directly from the Buddha as do his exoteric teachings reported in the original Pali canon.

Chapter Eight

1. For natural literalism and the distinction between it and conscious literalism, see Paul Tillich, *Dynamics of Faith* (New York: Harper and Row, 1957), chap. 3, esp. pp. 51–53. Conscious literalism, a modern development, is aware of challenges to a literal reading of the Bible and insists on literalistic interpretation. Fundamentalism, which emerged within American Protestantism early in the twentieth century, is an example of conscious literalism and is very different from the natural literalism of the premodern period.

2. See also my *Jesus in Contemporary Scholarship* (Valley Forge, Penn.: Trinity, 1994), pp. 175–176.

3. For a concise summary with bibliography, see J. C. Neill, "Biblical Criticism," in *The Anchor Bible Dictionary*, ed. David Noel Freedman, vol. 1, pp. 725–730 (New York: Doubleday, 1992). See also W. Neil, "The Criticism and Theological Use of the Bible, 1700–1950," in *The Cambridge History of the Bible*, ed. S. L. Greenslade, vol. 3, pp.

238–293 (Cambridge: University Press, 1963). For a brief treatment, see my essay "Profiles in Scholarly Courage," *Bible Review* (October 1994):40–45.

4. From Paul, our earliest New Testament writer: 1 Thessalonians 4.13–18, 1 Corinthians 15.51–52. In Mark: 9.1; 13.30, referring to the "things" mentioned from 13.4 onward, including especially 13.24–27. In Matthew: 10.23; 16.27–28; 24.33–34, referring to the section from 24.4 onward (taken over from Mark, with additions; note that imminent expectation remains). In Revelation: the whole of the book describes "what soon must take place" (1.1); "the time is near" (1.3, 22.10), for Jesus is "coming soon" (22.12, 20). A passage in 2 Peter (written in the second century) seems to respond to the fact that the second coming didn't occur as quickly as expected and therefore is indirect evidence that it was initially expected soon: 2 Peter 3.3–10.

5. What is commonly called the Old Testament in Christian circles is usually called in scholarly circles the Hebrew Bible (almost all of it is written in Hebrew; the New Testament is written in Greek). The reasons for preferring "Hebrew Bible" are twofold. The first has to do with Judaism: For Jewish people, the Hebrew Bible is not the "old" testament, but their Bible. The second has to do with Christianity: Namely, the terms *old* and *new* when applied to the two parts of the Christian Bible easily create the impression that the "old" is not very important compared to the "new"–that it is dated and has been replaced. In the mid-second century, a Christian teacher named Marcion explicitly rejected the Hebrew Bible as an inferior revelation; the early church then rejected Marcion and affirmed that the Hebrew Bible is, for Christians, sacred Scripture. Yet though the official Christian position is that both parts of the Bible are equally important, and though the church rejected Marcionitism, it has been common for Christians throughout the centuries to think of the New Testament as much more important. Calling the "Old" Testament "the Hebrew Bible" may help correct this tendency.

6. Still the most famous history of the quest is Albert Schweitzer's fascinating *The Quest of the Historical Jesus,* published in German in 1906 and in English in 1910 and available in several editions. Although Schweitzer began his book with Reimarus, Reimarus did have predecessors. See Colin Brown, *Jesus in European Protestant Thought: 1778–1860* (Grand Rapids, Mich.: Baker Book House, 1985); and N. Thomas Wright, "Jesus: Quest for the Historical," in *The Anchor Bible Dictionary,* vol. 3. pp. 796–802.

7. This is the distinction between the pre-Easter Jesus and the post-Easter Jesus that I develop in Chapter 2.

8. Because the word *myth* is commonly misunderstood, a compact clarification is in order. In common usage, myth often means simply false or mistaken belief and thus something that need not be taken seriously. In the academic discipline of religious studies, myth means something quite different: A myth is a story about the relationship between this world and the sacred. As such, myths can be powerfully true (even though not literally true). For example, the Genesis stories of creation are myths in this sense. On the one hand, they are ancient Israel's stories of creation, and their details are not literally true but are simply the way ancient Israel told the story. On the other hand, their central claims about the relationship between the sacred and this world (including the claim that everything that is has its source in God) can be true (and for a Jew or Christian are affirmed as true).

9. The other book is *The Mystery of the Kingdom of God,* published in 1901.

10. John H. Hayes, *Son of God to Super Star: Twentieth-Century Interpretations of Jesus* (Nashville, Tenn.: Abingdon, 1976), p. 61.

11. Since about 1980 there has been widespread scholarly questioning of apocalyptic eschatology as the proper paradigm within which to see Jesus, and there has been the articulation of alternative paradigms. The discipline is presently quite divided; and though one cannot speak of a new paradigm having replaced the apocalyptic paradigm, the near consensus that Jesus is to be understood within an apocalyptic framework is gone *as a consensus*. In this book, Alan Segal represents the older position, whereas Dom Crossan and I argue for a nonapocalyptic understanding of Jesus. For my own description of the issues, see *Jesus in Contemporary Scholarship*, pp. 47–96.

12. Josephus, *Jewish Antiquities* 18.3.3. For a careful analysis of the text and a persuasive case for its authenticity, see John Meier, *A Marginal Jew: Rethinking the Historical Jesus* (New York: Doubleday, 1991), pp. 56–88. For non-Christian references to Jesus in second-century authors, see pp. 89–111.

13. We are not certain of the name of the author of any of the Gospels. When the Gospels were written, they were "anonymous" documents; that is, the name of the author did not appear in (or on) them. Names were assigned (apparently in the second century), in part to distinguish among the Gospels. Generally, scholars strongly doubt that Matthew and John were written by the disciples Matthew and John. About the Gospels of Mark and Luke, the verdict is more divided, with probably at least a slight majority of scholars doubtful that they were written by persons named Mark and Luke. For convenience sake, I refer to the authors as Matthew, Mark, Luke, and John without implying that these are the names of the authors.

14. At an important point, the analogy breaks down: The classroom example involves plagiarism (whether deliberate or unwitting), which, of course, is a violation of academic ethical standards. In the ancient world, however, copying another source without acknowledgment was common and not considered blameworthy. Thus, the gospel writers are not being called plagiarists.

15. In the last ten years, a number of scholars have argued that it is possible to detect earlier and later layers within Q material (to which the designations Q1, Q2, and Q3 are then given). See John Kloppenborg, *The Formation of Q* (Philadelphia: Fortress, 1987); and Burton Mack, *The Lost Gospel: The Book of Q and Christian Origins* (San Francisco: HarperSanFrancisco, 1993). Although it seems a priori likely that the Q tradition developed and therefore includes earlier and later material, I am not convinced that it is possible to separate out the layers into successive "editions" of Q, and I am even more skeptical that it is then possible to build further hypotheses on the division of Q into layers.

16. There is a significant minority voice in contemporary scholarship that disagrees with both the priority of Mark and the Q hypothesis. It favors instead the priority of Matthew (with Luke then using Matthew and Mark then using both Matthew and Luke). See, especially, William R. Farmer, whose position is summarized in *The Gospel of Jesus: The Pastoral Relevance of the Synoptic Problem* (Louisville, Ky.: Westminster/John Knox, 1994). This way of seeing the relationships among the synoptics also eliminates the need for Q–the verses shared in common by Matthew and Luke are explained because Luke had a copy of Matthew. The percentage of today's scholars favoring this alternative understanding of the origin of the synoptics is difficult to estimate, but I would be surprised if it were over 10 percent.

17. For beginning students and the newly curious, a very readable and compact account of gospel origins is found in W. Barnes Tatum, *In Search of Jesus* (Atlanta: John Knox, 1982), pp. 11–59. For a chapter-length account, see Stephen Patterson, "Sources

for the Life of Jesus," in *The Search for Jesus: Modern Scholarship Looks at the Gospels*, ed. Hershel Shanks, pp. 9–34 (Washington, D.C.: Biblical Archaeology Society, 1994).

18. Mark has sixteen chapters and 661 verses; Matthew has twenty-eight chapters and 1,068 verses; Luke has twenty-four chapters and 1,149 verses. To use word count, Mark has approximately 11,000 words; Matthew, 18,000; and Luke, 19,000.

19. The teachings that are present are collected together in a few chapters (for example, Chapters 4 and 13), or are commonly embedded in narrative (for example, the classic Markan "pronouncement stories" in Mark 2.1–3.6, in which a story about Jesus ends with a climactic saying).

20. There is no scholarly consensus about whether the author of John knew any of the synoptic Gospels. My impression is that mainline scholars are about evenly divided.

21. On Thomas, see Stephen Patterson, *The Gospel of Thomas and Jesus* (Sonoma, Calif.: Polebridge, 1993); and Stephen Patterson and Helmut Koester, "The Gospel of Thomas: Does It Contain Authentic Sayings of Jesus?" *Bible Review* (April 1990):26–39. For a translation of Thomas with notes, see Marvin Meyer, *The Gospel of Thomas* (San Francisco: HarperSanFrancisco, 1992).

22. The easiest way to compare texts from the synoptic Gospels is by using a gospel parallels that prints the synoptics in parallel columns. A widely used version is B. H. Throckmorton, ed., *Gospel Parallels* (New York: Thomas Nelson, 1979).

23. Most English translations of Matthew 21.7 "lose their nerve" and soften the incongruous picture of a person riding two animals at the same time by translating "he sat on them" with "he sat *thereon*." But the Greek text has the plural pronoun: He sat on *them*.

24. An irony: In Hebrew, Zechariah 9.9 does not have two animals, only one. The Hebrew text reads: "Your king comes to you . . . humble and riding on a donkey, on a colt the foal of a donkey." The last phrase does not refer to a second animal but specifies what kind of a donkey (namely, a young donkey). Either the author of Matthew did not understand this, or he was using a Greek translation of the Hebrew Bible in which the misunderstanding had already occurred.

25. There are slight variations in wording. Matthew does this five times in his birth stories alone: 1.22–23, 2.5–6, 2.15, 2.17–18, 2.23.

26. I owe the phrases to John Dominic Crossan, who uses them in his essay "The Passion, Crucifixion, and Resurrection," in *The Search for Jesus*, ed. Shanks, pp. 109–132; and in his book *Who Killed Jesus? Exposing the Roots of Anti-Semitism in the Gospel Story of the Death of Jesus* (San Francisco: HarperSanFrancisco, 1995).

27. I put "prophecy" in quotation marks because most of the Hebrew Bible passages used by New Testament authors did not in their original context refer to future events associated with the coming of a messiah. A very obvious example is Matthew's use of Hosea 11.1 in Matthew 2.15. In Hosea, "Out of Egypt have I called my son" clearly refers backward to Israel at the time of the exodus, not forward to the time of Jesus.

28. In addition to the story of walking on water, there is the story of Jesus stilling a storm: Mark 4.35–41, Matthew 8.23–27, and Luke 8.22–25.

29. Jesus would have been scandalized: It is impossible to imagine that as a monotheistic Jew he would have accepted worship from his disciples. See Mark 10.17–18, where Jesus even refuses to be called "good." This is yet another reason that it is impossible to imagine Matthew's narrative as a scene from the lifetime of Jesus.

30. One can see this going on to a limited extent in the synoptic Gospels by carefully comparing what Luke and Matthew modify in texts taken over from Mark. The primary example of this tendency is, of course, the gospel of John.

31. For an extended case study of the Lord's Prayer as a way of comprehensively introducing the methods of the modern historical study of the Gospels, see Dennis Duling and Norman Perrin, *The New Testament: Proclamation and Parenesis, Myth and History*, 3d ed. (Fort Worth, Tex.: Harcourt Brace, 1994), pp. 1–33.

32. The English word *temptation* here does not really catch the meaning of "lead us not into temptation." It is best understood as "Do not put us to the test" in the sense of "keep us from trial or ordeal" (perhaps referring to persecution).

33. See Crossan's comments about *Didache* in "The Householders Talk Back," in Chapter 3.

34. For an explanation of the variation between forgiveness of "debts" and "trespasses," see Duling and Perrin, *The New Testament*, pp. 3–5.

35. A clarification: It is not difficult in general to imagine Luke shortening material he takes over from Mark or Q (he sometimes does); what is difficult to imagine is a motive for shortening the Lord's Prayer in particular.

36. Did the Lord's Prayer speak about forgiveness of debts (Matthew and *Didache*) or sins (Luke)? Probably debts. But then a further question arises: Is debts meant literally or metaphorically? Commonly, of course, debts has been understood as a metaphor for sins. But lately a number of scholars have suggested that debts may have been meant literally as mutual forgiveness of financial debt within an economically oppressed peasant community. The question is unresolved.

37. Adaptation of traditions about Jesus for the corporate life of the community is widely reflected in the Gospels. The very fact of writing a gospel reflects the corporate life of the community: It was felt desirable to collect together the traditions about Jesus for community use. To cite a more specific example, the collection of a large number of Jesus' short sayings in the Sermon on the Mount (Matt. 5–7) was likely intended for instructional (catechetical) use.

38. Beginning with Jesus' arrest in Gethsemane and ending with his burial, the passion story is found in Mark 14.43–15.47, Matthew 26.47–27.66, Luke 22.47–23.56, and John 18.1–19.42. I leave unaddressed the question of whether the gospel of Peter preserves an independent and earlier version, as John Dominic Crossan has argued in *The Cross That Spoke* (San Francisco: HarperSanFrancisco, 1988), and *Who Killed Jesus?*

39. Both groups have something in common, of course: They both systematically reject established authority.

40. I put the word *trial* in quotation marks because it is not clear that we should understand these as "official trials" before officially constituted courts.

41. I use the word *brigand* rather than the more familiar *thief* or *robber* because those crucified with Jesus were not common criminals (robbers or murderers) but persons convicted of insurrection. As mentioned previously, crucifixion was used not for just any kind of serious crime but specifically for political rebels.

42. The consequences of his changes have been tragically brutal for Jewish people throughout the centuries in ways that the author of Matthew could not have foreseen or intended. The passage from Matthew—"His blood be *upon us and our children*"–has been one of the texts justifying Christian anti-Semitism. In a somewhat different way but with similar effect, the portrait of Jesus' enemies as "the Jews" in John's gospel has also been a major factor.

To say the obvious, historically speaking, Jesus' enemies were not "the Jews"; not only was Jesus Jewish, but also all of his followers during his lifetime were, as were the majority of Christians throughout the first century. Thus, when John spoke of "the

Jews," he meant those Jews who did not respond to Jesus (just as a radical or marginal Christian sectarian movement today might speak negatively of "the Christians"). My point is not to exonerate Matthew and John (and other New Testament writers) for their indictments of their opponents, but to underline that the words did not originally mean what Christians in subsequent centuries have sometimes taken them to mean.

43. The majority of scholars are skeptical that there was a formal Jewish "trial" of Jesus at which the issue was whether he thought he was the Messiah, the Son of God. Most, however, grant that there may have been an ad hoc gathering of a small circle of the Jewish ruling elite that collaborated with Pilate in the arrest and execution of Jesus as (from its point of view) a potentially dangerous prophetic figure with a following who spoke of a kingdom other than the kingdom of Caesar.

44. See, especially, Amos 8.9. See also Jeremiah 15.9 and Isaiah 50.3.

45. How Mark understood the death of Jesus as accomplishing this opening is beyond the scope of this chapter. To mention some possibilities (and more than one meaning may be involved): It could be that Mark understood Jesus' death as a sacrifice that opened up access to God; or Mark understood the death of Jesus to be a judgment on the temple (as the "seat" of the Jewish authorities); or Mark understood Jesus' purpose (and not just his death) as bringing about immediacy of access to God, thereby nullifying the notion of a restricted or mediated access.

46. For an extended analysis of early Christian use of the Hebrew Bible and Jewish traditions in the creation of the passion stories, see, especially, Crossan, *Who Killed Jesus?;* and Crossan, "The Passion, Crucifixion, and Resurrection."

47. For a similar division of the first century into thirds, see Tatum, *In Search of Jesus,* pp. 17–19.

48. The exception, of course, is Q, which (as mentioned earlier) may have been put into writing as early as the 50s.

49. Preprint world refers to the world before the printing press. Preliterate audience refers to people who by and large do not have access to written documents, either because they are illiterate, or because they cannot afford written documents (which were very expensive before the invention of the printing press), or both. Preliterate thus is not the same as illiterate and has nothing to do with intelligence.

50. One-liner should not be taken too literally here. Sometimes these aphorisms were two, three, or four lines long; the point, however, is that like one-liners, they were arresting and memorable.

51. A classic example of this from modern times is provided by John Dominic Crossan, *In Fragments* (San Francisco: HarperSanFrancisco, 1983), p. 38. Recalling Franklin Roosevelt's memorable saying about having nothing to fear but fear itself, Crossan then asks what Roosevelt really said. Did he say "The only thing we have to fear is fear itself," "The only thing you have to fear is fear itself," "The only thing there is to fear is fear itself," "We have nothing to fear but fear itself," "You have nothing to fear but fear itself," or "There is nothing to fear but fear itself." One realizes that one doesn't know (and also that it really doesn't matter). But we all know the gist of the saying.

52. A word of clarification: Some of the parables of Jesus are very short and thus are more like one-liners. Examples from Matthew 13: the parables of the woman and leaven (33), treasure hidden in a field (44), and merchant in search of pearls (45). My comments in the rest of this section about the parables as "short stories" are about the longer narrative parables.

53. Other examples in John where one cannot imagine this are 5.19–47, 6.25–58, and 8.12–59.

54. When an extended teaching is a collection of short sayings that could stand alone (such as Matthew's three-chapter-long Sermon on the Mount in Matt. 5–7), one can imagine that some or many of the individual sayings go back to Jesus, even though one cannot imagine the Sermon on the Mount as a whole delivered as a connected discourse and then preserved by oral tradition.

55. To clarify: I do not mean that all allusions to the Hebrew Bible must be ruled out. Whether or not Jesus had the degree of scribal literacy necessary to read the Hebrew Bible as a text, I assume that he knew its central stories and important figures from having grown up Jewish. But when a story or saying depends upon knowledge of the written text of the Hebrew Bible, we need to be cautious about attributing it to Jesus.

56. I owe this phrase to Walter Wink, "Jesus and the Domination System," in *1991 SBL Seminar Papers,* ed. Eugene Lovering Jr. (Atlanta: Scholars Press, 1991), p. 285.

57. Crossan in Chapter 3 provides a compact description of its central features as a two-class preindustrial agrarian society divided between exploited rural peasants and exploiting urban elites. His book *The Historical Jesus: The Life of a Mediterranean Jewish Peasant* (San Francisco: HarperSanFrancisco, 1991) is a model of the interdisciplinary approach to constructing the social world of Jesus. For my own chapter-length summary, see "The Palestinian Background for a Life of Jesus," in *The Search for Jesus,* ed. Shanks, pp. 37–57. See also "Resources for the Study of Jesus" in the backmatter of this book.

58. I owe the language of "religious classic" to David Tracy, *The Analogical Imagination* (New York: Crossroad, 1987).

Resources for the Study of Jesus

This list of resources for further study and reading is intended for the newly curious, whether in colleges and universities, in churches, or among the general public.

Primary Sources

B. H. Throckmorton, ed., *Gospel Parallels* (New York: Thomas Nelson, 1979; current edition recommended, though earlier editions are okay). Texts of the synoptic Gospels arranged in three parallel columns. Greatly aids comparisons and the study of development.

Robert J. Miller, ed., *The Complete Gospels,* rev. ed. (San Francisco: Polebridge and HarperSanFrancisco, 1994). Contains all canonical and noncanonical Gospels and gospel fragments, as well as a reconstruction of "Q" and a "Signs Gospel."

Robert Funk and Roy Hoover, eds., *The Five Gospels* (New York: Macmillan, 1993). The Jesus Seminar's edition of the texts of the four New Testament Gospels plus the Gospel of Thomas, printed in four colors (with introductory essay and commentary).

For the Bible as a whole (Hebrew Bible plus Christian Testament), the New Revised Standard Version (NRSV). Two excellent study Bibles (both NRSV, with introductions to each book and extensive explanatory footnotes) are *The New Oxford Annotated Bible* and *The Harper Collins Study Bible.*

Bible Dictionaries

More like "encyclopedias," these books contain short articles on topics relevant to the study of the Bible (books, persons, places, things, events mentioned in the Bible, aspects of biblical interpretation). Very helpful as a library resource.

The Anchor Bible Dictionary, ed. David Noel Freedman (New York: Doubleday, 1992). Six volumes; the most complete, important, and up-to-date Bible dictionary.

Harper Bible Dictionary, ed. Paul Achtemeier (San Francisco: Harper and Row, 1985). The best one-volume dictionary.

Interpreter's Dictionary of the Bible, ed. George Buttrick (Nashville, Tenn.: Abingdon, 1962, 1976). Four volumes, plus supplement in 1976. Though dated, still of value.

Magazines

Two popular-level magazines often contain articles of interest in the study of Jesus and Christian origins.

Bible Review, published by Biblical Archaeology Society, Washington, D.C.
The Fourth R (the magazine of the Jesus Seminar), published by Westar Institute, Sonoma, Calif.

Introductions to the Gospels and/or the New Testament

W. Barnes Tatum, *In Search of Jesus* (Atlanta: John Knox, 1982). Though beginning to be dated, a very clear and able introduction to the study of the Gospels and the historical Jesus.

Dennis Duling and Norman Perrin, *The New Testament*, 3d ed. (Fort Worth, Tex.: Harcourt Brace, 1994). Highly recommended for advanced undergraduates and seminarians and also useful as a resource book for general readers.

Luke Timothy Johnson, *The Writings of the New Testament* (Philadelphia: Fortress, 1986). Recommended for advanced undergraduates, seminarians, and general readers.

Stevan L. Davies, *New Testament Fundamentals*, rev. ed. (Sonoma, Calif.: Polebridge, 1994). A shorter and more accessible introduction than the two previously mentioned.

Resources for the Study of Jesus' Social World

Bruce J. Malina, *The New Testament World*, rev. ed. (Louisville, Ky.: Westminster/John Knox, 1993).

Bruce J. Malina and Richard L. Rohrbaugh, *Social-Scientific Commentary on the Synoptic Gospels* (Minneapolis: Fortress, 1992).

John J. Pilch and Bruce J. Malina, eds., *Biblical Social Values and Their Meanings* (Peabody, Mass.: Hendrickson, 1993).

John J. Rousseau and Rami Arav, *Jesus and His World: An Archaeological and Cultural Dictionary* (Minneapolis: Fortress, 1995).

John Dominic Crossan, *The Historical Jesus: The Life of a Mediterranean Jewish Peasant* (San Francisco: HarperSanFrancisco, 1991).

Richard Horsley, *Jesus and the Spiral of Violence* (San Francisco: HarperSanFrancisco, 1987).

Richard Horsley, *The Liberation of Christmas: The Infancy Narratives in Social Context* (New York: Crossroad, 1989).

Contemporary Books on Jesus

Marcus Borg, *Jesus in Contemporary Scholarship* (Valley Forge, Penn.: Trinity, 1994). An overview of what is happening in the discipline.

Marcus Borg, *Jesus: A New Vision* (San Francisco: HarperSanFrancisco, 1987); and Marcus Borg, *Meeting Jesus Again for the First Time* (San Francisco: HarperSanFrancisco, 1994). Argues that Jesus was a Spirit person, healer, wisdom teacher, social prophet, and movement initiator.

John Dominic Crossan, *The Historical Jesus: The Life of a Mediterranean Jewish Peasant* (San Francisco: HarperSanFrancisco, 1991); and John Dominic Crossan, *Jesus: A Revolutionary Biography* (San Francisco: HarperSanFrancisco, 1994). Scholarly and popular versions of Crossan's interdisciplinary sketch of Jesus as a voice of peasant social protest whose practice of free healing and inclusive eating imaged a radically egalitarian social order. See also John Dominic Crossan, *The Essential Jesus: Original Sayings and Earliest Images* (San Francisco: HarperSanFrancisco, 1994).

Stevan L. Davies, *Jesus the Healer: Possession, Trance, and the Origins of Christianity* (New York: Continuum, 1995). Argues that Jesus as healer is the central category for glimpsing Jesus.

Elisabeth Schüssler Fiorenza, *In Memory of Her*, rev. ed. (New York: Crossroad, 1994; originally published in 1983); and Elisabeth Schüssler Fiorenza, *Jesus: Miriam's Child, Sophia's Prophet* (New York: Continuum, 1994). Though focused more on the early Christian movement than on Jesus himself, a sketch of Jesus as an egalitarian wisdom prophet emerges.

Robert Funk, *Honest to Jesus* (San Francisco: HarperSanFrancisco, forthcoming). A treatment of the historical Jesus by the founder of the Jesus Seminar.

Richard Horsley, *Jesus and the Spiral of Violence* (San Francisco: HarperSanFrancisco, 1987). Argues that Jesus was an Elijah-style social prophet who sought to create communities of solidarity in a peasant society.

Luke Timothy Johnson, *The Real Jesus: The Misguided Quest for the Historical Jesus and the Truth of the Traditional Gospels* (San Francisco: HarperSanFrancisco, 1995). An attack on much of contemporary Jesus scholarship, arguing that it is flawed and that the quest as a whole is unnecessary.

Burton Mack, *The Lost Gospel: The Book of Q and Christian Origins* (San Francisco: HarperSanFrancisco, 1993). Using the earliest layer of Q as his primary source, argues that Jesus was a Cynic-like sage.

John P. Meier, *A Marginal Jew: Rethinking the Historical Jesus*, two vols., with a third forthcoming (New York: Doubleday, 1991, 1994). Already sixteen hundred pages long, this massive work by a moderate Roman Catholic scholar is especially valuable for its full argumentation and bibliographies.

E. P. Sanders, *Jesus and Judaism* (Philadelphia: Fortress, 1985); and E. P. Sanders, *The Historical Figure of Jesus* (London: Penguin, 1993). Sees Jesus within the framework of apocalyptic eschatology (specifically, temple restoration eschatology).

Paula Fredriksen, *From Jesus to Christ* (New Haven: Yale University Press, 1988). Argues similarly to Sanders.

Walter Wink, *Engaging the Powers* (Minneapolis: Fortress, 1992). Pages 109–193 argue that Jesus actively and nonviolently challenged the domination system of his day.

N. Thomas Wright, *The New Testament and the People of God* (Minneapolis: Fortress, 1992); and N. Thomas Wright, *Jesus and the Victory of God* (Minneapolis: Augsburg Fortress, forthcoming). Argues that Jesus saw himself and his mission as the decisive climax of Israel's history and vocation.

About the Book and Editor

On February 9 and 10, 1996, six internationally known Jesus scholars participated in the first national symposium to commemorate the 2,000th anniversary of the birth of Jesus. Talking about the historical, religious, and cultural significance of Jesus, these scholars drew mass media attention and inspired a phenomenally successful follow-up discussion group on the Internet. *Jesus at 2000* makes the symposium available to those seeking an introduction to the controversial historical study of Jesus and Christian origins and to those wishing to examine the intricacies of this New Testament scholarship more carefully.

In addition to the papers presented by Marcus Borg, John Dominic Crossan, Alan Segal, Karen Jo Torjesen, Harvey Cox, and Huston Smith, this book includes questions from the symposium as well as a concluding chapter that introduces the historical study of Jesus and Christian origins to the newly curious. Readers will appreciate the wide range of perspectives offered, from historical Jesus scholarship to Jewish studies, early Christian history, world religions, and religion and culture. Written for a general audience, the book will be useful in both academic and church settings for those wanting to know what the academy is saying about Jesus.

Marcus J. Borg is Hundere Distinguished Professor of Religion and Culture at Oregon State University. He is the author of seven books, including the best-selling *Jesus: A New Vision* and *Meeting Jesus Again for the First Time.*